This is a highly interesting, original, and intelligently written study. Martin Beckstein has utilized some of the latest cutting-edge analyses in political and social theory to reinterpret fundamental economic practices and categories. The book ranges widely across economic practices with a critical eye and teases out intentional and hidden political significance embodied in them. By combining sophisticated theory with often entertaining examples, Beckstein contrives to make the book both challenging and very readable.

Michael Freeden, *The University of Nottingham, UK*

The economic colonization of society and politics has been one of the great themes of modern social theory. Martin Beckstein reverses this perspective, asking how far in today's world everyday economic practices such as consumption or work may contain the potential for new forms of democratic political expression and contestation. Based on a micro-political approach emphasizing the view "from below" and on numerous examples richly illustrating his argument Beckstein makes an important contribution to a subject that has not so far received sufficient attention.

Roland Kley, *University of St. Gallen, Switzerland*

The Politics of Economic Life

In recent years, economic life has become increasingly politicized: now, every company has a 'philosophy', promising its customers some ethical surplus in return for buying their products; consumers shop for change; workers engage in individualized forms of employee activism such as whistleblowing; and governments contribute to the re-configuration of the economic sphere as a site of political contestation by reminding corporate and private economic actors of their duty to 'do their bit'. *The Politics of Economic Life* addresses this trend by exploring the ways in which practices of consumption, work, production, and entrepreneurship are imbued with political strategy and ideology, and assesses the potentials and perils of the politicization of economic activity for democracy in the 21st century.

Martin Beckstein is Postdoctoral Assistant for Political Theory at the University of Zurich.

Routledge Innovations in Political Theory

1 **A Radical Green Political Theory**
Alan Carter

2 **Rational Woman**
A Feminist Critique of Dualism
Raia Prokhovnik

3 **Rethinking State Theory**
Mark J. Smith

4 **Gramsci and Contemporary Politics**
Beyond Pessimism of the Intellect
Anne Showstack Sassoon

5 **Post-Ecologist Politics**
Social Theory and the Abdication of the Ecologist Paradigm
Ingolfur Blühdorn

6 **Ecological Relations**
Susan Board

7 **The Political Theory of Global Citizenship**
April Carter

8 **Democracy and National Pluralism**
Edited by Ferran Requejo

9 **Civil Society and Democratic Theory**
Alternative Voices
Gideon Baker

10 **Ethics and Politics in Contemporary Theory**
Between Critical Theory and Post-Marxism
Mark Devenney

11 **Citizenship and Identity**
Towards a New Republic
John Schwarzmantel

12 **Multiculturalism, Identity and Rights**
Edited by Bruce Haddock and Peter Sutch

13 **Political Theory of Global Justice**
A Cosmopolitan Case for the World State
Luis Cabrera

14 **Democracy, Nationalism and Multiculturalism**
Edited by Ramón Maiz and Ferrán Requejo

15 **Political Reconciliation**
Andrew Schaap

16 **National Cultural Autonomy and Its Contemporary Critics**
Edited by Ephraim Nimni

17 **Power and Politics in Poststructuralist Thought**
New Theories of the Political
Saul Newman

18 **Capabilities Equality**
Basic Issues and Problems
Edited by Alexander Kaufman

19 **Morality and Nationalism**
Catherine Frost

20 **Principles and Political Order**
The Challenge of Diversity
Edited by Bruce Haddock, Peri Roberts and Peter Sutch

21 **European Integration and the Nationalities Question**
Edited by John McGarry and Michael Keating

22 **Deliberation, Social Choice and Absolutist Democracy**
David van Mill

23 **Sexual Justice/Cultural Justice**
Critical Perspectives in Political Theory and Practice
Edited by Barbara Arneil, Monique Deveaux, Rita Dhamoon and Avigail Eisenberg

24 **The International Political Thought of Carl Schmitt**
Terror, Liberal War and the Crisis of Global Order
Edited by Louiza Odysseos and Fabio Petito

25 **In Defense of Human Rights**
A Non-Religious Grounding in a Pluralistic World
Ari Kohen

26 **Logics of Critical Explanation in Social and Political Theory**
Jason Glynos and David Howarth

27 **Political Constructivism**
Peri Roberts

28 **The New Politics of Masculinity**
Men, Power and Resistance
Fidelma Ashe

29 **Citizens and the State**
Attitudes in Western Europe and East and Southeast Asia
Takashi Inoguchi and Jean Blondel

30 **Political Language and Metaphor**
Interpreting and Changing the World
Edited by Terrell Carver and Jernej Pikalo

31 **Political Pluralism and the State**
Beyond Sovereignty
Marcel Wissenburg

32 **Political Evil in a Global Age**
Hannah Arendt and International Theory
Patrick Hayden

33 **Gramsci and Global Politics**
Hegemony and Resistance
Mark McNally and John Schwarzmantel

34 **Democracy and Pluralism**
The Political Thought of William E. Connolly
Edited by Alan Finlayson

35 **Multiculturalism and Moral Conflict**
Edited by Maria Dimova-Cookson and Peter Stirk

36 **John Stuart Mill—Thought and Influence**
The Saint of Rationalism
Edited by Georgios Varouxakis and Paul Kelly

37 **Rethinking Gramsci**
Edited by Marcus E. Green

38 **Autonomy and Identity**
The Politics of Who We Are
Ros Hague

39 **Dialectics and Contemporary Politics**
Critique and Ttansformation from Hegel through Post-Marxism
John Grant

40 **Liberal Democracy as the End of History**
Fukuyama and Postmodern Challenges
Chris Hughes

41 **Deleuze and World Politics**
Alter-globalizations and Nomad Science
Peter Lenco

42 **Utopian Politics**
Citizenship and Practice
Rhiannon Firth

43 **Kant and International Relations Theory**
Cosmopolitan Community Building
Dora Ion

44 **Ethnic Diversity and the Nation State**
National Cultural Autonomy Revisited
David J. Smith and John Hiden

45 **Tensions of Modernity**
Las Casas and His Legacy in the French Enlightenment
Daniel R. Brunstetter

46 **Honor**
A Phenomenology
Robert L. Oprisko

47 **Critical Theory and Democracy**
Essays in Honour of Andrew Arato
Edited by Enrique Peruzzotti and Martin Plot

48 **Sophocles and the Politics of Tragedy**
Cities and Transcendence
Jonathan N. Badger

49 **Isaiah Berlin and the Politics of Freedom**
"Two Concepts of Liberty" 50 Years Later
Edited by Bruce Baum and Robert Nichols

50 **Popular Sovereignty in the West**
Polities, Contention, and Ideas
Geneviève Nootens

51 **Pliny's Defense of Empire**
Thomas R. Laehn

52 **Class, States and International Relations**
A Critical Appraisal of Robert Cox and Neo-Gramscian Theory
Adrian Budd

53 **Civil Disobedience and Deliberative Democracy**
William Smith

54 **Untangling Heroism**
Classical Philosophy and the Concept of the Hero
Ari Kohen

55 **Rethinking the Politics of Absurdity**
Albert Camus, Postmodernity, and the Survival of Innocence
Matthew H. Bowker

56 **Kantian Theory and Human Rights**
Edited by Reidar Maliks and Andreas Follesdal

57 **The Political Philosophy of Judith Butler**
Birgit Schippers

58 **Hegel and the Metaphysical Frontiers of Political Theory**
Eric Lee Goodfield

59 **Time, Memory, and the Politics of Contingency**
Smita A. Rahman

60 **Michael A. Weinstein**
Action, Contemplation, Vitalism
Edited by Robert L. Oprisko and Diane Rubenstein

61 **Deep Cosmopolis**
Rethinking World Politics and Globalisation
Edited by Adam K. Webb

62 **Political Philosophy, Empathy and Political Justice**
Matt Edge

63 **The Politics of Economic Life**
Martin Beckstein

The Politics of Economic Life

Martin Beckstein

Routledge
Taylor & Francis Group
LONDON AND NEW YORK

First published 2016 by Routledge

2 Park Square, Milton Park, Abingdon, Oxfordshire OX14 4RN
711 Third Avenue, New York, NY 10017

Routledge is an imprint of the Taylor & Francis Group, an informa business

First issued in paperback 2017

Library of Congress Cataloging-in-Publication Data
Beckstein, Martin.
The politics of economic life / Martin Beckstein. — 1 Edition.
pages cm. — (Routledge innovations in political theory ; 63)
Includes bibliographical references and index.
1. Economics. 2. Political science. I. Title.
HB171.B345 2015
320—dc23
2015013383

ISBN: 978-1-138-91555-8 (hbk)
ISBN: 978-0-8153-7022-2 (pbk)

Typeset in Sabon
by Apex CoVantage, LLC

Contents

Acknowledgments

This project has benefited from the assistance of many people and institutions, without whom it would not have been possible.

The Swiss National Science Foundation generously funded a two-year visiting scholarship at the University of Oxford's Department of Politics and International Relations. The stimulating environment at Oxford perfectly complemented the input I received at the University of St. Gallen. I also gratefully acknowledge the University of Zurich's Research Priority Program for Ethics' generosity in covering the cost of permissions and copyrights on the pictures reproduced in this book. *Nations and Nationalism* and *Studies in Social and Political Thought* kindly permitted me to use parts of two articles they had previously published.

Moreover, the project benefited greatly from encouraging remarks and constructive criticism provided by two anonymous reviewers, as well as from professional and amiable collaboration with Nicole Osborne and Natalja Mortensen and Lillian Rand of Routledge.

Finally, I owe my deep gratitude to Roland Kley, Michael Freeden, Oliver Marchart, Ursula Jasper, Eckhart Dietzfelbinger, Sharon Macdonald, Doreen Massey, Dana Mills, Eno Trimcev, Kaspar Schiltz, Bernd Bucher, and Ralph Weber for their scholarly advice and intellectual as well as emotional support.

1 The Politicization of Economic Activity

Many people inside and outside of academia feel that a process of economization has taken hold of liberal-democratic societies in recent decades: the leaders of the most powerful nation-states have relinquished the political stage to business, referring to factual constraints; transnational corporations are at the helm of globalization, evading national legislation and propelling deregulation through the ever-present threat of exit; the logic of the market has thoroughly penetrated public affairs; personal relationships are increasingly becoming commercialized; governments privatize public services, restrict the welfare state, and contract policy-making out to the private sector; election campaigns degenerate into politainment; citizens buy public goods rather than negotiating policies that fit into a collective project and—cause or consequence—have been recast as customers by public administrations. It is only logical, or so it appears, that economists have rather successfully applied neoclassical methods to explain all sorts of behaviour outside the economic sphere, including political activity. 'Economic imperialism', as they themselves have labelled their research programme (Fine 2001, Lazear 2000, Radnitzky and Bernholz 1987), recommends grasping family members, lovers, or citizens as egoistic utility-maximizers and caring, loving, or voting rather literally as a shopping expedition. To the extent that a process of economization has indeed gained a foothold, it is certainly a cause for concern and should be analysed in detail.

However, as the 21st century unfolds, and in particular after the financial crisis of 2007–08, it becomes ever more apparent that along with the economization of social life comes an inverted trend by which economic life is increasingly becoming politicized: companies are redefined as (corporate) citizens; they all have their own 'philosophies' that assert a willingness to assume social responsibility and promise customers a humanitarian, ecological, or otherwise ethical surplus when buying their products; consumers, in turn, boycott, shame, and shop for change; while strikes have forfeited some of their popularity, individualized forms of workplace resistance such as whistleblowing are very much in vogue and talked about. The economic sphere, it seems, has become a site of political contestation in addition to economic competition and, again, public political authorities are not innocent bystanders but, like private economic actors, actively promote the trend.

There have, of course, been occasional experiments in the politicization of economic activity. Having already decided in 1887 that products should visibly declare their country of origin, the British government sharpened the Merchandise Marks Act during World War I in order to propagate the idea of 'buying British' and to trigger consumer boycotts against the central powers. Applying a similar ruse in the war against the 'inner enemy' in 1933, the Nazi regime turned the public against Jewish businesses with the slogan 'Do not buy from Jews'. Tellingly, for these early examples of experimental politicization, neither effort worked in the respective governments' interest. 'Made in Germany' soon came to be associated with product reliability and quality, and the Nazi press was compelled to admit that propaganda had, if anything, been pushing, not decreasing, the sales of Jewish shops (Friedländer 2007: 34, Holst and Bräunlein 2008). One business that did incur losses from the Nazi boycott—to give a similarly ironic example of politicized corporate activity—was the Coca Cola Company. A competitor (Karl Flach, Principal of Afri-Cola) distributed Coca Cola bottle caps with Hebrew 'kosher' labels from New York in order to defame the company as a Jewish intruder in the German market. Though the Coca Cola brand suffered considerable damage in the short term, the company's reputation was soon more than restored. Under Max Keith, Coca Cola managed to market their drink as a truly German, in fact, *völkisch* product. Coca Cola placed advertisements in fascist periodicals such as *Die Wehrmacht* or *Der Stürmer*, and Coca Cola kiosks offered the 'brown' soda to the participants of Nazi-party rallies. That the Coca Cola logo rested comfortably next to the swastika in the Third Reich, ironically again, did not affect the product's image in the Allied countries, where it symbolized American freedom (Pendergrast 2004: 213–26, Schutts 2007: 161–71).

History, both recent and remote, has witnessed a plethora of impromptu tactics, situational ruses, or tentative attempts to politicize economic life. Today, however, we see systematic patterns, elaborate strategies, and programmatic policies. Moreover, today these are not framed as an extraordinary continuation of war by other means, but seamlessly blend with the routinized implementation of corporate philosophies and manifestos of smart governance. Consider, for instance, the Third Way's vision of politics, as it unfolded in Britain and Germany at the turn of the millennium. Anchored in the quadrangular scheme of the concepts of 'de-bureaucratization', 'cooperative self-help', 'stakeholder empowerment', and 'no rights without responsibilities', the Third Way articulates an attempt to reinvent political governance in times of globalization. The idea is not simply to restore the authority of nation-states by scaling back governmental activity and unburdening the welfare state. Rather, governmental competencies are placed at arm's length from the administration's main remit by employing actors from other sectors with the performance of public tasks (Burnham 2001, Freeden 2002). Economic actors play a central role in the Third Way's paradigm of multi-sectoral governance. Business is to be implicated in policy-making and consumers entrusted with the tasks of monitoring and implementation. Gerhard Schröder's social democratic-green coalition in Germany accordingly spent €3.3 million in 2003 to inform consumers that 'Fair Feels Good'. In the following years, additional campaigns (e.g. 'Echt gerecht. Clever kaufen') were initiated (Kneip and Niesyto 2007: 156, 174). The conservative-liberal Merkel administration invigorated these efforts rather than scaling back the double strategy of simultaneously economizing public affairs and politicizing economic life. Lest the 'fair and task-oriented dialogue between business and consumers' founder on the 'passivity of consumers', the Ministry for Consumer Affairs budgeted another three-quarters of a million euros in 2011 to establish an Internet platform where consumers were called upon to 'actively participate in the deliberations about product identification'.[1]

The Labour administration under Tony Blair, for its part, launched a range of initiatives to politicize various kinds of economic activity, one of which was a nationwide £10 million advertising campaign in 1999 to remind hesitant ethical consumers about their responsibility to 'do their bit' (cf. Hobson 2004: 126). Under Cameron, the British Department of Health contracted out policy-making on alcohol and diet-related diseases in 2010 to drink manufacturers and fast-food companies such as Diageo, PepsiCo, McDonald's, and Kentucky Fried Chicken (Lawrence 2010; Milne 2010). As stated by Peter Burnham (2001: 136), the strategy of simultaneous economization of politics and the politicization of economic life banks not so much on the expectation that the government will ultimately manage to retain control and keep market actors on a leash. Rather, the intention is to renegotiate the question of 'Who is responsible for responsibility?' and redistribute accountability for societal regulation. Offloading responsibility for policy direction and success, governments apparently intend to shift some ground for contestation to the marketplace. By politicizing economic activity, politicians de-contest their own policies, and drag a set of other actors onto the firing line.

Governments discharge responsibilities in order to regain power and adapt to the age of global networks and flows, hoping to become more agile and less tangible, to become 'liquid' themselves. Business actors declaim to render services to the community because they prefer setting standards themselves rather than having them imposed, and because they prefer negotiating with consumers rather than governments and parties where money is drained away rather than coming in. Consumers and workers try to unlock potentials for politics in the marketplace in order to extend active citizenship or because they flee from traditional channels of democratic articulation. The politicization of economic life is too ubiquitous a trend to be overlooked. Yet is the politicization of economic life just a discursive hype? Are companies really becoming politically active, or do they simply pursue pseudo-political strategies in addition to conventional ones in order to maximize their profits? Can consumers and workers reasonably hope to avail themselves with opportunities for politics in the marketplace or can only better-off citizens find a novel way to feel (rather than do) good? Is the politics of economic life a yuppie idea of political activism, a scholarly quibble, or might it actually be a matter of real politics?

The present study addresses these and other questions in order to enhance our understanding of the potentials and perils of the politicization of economic activity. It provides an empirically-informed theoretical inquiry into the economic sphere as a site of political contestation and asks—inverting the slogan of economic theories of politics, as it were—under what conditions and to what extent practices of shopping, work, production, and entrepreneurship can be regarded as an expedition in voting.

1.1 Economic Life in Political Thought

Political theorists never ignore economic matters for any length of time. The view that a proper understanding of what happens in the economic sphere of society requires 'pure economics', which only sees relationships among things, not people (Walras 2003: 225) or the view that economic interaction is a 'solved political problem' (Lerner 1972: 259) is not common in political theory. On the contrary, authors such as Karl Polanyi, Robert A. Dahl, and Charles E. Lindblom have pointed out the empirical and normative contingency of Western market economies (Dahl and Lindblom 1976: 35, Dahl 1989: 323, 2000: 173–7, Polanyi 1957, 1977: 6–10). Their work strongly suggests that the interplay between supply and demand necessarily requires governmental regulation, and therefore is not as spontaneous as we might think. They have questioned the expectation that economic market systems provide fair opportunities, have trickle-down effects that benefit everybody, and guarantee stability. Furthermore, they have endeavoured to remove the sacrosanctity and inevitability that non-political accounts see in market-economic systems when studying the economic architecture not in terms of choice, but in terms of quasi-natural laws. By thinking politically about phenomena in the economic sphere, political theorists have thus laid the groundwork for approaching markets and economic institutions neither as unfolding nature nor solved political problems, but rather as contentious issues that require debate and democratic revision.

Still, as Stephen L. Elkin (2006: 792) points out in the *Oxford Handbook of Political Theory*, the economy is still an understudied subject, in a number of regards, in political theory. One such important research gap is the individual behaviour of actors in the economic sphere, associated respectively with the political significance of acts of consumption, production, entrepreneurship, and work. Marcel Wissenburg notes accordingly that the practice of economic life is 'virtually ignored' in political theory: '[e]ven in Marxist thought, the role of the economy and economic actors [. . .] is analysed only at a very general, abstract, macro level' (Wissenburg 2009: 172). As suggested by this quotation, and as will be tracked in greater detail in Chapter 2, this neglect is contingent on the methodological 'macro' focus that is traditionally adopted by political theorists in the study of economic matters. Contributions to political economy such as those aforementioned typically approach the economy as a system, a structure of interdependent institutions and incentives, and thus inadvertently tend to render the economy as an object of politics all-too effectively: the economy is grasped as a machine that, on moderate accounts, is a fairly responsive target of governmental regulation and, in more extreme accounts, mutates into a non-human actor that ruthlessly imposes its logic upon society and engenders relations of super- and subordination all by itself. In either case little attention seem to be given to the fact the alleged machinery is not only run by human beings, but is in fact constituted by their very conduct. The concern of traditional macro approaches with the economic system and its institutions comes at the expense of a neglect of the concrete interactions within that very system. These approaches help to illuminate issues of economic polity, and to explore the possibilities of economic policy; yet they blind the scholar to the phenomenon of economic politics.

Very few scholars, mostly from Marxist, feminist, or neo-Gramscian backgrounds, have brought the political dimensions of the economy, at a micro level, into focus, and thus contributed to a political theory of economic life rather than a political theory of the economy. Samuel Bowles and Herbert Gintis's (1990) work stands out from other Marxist scholarship that seeks to meet Adam Przeworski's (1993: 234) demand that a 'Marxist economic theory must be a political theory of the economy'. By acknowledging the role of power and ideology in capitalist exchanges, Bowles and Gintis set out to challenge the 'micro-foundations' of economics. J.K. Gibson-Graham (2006a, 2006b) provides an astute criticism of what she calls 'capitalocentrism' in accounts of the economy, bringing the diversity of economic practices that are in operation in industrialized societies today to the fore, and discussing their political significance. Similarly, Evan Watkins (1998) and Jacinda Swanson (2002, 2007a, 2007b, 2008) expose the theoretical problems of conventional macro approaches, destabilize images of a monolithic, uniform capitalist economy, and give space to the transformative potentials of the practice of economic life (see also Cameron and Gibson-Graham 2003, Diskin and Sandler 1993).

Characteristic of these contributions is, besides a micro approach, a marked anti-capitalist agenda. Deconstruction of the economy is undertaken for the purpose of breaking up alternative economic organization into many localizable efforts, thus making the seemingly insurmountable task of overcoming capitalism manageable (Cameron and Gibson-Graham 2003, Gibson-Graham 2006b: 4, Swanson 2007b: 8, Watkins 1998: 34; see also Kogl 2008: 1–2). The anti-capitalist agenda does not lessen the theoretical value of these studies, which is considerable even for scholars who are less critical of the prevailing economic status quo; but it has the consequence that only those political potentials in the marketplace that might serve the purpose of altering the economic status quo and abolishing 'exploitative' and 'unjust' practices from within the economic sphere are given attention (Swanson 2007b: 4). The politics of economic life are analysed neither systematically (in regard to the potentials of practices of consumption, production, entrepreneurship, and work to make a political impact), nor generally (in regard to the various ideological causes, anti-capitalist or else, that economic politics may help to further).

While further inspiration for the present study can be drawn from a book edited by Patricia Fernández-Kelley and Jon Shefner (2006) that sets out to reveal the political dimensions of economic activity in informal economies in Latin America, Virginia Sapiro's (2000) 'Economic Activity as Political Activity' is an existing attempt to develop a systematic and general micro approach to the politics of economic life. The strength of Sapiro's framework is that it manages to get a grip on the ways by which economic activity fuels conventional politics (e.g. voluntary work in election campaigns) as well as how private money impacts interactions on the stage of politics (e.g. party donations). It does not, however, provide an adequate framework for studying the political effects that emanate from the marketplace through economic practices themselves. Moreover, Sapiro's approach to studying the political significance of economic activity through actors and their intentions runs into methodological problems. Intentions are notoriously difficult to verify because it is often unclear exactly who the author of an action actually is (e.g. is it the legal person of the firm, firm owners, managers, or all staff?). Moreover, it is disputable whether intentions are a decisive factor for the political quality of an action. The basic theoretical framework for the study of the political significance of economic life developed in Chapter 3 seeks to avoid these problems by focusing on conduct and consequences rather than actors and intentions.

In addition to these comparably few contributions to the development of a micro-political approach to economic life, a large number of studies exist that engage with the political dimensions of specific individual economic activities. Practices of production have recently aroused multifarious scholarly interest in connection with the issue of corporate social responsibility. Work has been discussed in consultancy studies against the backdrop of organizational efficiency, while industrial sociologists have looked at this in terms of resistance against intra-firm governmentality.

Entrepreneurship has become a contested subject in normative political philosophy, such as for instance in debate about whether the principle of collective self-rule also applies to the managerial control of companies ('industrial democracy'). Research on consumption and its ethical implications by economists, political scientists, and scholars of cultural studies, among others, has produced scores of articles, edited books, monographs, and even journals. An important task for the present study therefore consists in taking stock and connecting these diverse pieces of research that are scattered across scholarly subjects and disciplines, gather comparative insights, and draw tentative conclusions about the potentials for politics in the marketplace.

Meeting this challenge requires us to embark on a diverse set of issues and concepts in the discursive field of politicized economic activity, and to remain open to eclecticism while incrementally developing the account, instead of pressing any findings into a ready-made theoretical model—just as it is necessary to proceed inductively on occasion, to interpret empirical examples, and to be prepared to become cognitively involved with the concrete manifestations of economic life, all its variety, creativity, paradoxes, and, to some extent, with the jargon spoken in the marketplace. Accordingly, the present study is intended as a critical scholarly exploration rather than a critical intervention. While fully immersing the reader in the subject matter by looking at economic activity through a political lens, value is also placed upon regular self-reflection on the account's theoretical expenditures and practical relevance. The book aims to contribute to a political theory of economic life by thinking politically about economic matters below the systems level without claiming to be a comprehensive theory. And just as it cannot hope to offer the first word on a topic that is attracting increasing interest inside and outside of academia without having received sufficient systematic consideration, it does not wish to offer the last.

1.2 Focus of the Study

In casting a political perspective on economic life, this study limits itself to 'affluent' Western societies. Economic life in these societies will be heuristically differentiated into four economic activities: work, consumption, production, and entrepreneurship. The activities of economic life could be differentiated in alternative ways. Leaving aside more complex taxonomies that distinguish a significantly higher number of different economic activities, one might argue that at least exchange and distribution should be included as distinct types of economic activity.[2] Or one might prefer an even simpler heuristic that for instance subsumes entrepreneurship and work under the category of production. It is, accordingly, often suggested that economic life is best captured in a binary scheme that distinguishes practices of production from practices of consumption or distribution.[3]

Alternatively again, observations of the transformation of economic life might be taken as exhortation to rethink and perhaps replace traditional categories of economic activity with more timely ones (e.g. 'prosumption').[4] And one may wish to see the particularity of the processes of financial markets better reflected in the heuristic. Given these alternative options it is clear that the investigation of practices of work, consumption, production, and entrepreneurship is neither capable of capturing economic life in all of its manifestations nor of proving the best choice for all scholarly interests. However, the four-fold scheme adopted in this study might be sufficiently nuanced to illuminate a variety of economic processes, sufficiently straightforward to be accessible, and sufficiently simple to keep the research task manageable.

By investigating the political significance of practices of work, consumption, production, and entrepreneurship, insights can be gained about the inner life of the economy that traditional macro approaches have foregone for the sake of systemic findings. As a result, we may realize that the phenomena we have been using to describe and analyse in economic terms should additionally be described and analysed in political terms. Relatedly, we may come to see that politics can be found in places we have not been used to looking, and takes forms we have not sufficiently recognized. Colin Hay has recently underscored the promising nature of such an endeavour:

> To associate politics with the capacity for agency is not, of course, to deny that such a capacity is displayed in arenas—such as the market—conventionally described in non-political terms. Indeed, if anything, it is to point to the potential value of a political analysis of arenas such as the market, complementing the modes of analysis (here, economic) with which they are more conventionally associated.
>
> (Hay 2007: 165 n. 2)

More specifically, the investigation of the politics of economic life adds to recent attempts to chart existing channels of political articulation and develop plausible scenarios of the becoming-other of politics (Arditi 2003: 307, Tilly 1995, Tilly and Tarrow 2007, Wenman 2003: 63). Tackling the changing nature of politics is particularly important in the context of discussions about the future of liberal democracy. Large strands of literature have articulated the anxiety that the democratic project has come under pressure in the past few decades. Most trenchantly, Colin Crouch (2004: 6) has concluded that democracies in Western Europe and the United States are far past the peak of democratization, arguing that mere forms of democracy are fully in place today, whereas in their inner substance they have degenerated into 'post-democracies'. Such pessimistic assessments have been fuelled by warnings that citizen apathy and a growing feeling of powerlessness are the necessary consequences of these developments (e.g. Putnam 2007). However, it is important to realize that low voter turnout and declining membership of political parties and unions do not necessarily amount to a general disaffection with democracy. The present era might nevertheless not be quite 'post-democratic', which refers to a scenario where 'politics is really shaped in private' (Crouch 2004: 4). We may just have entered a 'post-electoral era' (Ginsberg and Shefler 1990: 1) where election outcomes fail to stand in causal relation to governmental decision-making. Furthermore, disenchantment with conventional channels of political articulation is not the same thing as a general feeling of powerlessness. Upright concern about the shape of established liberal democracies runs the danger of blending with paralysing pessimism if assessments take into consideration only conventional forms of politics, meanwhile neglecting the examination of changes over time in the repertoire of contention available to citizens. Following William Connolly (1995: xxi, 1999: 146, 2005: 152), therefore, we would be well advised to acquire a timely vocabulary and to 'pluralize' political action. Alongside Michael Walzer (1999: 58) we need to ask: 'Deliberation, and what else?' We should keep in mind Michael Freeden's (2011: 1) suggestion that we also decode non-verbal features of the ideological struggle, as well as Ulrich Beck's (1996: esp. 99) recommendation that we look for politics in new places (see also Dryzek 1996: 4, Hitzler 2000). Investigating the politics of economic life, neglected as economic activity has remained in political theorizing, significantly contributes to this research programme. It will help us to know whether these non-conventional forms of politics can replenish or supplement the repertoire of political participation open to democratic citizens, and relatedly, to enliven our democratic imagination.

Additionally, it is hoped that this study will contribute to contemporary scholarship on politics in regard to the ontological side of the 'political difference' and thus sharpen—from the margins, as it were—the concept of the political. Post-foundational political theorizing has done a good job in overcoming conceptions of politics that identify it with processes existing within a specific historically-established order (e.g. the government-related politics of the Westphalian nation-state). Politics, as has been pointed out, instead transcends and shapes the grounds on which it contingently takes place, reconfigures collective identities and notions of what is legitimate and illegitimate, and thus can be grasped as a process of reinstituting society (e.g. Laclau 1999: 146, Lefort 1988, Marchart 2007, Wenman 2003). However, more reflection is needed to avoid the heroification and romanticization of politics, or, as Oliver Marchart (2007: 131) calls it, the 'rarification of the political event': the tendency to recognize only sudden eruptions of epochal change such as the French Revolution as properly political. If the post-foundational conception of politics is to retain its theoretical value, we need to come to terms with the many small, but nevertheless constitutive, processes that bring about big events without resorting to the analytically useless truism that everything is political, thus banalizing the very concept of politics. The task is to develop a compelling conception of micropolitics that allows for specifying the conditions under which an intervention in the process of reinstituting society acquires a political quality. And with regard to this task, it is not far-fetched to say that an investigation of the politics of economic life has a strategic advantage. After all, the traditional association of economic life with private, non-political affairs should remind us that we need to be careful and think twice before attributing political significance to some act or practice. 'Everyone knows', Leo Strauss (1988: 14) reminds us accordingly, 'that buying a shirt, as distinguished from casting a vote, is not in itself a political action.' However, without developing a workable conception of micropolitics we cannot know whether buying a shirt might in fact be a political action under certain conditions, perhaps even more significant than casting a vote. And increasing our knowledge in this regard may foster our ability to differentiate between everyday market bustle with an ethical veneer and actual political activism in the marketplace.

1.3 The Structure of This Book

'Towards a Micropolitical Approach to Economic Life' (Chapter 2) analyses the outlook offered by traditional (macro) approaches to economic matters in political theory, and examines criticism launched against them in more recent scholarship. It is argued that micropolitical approaches to economic life should be grasped as alternative perspectives rather than as theoretical rivals, but that they are needed in order to challenge non-political descriptions of interactions 'within' the economy.

'The Marketplace as a Site of Politics' (Chapter 3) goes on to develop a basic theoretical framework for analysing the political significance of economic matters on a micro level. Such a perspective faces a tough challenge, as the ancient Greek dichotomy of *oikos* and *polis* has often been taken as an invitation in Western thought to juxtapose the political and the economic as internally unified and coherent contexts of meaning. I propose bifurcating both concepts into formal-topographical and function-related dimensions. The first suggests differentiating between economic activities with which we are familiar when moving and engaging in the marketplace, and political activities that we associate with government-related interactions on the stage of politics. The second dimension directs attention to the more substantial aspect of consequences, which, depending on the kind of consequences, justifies attributing to empirical acts economic or political qualities, or both. This splitting operation allows the compilation of a sufficiently clear theoretical grid for identifying economic politics in practice.

On this basis, Chapters 4–7 flesh out the micropolitical approach to economic life and incrementally extend the theoretical framework by surveying and discussing the variety of ways by which practices of work, consumption, production, and entrepreneurship may serve as vehicles for politics. 'Work and the World of Micropolitics' (Chapter 4) takes issue with collective and individualized forms of worker politics, and examines the pitfall, as can be observed in scholarly discussions of the latter, of celebrating any—however minuscule—recalcitrant behaviour at the workplace, as an act of resistance. If a micropolitical approach is not to dissolve into indiscrimination, a robust conception of micropolitics must be developed to differentiate between the *presque rien* and the *pas encore* of politics, i.e. the 'what is' and 'what is not (quite)' of political relevance. For this purpose three conceptions of micropolitics that can be found in the history of political thought—molecular politics (Gramsci), the politics of everyday life (De Certeau), and life politics (Giddens)—will be compared and amended by introducing an arithmetic criterion: in order to acquire a relevant political quality, an (economic) act must set off disproportionally strong effects on the process of reinstituting society.

'Shopping for Change?' (Chapter 5) portrays the realm of consumption as a space where normative visions, ideological antagonisms, arguments, theories, and strategies run together. Against scholarship that reduces political consumer activism to socially responsible shopping and a hobby for the better-off, the chapter argues that we need to remind ourselves of the rich diversity of consumption practices if we are to generate awareness of its political potentials—and political impasses.

'Political (By-)Products of Economic Production' (Chapter 6) addresses the hypothesis, explicitly or implicitly championed in much talk about business activity, that producers generally do not qualify as political actors. Taking issue with Ulrich Beck's theory of (passive) subpolitics, I argue that the denial of producer power, as well as the denial of political intentions among producers, is an unnecessary hindrance for activist strategizing in the marketplace.

'Entrepreneurial Space Production' (Chapter 7) focuses on practices of configuring the layout of a company's place of business as a non-verbal, yet all the more visible way of conveying political meaning. To illustrate and underscore the use of a micropolitical approach to economic life, an act of entrepreneurial space production is discussed in detail: the opening of a Burger King restaurant in a historical building on the former Nazi Party rally grounds in Nuremberg, Germany. We track how a local and seemingly minor act of setting up a fast-food outlet has unfolded and fed into a political discourse of real national significance, arguing that it in fact constitutes a remarkable intervention in the discourse on German nationhood. The findings contrast sharply with the interpretation of the political significance of entrepreneurial space production provided by macro accounts. They tend to disregard an individual branch as an instantiation of the parent company and suggest that multinational companies—'through' their subsidiaries—drain local sites of their specific social meaning and homogenize space by imposing the values of global capitalism. The macro account provided by George Ritzer (2008: 1) tellingly takes fast-food chains as the symbol of this alleged, unilateral top-down process, labelling it the 'McDonaldization of society'.

'Faraway, So Close' (Chapter 8) systematizes the insights gained through the development and application of the micropolitical approach to economic life. In addition some tentative considerations are made about whether the spread of economic forms of political activism might beneficially complement traditional channels of political articulation in the 21st century, rather than thwart the democratic process.

Notes

1. Source of quotations: Consumer Minister Ilse Aigner quoted from Lütge (2011: 29), and www.lebensmittelklarheit.de/ (accessed 10 September 2011). For a description of the Internet platform's mission, see the section 'Über Lebensmittelklarheit.de'. Regarding the government's role in the process of the politicization of economic life, see also Beckstein (2014).
2. J.K. Gibson-Graham (2006a: 59–68), for instance, highlights the importance of practices of transaction (besides labour and enterprise). Neva R. Goodwin et al. (2006) include distribution and resource maintenance in their classification of 'essential economic activities', in addition to production and consumption.
3. Production is often thought of in very broad terms as comprising any kind of economic activity except consumption, which is then understood as the final purchase of goods and services; otherwise consumption is rendered a residual category that encompasses everything except production, which is then understood as the design, fabrication, and marketing of goods and services. Stephen A. Resnick and Richard D. Wolff (1989: 20) classify economic activity in divergent but still binary manners into practices of production and distribution.
4. The portmanteau 'prosumption' was invented to indicate the blurring and merging of the roles of producers and consumers that has occurred since the late 20th century. The concurrence of these roles can be observed, for instance, when customers of online shops are expected to be their own cashier, or customers of fast-food restaurants are expected to work as their own waiter and clear their waste (Ritzer and Jurgenson 2010, Toffler 1980: 265).

2 Towards a Micropolitical Approach to Economic Life

George Pullman made a fortune as a gold broker near Golden, Colorado. He amassed even more money, and fame, by running the Pullman Palace Car Company, which developed luxury railroad sleeping, dining, and parlour cars. Founded in 1867, the company grew steadily, and to meet demand an expansion of the business soon became necessary. In 1880 Pullman therefore commissioned the architect Solon Beman to build a new set of factories at Lake Calumet, some twenty-four kilometres south of Chicago. Apart from factory buildings, dormitories and private houses for workers were also erected. Moreover, playgrounds and parks, a hotel, an arcade to host shops, a gymnasium, a library, a market, a bank, and a theatre were added, not to forget the schools, the church, and the administration building. A nice little town, designed from scratch and inhabited in its heyday by about 14,000 people, was erected and substantially completed within a couple of months. According to an anecdote, the architect Beman was so proud of his creation that he asked to name the company town after himself; Pullman reacted appreciatively, but added for consideration that it would be fairest to find a name that did justice to the efforts of both men. To account for his own initiative and financing as well as the architect's congenial realization of the project, Pullman proposed the Solomonian compromise of taking a syllable from each of their last names. Beman agreed with zest—a bit too hastily, perhaps, because swiftly the entrepreneur took the first syllable of his last name and the second syllable of the architect's: Pullman, Illinois, was founded.

At the Prague International Hygienic and Pharmaceutical Exposition of 1896, Pullman, Illinois, was awarded the title of 'the world's most perfect town'.[1] While the creation of a perfect town was exactly what George Pullman had aimed for, he enjoyed portraying his project as 'just another business venture' (Walzer 1983: 295). And an economic endeavour it was indeed: expenditures were calculated to be amortized in due course, and even secondary production facilities such as the Pullman Farm were devised to yield sure profits (The Pullman Company 1893: 30–2, cf. Lindsey 1939: 277). Yet in *People v. Pullman's Palace-Car Co.* (1898), the Illinois Supreme Court came to the conclusion that more than just business was going on: George Pullman had created a state within the state that levered out American democracy.

The verdict was not short of evidence. While formal authority and political jurisdiction for the company town lay with the Hyde Park Township and the State of Illinois, the entrepreneur *de facto* controlled the municipal government, as the company owned everything, refused to sell either land or houses, and even employed the school board members (Ely 1885: 461). Company inspectors threatened fines if it was found that families who were 'accustomed to filth and squalor' failed to mend their ways despite living in superior housing (*St. Louis Spectator*, 30 September 1882; quoted from Buder 1967a: 7). A critical Catholic priest who saw in Pullman not an ordinary businessman, but a 'capitalistic czar; a man who ruled, crushed and oppressed by the force of money' (*Chicago Daily News*, 11 February 1887; quoted from Lindsey 1939: 284) was expelled from the town. Given that critical voices could disturb the orderly community, newspapers other than the semi-official *Pullman Journal* (which gave unfailing support to the entrepreneur's policies) were prohibited (Lindsey 1939: 279). In short, effective control was established over the township and Pullman, as a company official astutely noted, managed 'to govern them [the inhabitants] in the same way a man governs his house, his store, or his workshop' (Buder 1967b: 107). Finding this paternalism to be in conflict with the law, the Supreme Court ruled that the corporation had to sell off any of the town's property that was not needed for industrial production in order to restore the liberal-democratic order and ensure that employees regained citizen rights (Lindsey 1939: 288).

For Michael Walzer, too, Pullman's business venture constitutes an eminent political problem. Investigating the implications of the normative principles upon which liberal societies rest, he quickly comes to endorse the Supreme Court's verdict: civil liberties and democratic rights must not be sacrificed. Plato is right when he says that a skilled navigator is required to sail the ship of state safely through the waves. Yet government is essentially about the determination of goals and destinations, and the question 'Where to go?' cannot be answered by navigation. All passengers on the ship of state have a right to determine its port of call, and no single one of them is entitled to invest him- or herself with autocratic rule: 'If he [Pullman] wanted power, [. . .] he should have run for mayor' (Walzer 1983: 303). However, Walzer takes a further, more decisive step, arguing that the democratic norm also applies to managerial structures. Vision, technical expertise, or ownership does not legitimize the subjection of residents in territorial associations—why would they authorize somebody to erect an autocratic boss/worker relationship in an economic association? In fact, Walzer claims that they do not: if entrepreneurs like Pullman want to manage their company; they should have to run for leadership.

Walzer acknowledges that the Pullman case is historically unique, but his point is that capitalist firms, today just as then, constitute authoritarian 'private governments' (Walzer 1983: 294):

> The right to impose fines does the work of taxation; the right to evict tenants or discharge workers does (some of) the work of punishment. Rules are issued and enforced without public debate by appointed rather than by elected officials. There are no established judicial procedures, no legitimate forms of opposition, no channels for participation or even for protest. If this sort of thing is wrong for towns, then it is wrong for companies and factories, too.
>
> (Walzer 1983: 301)

The strength of liberalism, Walzer says, is its capacity to compartmentalize society and separate spheres of influence. Thus, church and state are divorced, and many things besides: 'Liberalism is a world of walls, and each one creates a new liberty' (Walzer 1984: 315). Liberalism's only deficit is that it has not gone far enough. As long as private firms are effectively allowed to exercise control over the destinations and risks of other people, Walzer argues, the economy is not sufficiently walled in.

Doubts remain concerning just how compelling Walzer's case for industrial democracy really is. Yet the validity of the normative argument is not a concern at this point.[2] Important for the present investigation is, rather, Walzer's perception that there is a problem with traditional understandings of the economy. '[I]n theory', he says, 'economic decisions are non-political', but what 'is important is that we know it to be political, the exercise of power' (Walzer 1983: 301–2).[3]

Of even greater importance for this study is that Walzer does not show, as one would expect from this quotation, exactly how and in what sense economic decisions are political. Strictly speaking, the only political dimension that his account reveals is what he calls the 'liberal art of separation' (Walzer 1984: 318), that is, the politics of governmental regulation. Walzer provides arguments for why the institution of the capitalist firm is political, and why liberal governments ought to reform the legal basis of managerial control of firms. He shows that the capitalist firm is political as such, but not that there is a political relevance in the actions of capitalist firms in particular. In fact, it is astounding that his attempt to ascribe a political quality to economic phenomena via the Pullman case consequently factors out most aspects of political interest that catch one's eye in the historical episode, including: Pullman's entrepreneurial founding act, which reads like a paternalist treatise on how to improve society, and which, unlike most political treatises, attracted a great deal of attention in the public discourse; his philanthropic realism, which informed how Pullman hoped to mitigate the downside of industrialization by improving working and living conditions, and to 'bette[r] the relations of capital and labor' (The Pullman Company 1893: 34); the ideological idiosyncrasy of believing that the 'value of the beautiful' (The Pullman Company 1893: 33) would pay off not just economically but socially, too, on account of its capacity to develop middle-class values in workers (The Pullman Company 1893: 31–2; cf. Buder 1967a: 3); the extensive set of behavioural regulations and surveillance methods implemented to maintain his personal utopia; the overall vision that inhabitants exploited in order to present themselves as victims of a failed dream in the years of national depression between 1893and 1894, as well as to gain more financial aid than other affected communities; and, last but not least, the diverse strategies and silent tactics of employees in reclaiming the town up to the present day (Reiff 2000).

In the following section I outline the major challenges that political theorists have posed against non-political accounts of the economy (Section 2.1). Although I cannot hope to do justice to all of these in equal measure, I believe that the oddity revealed in Walzer's discussion of the Pullman case is a rather good example of their contributions to political theory. Critics of non-political accounts of the economy such as Robert A. Dahl, Charles E. Lindblom, and Karl Polanyi provide approaches that allow us to look at economic phenomena through a political lens. This lens brings the economic system and its institutions into focus, but neglects to direct—or even further blurs—our view to the interactions inside them. To argue this point, I draw on arguments made by anti-essentialist scholars who claim that a truly political account of the economy would need to more rigorously de-reify the allegedly static nature of the economy (Sections 2.2 and 2.3). While much is to be gained from shifting the focus from the systems level to the level of economic activity, the point cannot be to rule out one kind of approach by appeal to another. Accordingly, I shall characterize the interest of the presented *micropolitical approach to economic life* as, in the main, complementary to, rather than intrinsically critical of, *macropolitical approaches to the economy* (Section 2.4).

2.1 The Critique of Non-Political Accounts of the Economy

Political theorists have directed sharp criticism towards accounts of the economy associated with neoclassical economics or provided by libertarian authors such as F.A. Hayek and Milton Friedman (e.g. Bowles and Gintis 1990, Dahl 1985, 2000, Dahl and Lindblom 1976, Kley 1994, Polanyi 1957, 1971, Unger 1997, Walzer 1983, 1984). In a nutshell, political theorists criticize these accounts for depicting the economy as a self-regulating market whose operations are guided by ahistorical laws. Such portrayals, it is claimed, are non-political in character because they fail to link the study of the economy to questions of contingency, ideology, and power. Dahl and Lindblom (1976: xlv) accordingly state that 'in formal theory today, politics and economics are frequently regarded as distant cousins not quite on speaking terms'.[4]

The neglect of contingency, ideology, and power in studies of economic matters—as claimed by political theorists—can be explained by reference to John Locke's *Second Treatise on Government*. Here one can find an early depiction of the economy as an essentially free market based on private property. Private property comes into existence, the rationale goes, by mixing one's labour with natural resources. Fruit on trees or the land on which they grow are goods that can be freely appropriated as long as they have not been appropriated by somebody else beforehand: 'The labour that was mine, removing them out of that common state they were in, hath fixed my Property in them' (Locke 1988: [§28] 289). In order to meet biological needs, of course, human beings must be entitled to imbibe goods, but Locke's point here is that goods can be rightfully appropriated, regardless of whether their appropriation satisfies immediate biological needs or serves to assure a decent livelihood in the future. This brings humans into a position to trade goods and divide labour, and to use money to facilitate exchange, so that eventually productivity is increased and wealth created, which benefits society as a whole.

Locke does not seem to be aware that his account could be controversial. Yet the precise 'mixing ratio' for the acquisition of property when blending one's labour with natural resources is hardly straightforward. It sounds plausible that in order to acquire the property of an apple on an unowned tree, I need to pick it. But a moment's reflection reveals that it is not clear whether I additionally need to eat it. Neither is it straightforward whether simply being the first to find the apple already constitutes a sufficient property claim. Milton Friedman (1962: 165) champions such a radicalized 'finders keepers' (Kogl 2008: 53 n. 6) account of appropriation, for instance. Offering the example of three shipwrecked individuals landing on three separate but mutually accessible islands, he finds no reason why the lucky person that lands on an island that is well endowed with natural resources should share 'his' wealth with the unlucky others who land on barren islands. Matters become even more complicated once we consider goods such as land, labour, or ideas, and ask, for instance, whether it is enough to sink a well in order to appropriate a spring of water. Why should one expect to gain property for oneself, rather than donate to the community, when deploying labour and building materials to harness natural resources? It might actually be more plausible to say that a person wastes energy, as well as personal property, when proceeding as Locke suggests. Taking this line, Robert Nozick (2003: 174) reduces Locke's theory to absurdity by wondering whether spilling an individually and rightfully-owned can of tomato juice into the sea means that one acquires the ocean itself as one's legitimate property.

It turns out that Locke does not merely fail to consider alternative answers regarding the 'mixing ratio' between labour and natural resources;

he also systematically disregards social relations. Locke does not merely assume that God has given the earth to be subdued; he also assumes that God commissioned the human being individually, rather than humankind as a whole. Rejecting the second assumption, however, leads to the idea that the appropriation of scarce goods requires the exclusion of others—a detail that, if emphasized, might lead to the conclusion that the individual *takes* the liberty of appropriating, rather than naturally having it. Hence, private appropriation and the subsequent exchange of goods and labour is unproblematic for Locke because, before markets emerge and conflict about resources can arise in economic life, the human being is placed in a direct and asocial relationship with nature. Not only is 'Locke's implicitly male individual alone, neither dependent nor depended upon by others, apparently not participating in the family economy, which regularly shares "property"—e.g. food—among members' (Kogl 2008: 35), neither does he deem it necessary to relativize, define, or agree upon property rights in interpersonal relations. '[T]he ore I have digged', for Locke 'become[s] my property' just like 'the grass my horse has bit [or] the turfs my servant has cut'. These things 'become my property, without the assignation or consent of any body' (Locke 1988: [§28] 289).

Appropriation does not require consent from others on Locke's account because private property is built upon a higher authority than intersubjective agreement. In part it builds upon biological imperatives, yet characteristically also upon principles that are grounded in Christian ontology. Human life is placed in the here and now, but this here and now is the intermezzo of temporality, the *saeculum* ('century'), which is logically embedded in a reality that lies beyond time. Earthly affairs, and with them the ontological foundations of property and the economy, are presumed to be stably fixed in another world. Neither its discursive definition nor its practical maintenance is dependent on, or the result of, politics. Reminiscent of medieval understandings, where secular rule was grasped as *ministerium* ('service') to He who installed order, government in Locke's account may administer affairs in society, try to increase social harmony, and make laws to implement and inculcate justice. But as the principles of social organization precede both society and human life on earth, order itself is not open to debate. The social order is always already established; it cannot be modified, only violated. The economic order, therefore, is likewise not a matter of contestation but enforcement; not of politics, but of police.

In non-political accounts of the economy explicit reference to an eschatological context is the exception. We are seldom confronted with assertions such as Lloyd Blankfein's claim after the financial crisis of 2007–2008 that bankers were 'just doing God's work' (Blankfein, quoted from Arlidge 2009). Yet the organization of the economy can easily be placed out of human reach in logically similar ways. The economy may be conceived as naturally and spontaneously evolving in the form of a market, as being structured by ahistorical laws and anthropological constants, and—insofar as governments do not disturb its processes—also to be free. While it is assumed that contingency, ideology, and power are not intrinsic to the market, a beneficial functionality is simultaneously assumed to exist. Thus, an unencumbered market appears to provide society with a perfectly neutral means of allocating resources. The supposedly unregulated play of supply and demand seems to guide resource allocation by itself towards efficiency, stability, and, if not towards equality, then it is at least expected to ensure trickle-down effects by itself.

According to Polanyi (1977: 6–10), such an account of the economy was anticipated to some extent by both the French physiocrats and Adam Smith; it emerged as a non-political doctrine in the stricter sense in the 19th century, and thenceforth took firm hold as common sense in the Western world. There is some reason to believe that the account of the economy as a spontaneously-evolving free market is present in today's discourse as common sense rather than as a standpoint that was explicitly championed. However, Hayek (1956) and Friedman (1962) certainly come close to affirming this view. At any rate, political theorists consider non-political accounts of the economy sufficiently influential to level thorough criticism and affirm, as Dahl does when he states that:

> Competitive markets, ownership of economic entities, enforcing contracts, preventing monopolies, protecting property rights [. . .] and other aspects of market capitalism depend wholly on laws, policies, orders, and other actions carried out by governments.
>
> (Dahl 2000: 174)

The main reason for criticism seems to be the practical consequence of non-political accounts of the economy, namely that controversy is scotched and democracy quarantined from questions concerning alternative ways of economic organization. Where the economy is characterized as naturally self-regulating, any attempt to intervene through legislation must appear unnatural and, insofar as a beneficial functionality is assumed, also unwise and illegitimate (Massey 1998: 8). To challenge this discursive de-contestation of the economic status quo, critics claim that today's market economy is a contingent and markedly political development, and that therefore the organization of the economy is open to debate: be it with regard to single institutions such as private appropriation, the managerial structures of companies, as Walzer argued through the Pullman case, or the entire economic system.

2.2 Reification and the Strictures of Objectivity

Details of these critiques of non-political accounts of the economy will not be of further concern here. Instead, I will reflect more closely on the underlying argumentation, as well as the critique's more subtle implications. We will see that despite the abundance of practical reasons for providing a political account of the economy, scholars frequently insist on carrying out their critique in the name of an urgency to purge fallacious theorizing. Moreover, there is reason to believe that critics of non-political accounts of the economy fail to overcome the (alleged) cognitive fallacy themselves.

It is easy to see that non-political accounts of the economy may serve practical purposes in daily politics. Words like Margret Thatcher's 'there is no alternative' (quoted from Jay 1996: 361) or Bill Clinton's remark that resistance to the current forces of economic globalization is just as pointless as resistance to the force of gravity (quoted from Massey 2005: 5) frequently feature in public debate about the economy because they help to de-contest liberalization policies. Yet critics locate the primary problem with non-political accounts of the economy at a deeper level than simple rhetoric and ideological instrumentalization. It is one thing when politicians present their course of action as axiomatic and deny alternative ways of regulating the economy; '[i]t is quite another thing', Lindblom tells us, when:

> those academics and other scholars, analysts, and critics who are trying to think constructively about the options open to us often themselves cannot see the market as a variable but treat it as the fixed element around which policy must be fashioned.
>
> (Lindblom 1982: 333; see also Kogl 2007: 27)

Despite occasional instrumentalization for political purposes, the primary problem identified in non-political accounts of the economy is theoretical in character. Polanyi (1977: 6) speaks of an 'economistic fallacy'; 'the error [of] equating the human economy in general with its market form'. Roberto Mangabeira Unger (2004: 41, 200) calls this a belief in 'false necessity': the ingrained inability to imagine credible alternatives, stemming from an 'experience of acquiescence without commitment' to the factual. And a variety of other labels are offered, for instance: the 'naturalization' or 'de-politicization' of the economy (e.g. Magnusson and Stråth 2001: 27, Kogl 2007, Swanson 2008), the 'doctrine of economic neutrality (Teivainen 2002: 1), 'economic essentialism', 'economic determinism' (Laclau and Mouffe 1985: 76, Ozselcuk 2009: 20 n. 13, Swanson 2007b), or simply 'economism' (Miliband 2004: 9). All these labels, however, allude to the comparatively traditional notion of reification, which, in the words of Thomas Luckmann and Peter L. Berger, denotes a taking-for-granted as inevitable what in fact is the product of human action:

> [R]eification is the apprehension of the products of human activity as if they were something other than human products—such as facts of

> nature, results of cosmic laws, or manifestations of divine will. Reification implies that man is capable of forgetting his own authorship of the human world, and, further, that the dialectic between man, the producer, and his products is lost to consciousness. The reified world is, by definition, a dehumanized world. It is experienced by man as a strange facticity, an *opus alienum* about which he has no control rather than as *the opus proprium* of his own productive activity.
> (Luckmann and Berger 1991: 89)

Notably, critics see the theoretical pitfall not in descriptions that fail to correspond to empirical reality, but rather in that habituation to the status quo, combined with an underestimation of human capability to shape the social world, tempts politicians and theorists to erroneously attribute an undue solidity and durability to the economy. While investigating objectivity, critics suggest, politicians and theorists fail to retain awareness of the human capacity to objectify, and accordingly mistake our own products for inert facticity.

The intricate relationship of cognitive reification and empirical facticity (as well as the ambivalent conclusions that may be drawn from it) comes out clearly in Karl Marx's critique of bourgeois economics, especially in Georg Lukács's interpretation thereof.[5] Bourgeois economists, Lukács tells us, suggest considering productive relations as being between objects that are exchanged, namely commodities. They treat not only goods and money as commodities to be traded in a market of supply and demand, but even land and labour, which is why Marx calls them 'commodity fetishists' (Lukács 1999: 83–6). Besides this normative disagreement, Lukács goes on to argue that bourgeois economists let themselves get carried away in believing that economic relations are necessarily constituted by commodities that are subject to impersonal market forces such as inflation, depression, or the law of supply and demand. Commodity exchange appears to them 'as much a self-evident and nature-imposed necessity as productive labor itself' (Marx 1990: 327). Erroneously, the economy's market form is expected to be timeless and universal; it is 'mystified' and acquires a 'phantom objectivity' on their account, claims Lukács (1999: 83; see also Marx 1993a: 969–70).

Lukács underlines, however, that it would be a great mistake to believe that the commodity structure is a fiction; the market and commodities are 'by no means merely forms of thought' (Lukács 1999: 177). Marx stresses this point over and over again, for instance, by saying that this is the crucial difference between his lesson about economic affairs and Feuerbach's narrative on religion: whereas the gods of clerics are imaginary, the market of bourgeois economists is not; it is real and its power actually constrains. And whereas religion can be ended by insight, the conversion of economic affairs as the exchange of things into human relationships is 'an historical and not a mental act' (Marx and Engels

2004: 61). Markets and commodities are a reality; they 'are the forms in which contemporary bourgeois society is objectified' (Lukács 1999: 177). For 'objectively [under capitalism, . . .] a world of finished objects and of relationships among things comes into being (the world of commodities and their movement on the market)' (Lukács 1999: 87). Bourgeois economists are wrong insofar as they mistake the given world for the truth of the world, and present as nature what is a contingent historical product. Nevertheless, they (cognitively) reify only what earlier generations have (materially) objectified. Startlingly, their ontological 'mystification' turns out to be simple realism with regard to the ontic presence of the economy in its current form (see also Marx 1993a: 969–70).

It is well known that Marx is torn regarding the relationship between human beings and their historical environment. Marx, the scientist and historical materialist, attaches the conditions for overcoming capitalism to opaque historical forces that also gave birth to it in the first place. Marx, the activist and humanist, in contrast, is enthusiastic about the human capacity to build and produce, and eagerly searches for strategies to refashion the economic and social status quo (Pitkin 1998: 128–37). Still, even for the latter the manacles of facticity are no less rigid than the shackles of the mind are tight. Even Marx the activist appears to have believed that the construction of the economy was accomplished in a way that leaves little room for implementing change (Walzer 1984: 318). He affirms that 'individuals have [. . .] become more and more enslaved under a power alien to them, [. . .] a power which has become more and more enormous and, in the last instance, turns out to be the world market' (Marx and Engels 2004: 55). Though the laws of the market may not always and everywhere be valid, they are real enough in the present conjuncture to strike us 'as inexorable, independently functioning powers' (Lukács 1999: 87). Not even the capitalist class, which profits from the unfolding of the commodity structure, has control over the market. 'Modern bourgeois society', we read in *The Communist Manifesto*, is 'like a sorcerer who is no longer able to control the powers of the nether world whom he has called up by his spells' (Marx and Engels 2002: 225).

It is just one quirk of history that Marx was born in 1818, the same year in which Mary Shelley's *Frankenstein or The Modern Prometheus* first saw the light. But Marx's perception of an unleashed market gives us sufficient reason to entertain the idea that Shelley's *Frankenstein* and his critique of capitalism grew out of the same zeitgeist of Western civilization. The 'promethean shame' (Anders 2009: 31) that homo faber experiences when he is overshadowed by his own creations, and which pushes theorists to repress the human authorship of economic organization, in Marx is switched to a distinctively humanist concern: the anxiety that man–the–creator and altruistic fire-bringer has turned out to be a theomachic rebel whose creations have slipped out of control, and who is not in the slightest bit capable of undoing, containing, or even foreseeing the consequences of his deeds. While Marx the activist may not be much more representative than Marx the scientist for 20th-century critics of non-political accounts of the economy, and while there surely is plenty of disagreement in opinion and nerve about the benefits, problems, and injustices of a market-based economic order as well as the possibilities and strategies for shaping it, the humanist fear characteristic of *The Communist Manifesto* is today reaffirmed frequently with unabated vehemence.[6]

Against our intuition, the critical de-reification of markets and the commodity structure from nature into a human product does not necessarily spur optimism about the possibilities for economic reorganization. Polanyi (1971: 148) fiercely criticizes views that fail to grasp the economy as embedded and enmeshed in social relations and contingent institutions. But when analysing the economy of his day he actually finds that it is disembedded from social relations. At a certain point in history, Polanyi (1977: 10, 1957: 57) tells us, the economy was 'transmuted into a self-regulating system of markets' with the result that '[i]nstead of economy being embedded in social relations, social relations are embedded in the economic system'. The late modern market economy, he concludes, is 'an economic system controlled, regulated, and directed by markets alone', and 'order in the production and distribution of goods is entrusted to this self-regulating mechanism' (Polanyi 1957: 68; cf. Lie 1991).[7]

Dahl rejects the depiction of the economy as a self-regulating market as a myth, but then finds that the US economy has become 'an unregulated external force' (Dahl 1985: 101; cf. Swanson 2007a: 213). Lindblom (1982: 327, 330) asserts that the market not only incarcerates reflection on economics and politics by prompting the latter's cognitive reification, but also that the market 'imprisons our attempts [. . .] to improve the social world', and 'punishes' us as soon as 'we begin to debate or undertake reform'. Ernesto Laclau and Chantal Mouffe (1985: 73–7, 161–2) at one point reject the 'false' view and '[l]ast redoubt of essentialism' that the economy is dominated by necessary laws and not susceptible to conscious regulation, but at another point disclose the existence of a 'logic of capitalist accumulation' that 'penetrate[s] into increasingly numerous spheres' and entails the almost complete commodification of social life. Other critics of non-political accounts of the economy conclude that '[t]he unleashing of market forces transforms the political framework itself, undermines the hegemonic power, and creates a new political environment to which the world must eventually adjust' (Gilpin 1987: 77); or state that '[t]he capitalist economy [. . .] developed a systemic logic of its own. The markets of goods, capital, and labor obey their own logic, independent of the intentions of human subjects' (Habermas 2004: 500); some even worry that capitalism might indeed have come close to 'imposing its rule upon the entire world' (Dunn 2007: 6). By all appearances, then, fear of an unleashed market does not fall short of the terror experienced by individuals encountering Frankenstein's monster.

2.3 The Anti-Essentialist Critique of the Critique

As such, the humanist fear of losing control over one's creations is not unreasonable. Soberly considered, Luckmann and Berger's (1991: 89) assertion that, 'however objectivated, the social world was made by men—and, therefore, can be remade by them', appears to be too hasty a conclusion, because it rests on the assumption that human-made equals humanly changeable, whereas nature is unalterable (Pitkin 1987: 281). Our experience with the anthropogenic influence on the global climate, to give just one example, strongly suggests that both sides of the assumption are flawed. Remaking the results of human action is not always a matter of voluntary choice, and there is more than one logical step between accepting the economy in its present form as a human product and concluding that it is still a responsive target of politics.

However, the economy is not simply a fabricated artefact. Even the portrayal of the market economy as a mechanism that operates independently of us is misleading. We should think of the economy rather in terms of a social institution, which is to say an ongoing human production rather than a finished human product.[8] The ontological peculiarity of a social institution is that it consists of a web of relationships and orchestrated patterns of human activity. It 'is not a building or a bus, into and out of which people move. In a central sense, the institution is the conduct—the habitual, structured conduct—of people "in" it' (Pitkin 1998: 261; see also Collins 1981a, 1981b). The economy, accordingly, is not an external structure but rather a practice-based configuration that has no worldly existence apart from concrete economic interactions, such as acts of work, consumption, production, or entrepreneurship.[9]

Of course, there is some kind of structurality at issue when we study social institutions. The activities of people often display regularity. Informed by cultural and social norms as well as a legal framework, individual acts of work, consumption, production, and entrepreneurship become patterned 'institutionalized' practices. Social institutions may not quite have a logic of their own, and the economy is not an autonomous entity, but given social and legal orchestration, economic behaviour exhibits the signs of an inertia that stubbornly impedes sudden change. Although this apparent inertia is actually the conduct of people themselves, it can appear to be an alien force: like in a protest march, where the actions of individuals determine the process without any individual being able to steer it; people exercise power, as it were, without really having it. Hannah Arendt (1998: 40) describes this paradox as 'the rule of nobody', and affirms that this is not the same as an absence of rule. Sometimes, she says, 'the rule of nobody' turns out to be one of the 'cruelest and most tyrannical forms of rule'. So there is some kind of structurality inherent to social institutions. At the same time, it must not be forgotten that social institutions such as the economy nevertheless change as soon as people alter their conduct. Without stressing this proviso, the structurality of social institutions is easily reified into a non-human structure, and the rule of nobody specific transforms into the rule of a specific Nobody.[10]

Relying on practice-based ontologies, a new generation of political theorists has recently set out to turn the theoretical challenge posed by traditional critics of non-political accounts of the economy against themselves. If attributing an objectivity to the economy and considering it independent of human interaction really is the decisive lapse of non-political accounts, then grave doubts arise as to whether Dahl, Lindblom, Laclau and Mouffe, and others, are fully free of what they criticize. Humanly crafted, but non-human in its persistence, and in this sense understood as a finished product, the economy appears almost as intransigently reified as it does in accounts that portray the economy as naturally ordered. Accordingly, in spite of capitalizing on the constructed and political character of the economy, political accounts so far might themselves cling to reifications and essentialisms by suggesting a simplicity and stability where a high degree of complexity and instability might be more fitting. Naeem Inayatullah and David L. Blaney (1997: 66) confirm this impression, arguing that conventional critiques inadvertently 'fix' instead of 'de-reifying' economism. And Jacinda Swanson accordingly asks 'Why is it that so many political theorists fail to extend consistently their ruthless theoretical critiques of essentialist and determinist approaches [. . .] to their own conceptualizations of economic phenomena?' (Swanson 2007b: 5; see also Diskin and Sandler 1993: 30, Gibson-Graham 2006a: 6 n. 12, 2006b: 1–11, Swanson 2007a: 213, Teivainen 2002: 8).

While the essentialist hold on biological or psychological universals or identity has been loosened through studies informed by post-structuralism in the past few decades, anti-essentialist scholars argue that (re-)politicized accounts of the economy are still imbued with a simplicity emanating from its core. New approaches are required in political theory, approaches that more systematically deconstruct non-political accounts of the economy, portray it in terms of an on-going production, and reveal the power-related and ideological aspects of behavioural foundations. The task is to stop analysing economic processes 'through unnecessarily depoliticized lenses' (Teivainen 2002: 8), and 'steer clear of all forms of determinism and essentialism' (Swanson 2008: 58, 66 n. 3; see also Diskin and Sandler 1993: 29).

Anti-essentialists have a point. Confronted by understandings of the economy which, however critical they may be, take refuge in imageries of materiality, intrinsic logics, and autonomy, there is some reason to believe that political theorists have so far only halfway de-reified accounts of the economy. Nevertheless, we must ask ourselves whether the best way to proceed is under the auspices of anti-essentialism. While anti-essentialist approaches undeniably facilitate a fresh take on the economy with a view to politics, the underlying attitude might guide us to challenge the wrong adversaries on the wrong battlefield.

The reason for this concern is twofold. First, it is important to bear in mind that essentialisms may simply serve the linguistic function of metaphorical presentation. It is true that hypostasizing portrayals have haunted discussions on the economy in naturalizing, substantializing, deifying, demonizing, or anthropomorphizing variants; and it is true that these have often served to bring reckless claims to the fore. The great debate on democracy and capitalism, for instance, has revolved almost invariably around the trope of 'elective affinity', by which it is suggested that economic and political systems are chemical elements that automatically combine on the basis of their intrinsic properties. One conclusion was that democracy naturally attracts a market-economic order and that decentralization in post-Soviet countries would automatically bring democracy along with it.[11] No doubt, such depictions encourage jumping to audacious conclusions. Yet it is a rather complicated question whether, by resorting to essentialist depictions, authors imply a serious claim to the true essence of economic phenomena or not.

In the business section of newspapers, the economy is commonly likened to a body, of which some say that it requires medical care if ailing, whereas others are confident that it will recover on its own and warn against the risk of overdose. These are obvious rhetorical figures of speech. An analogy is drawn to make an issue accessible and to explain it, by projecting knowledge from one known field onto another in a manner of 'creative illumination rather than correct assertion' (Michael Freeden, quoted from Whitehead 2002: 38). In fact it is the nature of an analogy to enhance understanding by stating something that is, strictly speaking, wrong. In the case of 'elective affinity', the absurdity is even inherent in the term: a choice is posited in matters that are determinate by way of oxymoron ('Verwandtschaft', in the 18th century, denoted blood relationship; Howe 1978: 371). In addition, metaphors are used as cognitive shortcuts. Terms such as 'elective affinity', Charles Darwin (1872: 63) affirms, 'are almost necessary for brevity'.[12] It is no wonder, therefore, that even anti-essentialist scholars draw upon seemingly essentialist expressions themselves. Swanson, for instance, unhesitatingly integrates a quotation by Judith Butler into her argumentation that is loaded with reifying metaphors: 'any theory that fails to think the possibilities of transformation from within that "systemic" formation is itself complicit with the idea of the "eternal" character of capital that capital so readily produces' (Butler 1997: 13–14, emphases added; quoted from Swanson 2007b: 9).

One comes to see from reifying language that it is difficult to avoid relying upon reified and essentialist concepts. One may explain Butler's statement by saying that the theorist (rather than the theory) fails to think, and that the eternal character of capital is produced by human action (rather than by an autonomous entity called capital); but it is doubtful whether the solidifying reduction of processual complexity is thus not just displaced to another level, and thereby slips into the concepts of discourse, ideas, practices, or individuals:

> It seems inconceivable that any theory of reification [. . .] could avoid succumbing to its own critique. The ante is upped continually as a matter of course; what is presumed by the concept to be non-reified is inevitably reified in the moment of that presumption [. . .] the analysis of reification is structurally disposed to find itself waiting at the end of every investigation into its most elusive manifestations.
> (Bewes 2002: 95)[13]

It is simply not sufficient to add in a footnote, as Swanson (2008: 66 n. 4) does, that 'antiessentialism can only ever be a partial affair, an effort, and never a full achievement because of the impossibility of simultaneously questioning all languages, practices, identities, and so on' because this means suggesting that the persistence of simplifications and solidifications in theories were due to limited capacities of information processing. The point, rather, seems to be that we deliberately condone the simplification of some aspects of our understanding of the world in order to rethink other aspects that we were accustomed to taking for granted (cf. also Oakeshott 1990: 25). Theorizing, after all, requires the cognitive fixation of meaning, at least for the moment, and from the outset the determination of an object of analysis ushers in an oblivion of greater complexity. And on this basis, reification and de-reification correspond to simplification and problematization, and are better thought of as two sides of one contextually conditioned cognitive operation rather than two temporarily separated and qualitatively opposed modalities of consciousness.[14]

2.4 Dividing Work and Switching Lenses

An obsessive concern with eradicating essentialisms and reification runs the danger of turning critique into an end in itself (Fuss 1990; cf. Brint et al. 1995). Haunted by 'the anxiety toward reification' (Bewes 2002: 115), we might end up as the pot 'calling the kettle black' and waste energy criticizing the critics of non-political accounts of the economy instead of concentrating on establishing alternative political accounts of the economy. While not renouncing the techniques of de-construction and de-reification, I suggest replacing the anti-essentialist attitude with that of pragmatism: the attitude 'of looking away from first things, principles, "categories", supposed necessities; and of looking towards last things, fruits, consequences, facts' (James 1996: 510).

Pragmatism does not grant theories intrinsic value; rather, theories are appreciated because of their capacity to deal with the world: 'Theories thus become instruments, not answers to enigmas, in which we can rest. We don't lie back upon them, we move forward, and, on occasion, make nature over again by their aid'. We can find out about the usefulness of theories, their 'practical cash-value', not by purely theoretical means, but only once they are set to work, and 'any one of them may from some point of view be useful' (James 1996: 509–11). The practice-test for theorists is like the corridor in a hotel through which guests have to pass if they want to get into or out of their rooms (Franke and Weber 2012); and in their rooms—the respective theories, ontologies, methodologies, conceptual models, and analytical grids—they are well advised to take temporary residence, not permanent refuge.

Taking a pragmatist stance instead of adopting the anti-essentialist attitude, we can demarcate conventional systemic perspectives from those that focus on the concrete interactions within the social institution of the economy. Instead of claiming the general theoretical superiority of one or the other, they should be conceived as different tools with which to belabour understanding. In sincere acknowledgement of their contingency and conditionality we should feel comfortable using different theories depending on the task to which we apply ourselves. At its simplest, then, the overarching conceptual poles of the methodological alternative I suggest may be characterized by demarcating a macropolitical approach to the economy from a micropolitical approach to economic life.[15]

Macropolitical approaches to the economy help disclose the workings of 'the rule of nobody' and explore the contingent normative and factual foundations on which today's economy rests as well as the ideological alternatives against which the economic space can be modelled. Macropolitical approaches, in a word, serve to reflect on how governmental regulation might channel economic behaviour towards more desirable directions, thus probing the possibilities for 'systemic transformation' and 'structural reform' (Dahl and Lindblom 1976: xliv) or 'institutional experimentalism' (Unger and West 1998: 11).

Naturally, the conceptual tools of macropolitical approaches are of little use when it comes to the subtleties of economic life. While the conceptual net captures patterned behaviour and systemic structures, it is too coarse to catch the concrete interactions and internal diversity within the economic space. Alexis de Tocqueville (2003: 820) highlights this dilemma, when he says that, unlike God, we humans cannot simultaneously survey 'the whole of mankind and each man in detail'. We face a trade-off between ascertaining the larger picture and discerning particular details; we are like the traveller that has left the city and looks back on it from a nearby hill:

> [H]is eye follows the contours of the city with greater ease and, for the first time, he grasps its overall shape [. . . But as] he moves away, the men he just left vanish before his gaze; their dwellings become a blur; public squares move out of sight; he has difficulty distinguishing the streets.
>
> (Tocqueville 2003: 479; argument reversed)

Macropolitical approaches provide a political take on the economy only as an object that is acted upon from the outside, from the realm of government, and perhaps to some extent from the broader public sphere. To provide an overall vista and establish the economy as a potential target of politics, though, these approaches are impelled to analytically condense the diversity of economic operations into one monologous practice. The effects emanating from within the economy, however massive they may seem, appear in the macro vista as one impersonal and homogeneous market power—as the unfolding of a logic, not as the result of human actions. The effects have a political character only insofar as they reflect the politics from bygone times and remind us of former governmental initiatives to organize the economy that continue to indirectly channel today's economic behaviour. Long before the economy can be depicted as a prison for the thoughts and deeds of politicians, it must be taken as a prison for economic agents. Macropolitical approaches are compelled to articulate a notion of the economy that 'appropriates individuals' (Grossberg 1992: 132) and turns them, in Marx's words, into 'social representatives' of economic relations; it leaves no room for substantial and ideologized individual acts, but only for 'inducements' (Lindblom 1982: 326).[16] Regardless of whether the analytical simplification of economic life is a deliberate methodological choice or undertaken out of a humanist fear, and regardless of whether non-economism occasionally appears to consort with a latent anti-economic inclination, the analytical consequence of macropolitical approaches in all these cases is a conceptual 'othering' of economic activity vis-à-vis politics.

A micropolitical approach, in contrast, sets out to investigate the economy not as an object of politics, but as a sphere that hosts interactions of potentially political significance. This approach does not take a distant look at the economy from the home territory of political theorists—the realm of government—but instead zooms in on life inside of the economic space. The focus of micropolitical approaches is not on economic structures but economic activities; not ready-made creations but rather ongoing social practices; not consumerism but acts of consumption; not labour but work. The focus is not upon the capitalist firm as a legal institution (as with Walzer's discussion of the Pullman case), but on the political working of particular firms. Thus, micropolitical approaches may still contribute to rendering the economy an object of politics—partially rather than holistically by fathoming possibilities to change the 'systemic' formation of the economy from within. Additionally, however, there is a broader interest in 'outward' effects. On closer inspection, the Pullman case suggests after all that economic acts can be politically interesting—not only with a view to the economic order, but also for social life more generally.

Notes

1. Source of quotation: website of the Historic Pullman Foundation, www.pullmanil.org/town.htm, accessed 19 July 2013). For an overview of sympathizers and critics, see Reiff (2000: 8) and Reiff and Hirsch (1989).
2. Robert Mayer (2001) finds Walzer's argument inconsistent because the subjection of residents in polities differs in one important aspect from that of employees in firms. That is, the liberal traditions to which Walzer commits himself suggest that membership in territorial associations is involuntary while membership in economic associations is voluntary. On the ship of state, citizens can only choose between staying and jumping overboard far out at sea (Hume 2006: 193). Firms rather resemble ferries, whose owners determine the course and destination port, enter the market to recruit a crew, and attract passengers who are willing to make the trip. Firms, therefore, approximate polities figuratively, not gradually, and captains of industry, unlike navigators of the ship of state, do not exercise governmental power. Though compelling to a large extent, Mayer's argument overlooks the fact that Walzer thinks liberalism is fundamentally flawed on this point, as he emphasizes that employees' choices when it comes to subjection are sometimes massively constrained. For instance, he suggests that the Pullman Corporation held a quasi-monopoly over jobs in the region even after having divested itself of all property not used for manufacturing purposes. People who needed to work to ensure their livelihood could choose only between working for Pullman and moving to another town, and if they stayed, they faced the risk that Pullman could choose to relocate the company should he deem taxes too high or confidence shaken in local authorities (Walzer 1983: 301). Walzer argues convincingly that the distinction between voluntary and involuntary subjection might be blurred in reality. The problem with Walzer's argument, therefore, seems to be rather that he cannot explain why this blurring should be the rule. Hence, his argument only serves to substantiate the claim that employees are to be included in management in those cases where allegedly voluntary membership is effectively involuntary, but it does not legitimate a general norm of industrial democracy.
3. Clearly against the backdrop of Plato's ship metaphor, Walzer (1983: 291) defines political power as 'sustained control over the destinations and risks of other people'.
4. For two studies that inquire into the ideological differences of non-political economic theories, see Marciano (2007) and Hoover (2003).
5. Lukács (1999) frames his interpretation of Marx's critique of bourgeois economics under the heading 'reification' ('Verdinglichung'), although Marx rarely employed the term. (Except in Marx [1993a: 969, 1020]. On a limited number of other occasions Marx [1990: 209, 1054, 1056] also employs the synonymous term 'Versachlichung'.) Because Lukács's usage is rather

ambiguous, and at times denotes cognitive and at other times material processes of objectification (Pitkin 1987: 264–71), I stick to the meaning offered by Berger and Luckmann.

6. Although I put emphasis on structuralist portrayals in this discussion, it should be noted that one can of course also find critics of non-political accounts of the economy who affirm that the economy as a human product is still perfectly responsive to government action. Benjamin Barber (1984: 6), for instance, argues that the people in a strong democracy are in a position to choose the economic system they deem desirable.
7. On the 'performativity' of economistic theories of the economy, see also Breslau (2003) and MacKenzie et al. (2007).
8. In this sense, Berger and Luckmann (1991: 52) clarify at a later point: 'The social order is a human product, or more precisely, an ongoing human production [. . . it] exists only insofar as human activity continues to produce it'.
9. For conceptions of the economy as a social institution, see e.g. Collins (1981b) and Fligstein (1996). It should be noted that physical objects such as resources, money, and bank buildings may also play a significant role in the functioning of social institutions. Warning against anthropocentric biases, sociological approaches such as the actor-network theory, developed by Michael Callon, Bruno Latour, and John Law, therefore suggest integrating non-human entities into the study of agency.
10. In her outstanding analysis of Arendt's concept of the social, Hannah Pitkin takes issue with the hypostasization of social institutions. Rarely, she finds, are social institutions sufficiently analysed against the backdrop of human practice, which is why political theory is frequently plagued by, as she calls it, 'attacks of the Blob' (Pitkin 1998: esp. 242).
11. 'Elective Affinity' is a concept borrowed from 18th-century chemistry, where it describes the tendency of two chemical compounds to interchange their elements once the two are brought into contact with each other. Starting with Max Weber, who introduced the term into the social sciences, political theorists have heatedly debated how the 'substances' of capitalism and democracy interact and whether or not there is an 'elective affinity' between them. Whereas Weber (1906: 347; cf. Swedberg and Agevall 2005: 83) rejected the hypothesis as 'utterly ridiculous', and Joseph Schumpeter (2006: esp. 296–302) believed that democracy would eventually dissolve from capitalism and reunite with socialism, many others (even Marxists) do not hesitate to reaffirm the hypothesis of an elective affinity between democracy and capitalism (e.g. Almond 1991: 467, Axtmann 2007: 112, Dunn 2007, Jessop 1978: 19, Robinson 2000: 355, Weitzman 2004). Friedrich A. Hayek's (1956) one-to-one transfer of the chemical concept to the 'compounds' of the Western and Eastern bloc is both elegant and problematic: capitalism and democracy gravitate towards each other, as do socialism and dictatorship; introduce elements of a planned economy in the West and you pave the way to serfdom. Geoffrey Ingham (2008: 60) also affirms the hypothesis without bothering to address the implications of the metaphor, and as if it were a clear sign of scientific progress, he assures students in his 2008 textbook that by now the hypothesis of an elective affinity between capitalism and democracy is no longer contested.
12. Darwin justifies the usage of terms like 'elective affinity' by referencing their capacity to foster understanding. However, he underlines the condition that '[e]veryone knows what is meant and implied by such metaphorical expressions' (Darwin 1872: 63). As it is questionable whether 'elective affinity' is still recognized useful an expression for a largely opaque relationship that is, in the strict sense, anything but causal, scholars are well advised to give

at least some indication as to what they mean when invoking the puzzling nature of this concept. Johann Wolfgang von Goethe, who allegorized and popularized the concept by applying it to human relationships in the novel *Die Wahlverwandtschaften* (*The Elective Affinities*), and from whom Weber took the term (Howe 1978: 371), can serve as a good example. In Goethe's novel, Charlotte and Eduard enjoy a secluded and idle life on the grounds of their rural estate. Things change as soon as they invite the Captain and Ottilie to live with them. During an evening conversation, Eduard takes pleasure in toying with the idea that human couples, once brought into contact, might be driven to dissolve and reunite in other combinations just like the elements of chemical compounds, because of their intrinsic constitution. By and by, Eduard actually falls head over heels in love with Ottilie, and Charlotte becomes fond of the Captain. Eduard eagerly takes the odd comparison as an exculpation of the imminent adultery and indulges his passions, but Charlotte stays in control and decidedly rebuffs the determinist analogy: 'These comparisons are very entertaining, everyone likes playing with analogies. But a human being is after all superior by several degrees to those natural substances, and having been rather lax in our use of the fine words "choice" and "elective affinity" we might do well to return to our inner selves and ask in all seriousness what the validity of such expressions in this context is.' Furthermore, she raises perceptive doubts against the chemical analogy: 'as for the natural substance you were speaking of, it seems to me that the only choice lies in the hands of the chemist himself, who brings them together' (Goethe 2008: 33–4).

13. The de-reification of one thing at the expense of reifying something else is palpable in Berger and Luckmann's discussion of de-reification. When they characterize de-reification as an ability of the mature and reflective individual who has not yet fallen into cognitive degeneration, one quickly perceives Western, patriarchal, and secularist undertones. On the one hand, reification is a function of naivety, both in humanity overall and in the individual more specifically, whose overcoming is 'a comparatively late development in history and in any individual biography'. Apart from naïveté, there is on the other hand a danger of mental involution, which results in the reification of the world out of inhabituation. Accordingly, the critical question for an individual becomes 'whether he still retains awareness that [. . .] the social world was made by men' (Berger and Luckmann 1991: 89–90). The stipulation of the possibility of an autonomous individual that breaks through the identification 'with his socially assigned typification' (Berger and Luckmann 1991: 91) and confronts the social world, as it were, from the outside, is certainly among the more solid and intransigent of reifications to which we are used to clinging (Bewes 2002: 197–8). Though deconstructionists are perceptive of this pitfall and take great pains to avoid it, in the wider intellectual sphere of deconstruction, reifying figures re-emerge in surprisingly overt ways. Teivo Teivainen (2002: 12), for instance, after making reference to deconstruction, goes on to dichotomize political reality and ideological concealment, serious politics, and spinning—a move that evokes the imagery of spatially-separated realms of true and false consciousness.
14. Methodologically speaking, it is also unclear how essentialisms or reifications could be identified. Burke Thomason (1982: 164) writes in his book about (de-)reification: 'our own methodological perspective suspends completely the ontological convictions which such condemnations clearly presuppose'. As the recipient is involved in the process of attaching meaning, the same sequence of words can fulfil opposed functions in different contexts. In other words, a non-essentialist theorizing that has taken the linguistic turn does not know of such a thing as essentially essentialist conceptions.

15. Drawing a distinction between micropolicial approaches to economic life and macropolitical approaches to the economy is attractive on the basis of its simplicity and intuitive character. Given the popularity of the micro/macro distinction (especially in sociology and economics), however, it comes as no surprise that it has been understood in ways I do not agree with. First, paradigm wars have been fought in the name of micro versus macro, where scholars insist that one focus is more fundamental than the other (Giddens 1986: 139). Second, it is widely understood that the commitment to a micro approach means focusing on the activities of allegedly free agents, whereas a macro approach can only grasp structural constraints. (David Throsby [2003: 2] criticizes such understandings as laying the foundation for the cognitive reification of the economy.) In contrast, I take the micro/macro distinction to refer to the different lenses through which we look at the world, rather than to different phenomena in the world. The respective approaches, therefore, might also be said to grasp the dynamics of complex social phenomena from either a top-down or a bottom-up perspective.
16. Throughout the three volumes of *Capital*, Marx stresses the insignificance of individuals and conjures up the image of an omnipotent economic structure (Marx 1990: 92, 254, 342, 739, 1053–4; 1992a: 197, 207; 1993a: 397, 403, 496, 958, 963, 1019–20). However, at one point at least he also unambiguously characterizes this grasp as a methodological choice: 'To prevent possible misunderstandings, let me say this. I do not by any means depict the capitalist and the landowner in rosy colours. But individuals are dealt with here only in so far as they are the personifications of economic categories, the bearers of particular class-relations and interests. My standpoint, from which the development of the economic formation of society is viewed as a process of natural history, can less than any other make the individual responsible for relations whose creature he remains, socially speaking, however much he may subjectively raise himself above them' (Marx 1990: 92).

3 The Marketplace as a Site of Politics

A micropolitical approach to economic matters, in contrast to macropolitical approaches, does not focus on the economic system and its institutions, but on the concrete interactions that constitute the 'system'. The occasional (re-)organization of economic systems and institutions through the democratic legislative process is obviously political. What can be said about the countless inconspicuous everyday interactions that make up economic life? What, if anything, might be of interest about them from the point of view of political theory? Just to get into a position from which one can hope to answer this question, a considerable theoretical obstacle must be overcome: 'the economic' is probably the most important concept of demarcation to have determined what 'politics' is in Western intellectual history since the ancient Greeks; yet the central assumption underlying the idea of a politics of economic life is that the economic and the political may well coincide.

In ancient Greek thought, Hannah Arendt (1998: 29) claims, economic matters were the constitutive outside of politics: 'whatever was "economic", related to the life of the individual and the survival of the species, was a non-political, household affair by definition'. This does not mean that economic affairs were entirely unrelated to political affairs, but the relationship was conceived of nearly exclusively in terms of a precondition. Labour and commerce assured people a living, and by leaving labour and commerce to women, metics, and slaves, citizens could realize the good life by devoting themselves to political affairs. The ancient Greeks were right to consider economic life indispensable for human subsistence and *a forteriori* as a precondition of politics. Any kind of human behaviour presupposes the ready availability of material and other resources that are produced by the economy. This is true for politics in particular because politics, far more than philosophical reflection, is a distinctly resource-consuming business. The effective wielding of coercive force requires an arms industry, and the dissemination of knowledge and propaganda require printing shops. Economic activity makes politics possible, and its yields can indirectly be converted into political influence. In addition to being a resource-generating precondition for politics, as pointed out in the macropolitical approaches to the economy mentioned in the previous chapter, economic activity is also conditioned (i.e., regulated) by politics. There is no theoretical difficulty in relating economic activity to politics; but the conceptual differentiation of the economic and the political seems to rule out the possibility of economic activity immediately and directly serving as a vehicle for politics.

Arendt, as is well known, affirmed this impossibility and stressed the non-coincidence of the economic and the political in her seminal work on human activity, *The Human Condition* (Arendt 1998). She conceptualizes labour (as the maintenance of one's biological existence) and work (as the fabrication of lasting things) as economic kinds of human engagement, in strict demarcation from action, which for her is constitutively political. Only through political action do people directly interact with each other and concern themselves with the world. Through work and labour they primarily confront nature and concern themselves with life. It is important to understand, though, that Arendt's philosophical categories of the economic and the political hardly match with empirical acts such as casting a ballot or working in a call centre. This failure of differentiation impels her to add rather elusive qualifications. She says, for instance, that 'while the public realm as exchange market corresponds most adequately to the activity of fabrication, exchange itself belongs in the field of action and is by no means a mere prolongation of production' (Arendt 1998: 209); or that '"economic man", when he makes his appearance on the market, is an acting being and neither exclusively a producer nor a trader and barterer' (Arendt 1998: 185). One may say that Arendt simply sorts out exchange from the field of economic activities, but this brings her argument into even greater trouble, given that empirical practices of economic activity in modern societies almost always—at least at some point and to some extent—involve moments of exchange. The problem with Arendt's (and the classical) conceptualization of the economic and the political is that it does not distinguish between formal and substantial understandings of each.

In Arendt's case, this neglect of differentiation might be condoned, as her interest is in identifying distinct kinds of engagement with one's environment rather than in economic life or in concrete forms of political action. For our present purposes, however, we must keep formal and substantial meanings of the economic and the political apart. The following sections undertake this double splitting operation in order to develop an analytical grid that makes intelligible the idea that an economic activity (formally understood) may qualify as political action (in the substantial sense). Section 3.1 proceeds with a differentiation of the economic and the political along the formal dimension, while Section 3.2 addresses the substantial meaning of these concepts, and Section 3.3 specifies the conceivable ways in which economic practices might serve as vehicles for politics.

3.1 Economic (and Political) Activity: A Formal-Topographical Definition

Economic activity commonly serves as umbrella term for practices such as buying groceries or going to work in everyday speech: 'Countless everyday practices are understood by countless numbers of people worldwide in perfectly ordinary ways as economic practices, with little need for epistemological contortions to justify that understanding' (Watkins 1998: 3). The same is true for practices of political activity, such as when we cast a ballot, observe candidates conducting election campaigns, watch parliamentary debates on television, or read in the newspaper about intricate diplomatic negotiations. People discuss economic and political activities without being informed by textbook definitions; and if one wished to elicit the underlying criterion, one would have a hard time finding anything more than a vaguely topographical one. As Giovanni Sartori (1973: 18, 21) says about political activities, they are defined 'in relation to the sites attributed to the "political system". [. . .] This is their political "nature"'.

This study relies on this ordinary understanding, with its topographical distinction between the political sphere—or, as I will call it, interchangeably, the *stage of politics*—and the economic sphere or *marketplace*. It uses this distinction to differentiate economic and political activities on a formal level as a heuristic device.[1] Practices that take place in the voting booth, parliament, or the seat of government, or other sites of the stage of politics accordingly are grasped political activities, whereas economic activities are those that occur in the corner shop, office, factory floor, or other corners of the marketplace. Thus, a general idea of what is and what is not the object of analysis should be provided.

However, on closer inspection, it turns out that ordinary understanding and the topographical criterion are rather vague. A moment's reflection reveals that the spatiality of the marketplace and the stage of politics cannot be grasped in terms of traditional geographies or by adding together a number of physical sites. Rather, the marketplace and the stage of politics have been moulded as socially-constituted landscapes that include non-territorial (such as electronic) spaces and temporally or symbolically divided territorial ones. The Agora in Athens was a stage for both politics and business, and the Penniless Bench, covering the whole length of the east wall of St. Martin's Church on Oxford's town square in the 17th century, served as a butter bench on market days and was the meticulously protocolled venue for meetings of the mayor, councillors, and freemen on Sundays and holidays (Postles 2004: 42 n. 7). Today, canvassing by political parties is conducted in shopping centres, while the floors of governmental buildings are paved with fast-food operations (e.g. the Pentagon, which has more than twenty of these). The topographical criterion, without embedding it in a substantial conception of the political (which will be undertaken in Section 3.2), is of limited use in clarifying ordinary understanding. Invoking it at this point as a metaphorical clue is justified only because it provides a rationale for disregarding a handful of practices such as lobbying and making party donations that some people would intuitively characterize as economic and others as political, and others as both, because they do not fall clearly into the realm of the marketplace. With the topographical criterion in mind, one is justified in considering lobbying as a formally political, rather than economic activity, because it is carried out in the symbolic space of politics. (The term 'lobbying', after all, refers to the hallways of the houses of parliament.) The same applies to the voluntary donation of money or labour to political parties (as we are used to speaking of work and money 'in politics'), the refusal to pay taxes, as well as less common political practices on the part of business actors such as Amazon's 2011 ballot initiative to roll back the online sales tax in California (Richtel and Kopytoff 2011).

As anticipated in Section 1.2, the various practices thus designated as economic activities can be classified into four categories: work, consumption, production, and entrepreneurship. Work points to the contribution of labour and services to productive processes for the purposes of making a living. It is helpful to think of the figure of the employee here, even though employment is not the universal form of work practice (others include, for instance, domestic work). Consumption refers to practices of appropriating, possessing, accumulating, and distributing—in a word, utilizing—physical goods and, insofar as it applies, intangible services. Production can be understood as (organizing) the conversion of resources into usable products, which may be either goods or services. I include moments of the economic process that, strictly speaking, chronologically precede the actual moment of resource-conversion (such as the acquisition of resources required for production) in this category as well as moments that follow this process (such as the advertising and distribution of products). Whereas production is linked to the running (the logistical, technical, and remunerative execution) of businesses, entrepreneurship finally refers to the setting-up of businesses, such as, for instance, by implementing a certain business model.

3.2 Political (and Economic) Action: A Post-foundational Conception

In the formal-topographical understanding, work, consumption, production, and entrepreneurship are economic activities, while voting, running for office, etc. are political activities. The characterization of economic and political action (or politics), on the other hand, must rely on more substantial motifs of contraposition. In most situations, there is no need to distinguish between the formal dimension and substantial qualities because the respective activities (in the formal sense) in practice usually exhibit the respective qualities (in the substantial sense). However, the central assumption of a micropolitical approach to economic matters is that this is not always the case: formally economic activities occasionally exhibit substantial political qualities instead of, or in addition to, substantial economic ones. The other side of the coin, but less relevant to this study, is that formally political activities occasionally exhibit substantial economic qualities instead of or in addition to political ones. After indicating the two most popular substantial conceptions of the economic, I will turn to substantial conceptions of the political and make transparent that the understanding of political action (or politics) adopted in this study stands in the tradition of post-foundational political thought.

The Concept of the Economic

Two rival conceptions of the economic in the substantial sense have been particularly influential in the past, the first of which emphasizes the results of action. An activity is ascribed an economic quality on account of its capacity to effectuate the satisfaction of needs or desires (Khalil 1996: 14–16, Marshall 1920: 1, Polanyi 1977: 20, Weber 1978: 63–4). Secondary criteria might be added. For instance, granted that basic needs are not the same as unmediated necessity, one might wish to include the elicitation of preferences. Or, one might demand, as Max Weber does, that an action's main impulse be oriented towards economic ends and that it be exercised without the use of force (Weber 1978: 67; cf. Swedberg 2000: 55–7). However, for simplicity's sake we may determine the core of this conception as relating to the satisfaction of needs and desires.

A second conception of the economic is constitutively linked to actors and their decisions. An action is identified as economic in nature when an actor is confronted with the task of allocating limited means among competing ends (Khalil 1996: 16–22, Robbins 1935, Throsby 2003: 1). This 'scarcity definition' underlines instrumental–rational decision-making for the purposes of utility maximization. Thus, it may contrast with the first conception in not only its rationale, but its sentiment as well. The slightly materialistic undertones of the first conception are replaced by an implicit exhortation to 'economize' and be 'economical'. Armand Salacrou once polemically expressed this tendency by saying that '[e]conomy is a way of spending money without getting any pleasure out of it' (Salacrou quoted from Lachmann 2006: 9).

The scarcity definition has been subject to fierce criticism; its lack of sensitivity to other kinds of reasoning than egoistic utility maximization, for instance, has met with disapproval. The general expectation of rational behaviour has also aroused the suspicion that rationality is at work primarily in the scholar who interprets any kind of behaviour (be it the donation of one's entire income to the homeless or any act whatsoever) in terms of utility maximization, therefore rationalizing it (Khalil 1996: 19, Sen 1977, Weber 1978: 65–6). In spite of criticisms faced by this view, its advocates praise the scarcity definition as having enabled 'economics to invade intellectual territory that was previously deemed to be outside the discipline's realm' (Lazear 2000: 99). Given its capacity to serve as 'unified framework for understanding all human behavior' (Becker 2008: 14), there is reason to consider this model as the mirror-image of the present micropolitical approach to economic life. Certainly it constitutes the best-known and most practiced scholarly approach to investigating substantial qualities (here, economic) in a number of different formally-viewed (i.e., non-economic) realms. Yet it is important to acknowledge that the first conception of the economic can be employed to interpret practices outside the marketplace with a view to economic qualities. Weber (1978: 64) accordingly states that 'every type of action [. . .] may be economically oriented' and thus aims at satisfying needs and desires.[2] Statements holding that client politics generally shape public policy or that wars are waged for oil rather than justice also show that this logic is not infrequently applied. Moreover, there is an important limit to the analogy. While the economic approach to social and political life based on the scarcity definition of the economic presupposes that political activity can always be advantageously explained in terms of egoistic utility maximization, the present micropolitical approach only claims that economic practices may occasionally and under certain circumstances (also) exhibit political qualities. One possibility of justifying this qualified claim can be expressed through the notion of overdetermination, which holds that social practices are constituted, contingently and to varying degrees, by economic, political, cultural, and other processes (Althusser 1969: 87–128, Resnick and Wolff 1989: 87–8, Swanson 2007b: 6). Accordingly, the quest for politics in the marketplace does not hope to unsettle expectations that formal economic activities serve economic functions. Economic activities do usually help satisfy needs and desires, even while economic actors might aim at maximizing utility, be self-interested, etc. If anything, the political approach to economic life attempts to dislodge the depiction of the marketplace as a site from which exclusively economic effects emanate, and to explore the conditions under which the exercise of economic activity might simultaneously take on aspects of the political.

The Concept of the Political

Substantial conceptions of the political have been carved out in contraposition to the economic. The most important motifs of contraposition are, among others, that political action is motivated by essentially non-economic intentions or carried out in non-economic modalities of action; and that political action yields effects that are distinct from the effects caused by economic action or that different kinds of rationality are applied. For instance, the defining elements of politics are considered to be its being is driven by a public-spirited mentality rather than private self-interest, that it takes the form of deliberation or contestation rather than competition and deals, that it serves to realize the good life rather than warranting survival, or that value rationality rather than instrumental rationality is deployed by political actors. Among the variety of conceptions of the political—whose discussion falls beyond the scope of this study—post-foundational political thought provides a particularly promising model. Post-foundationalism typically bifurcates the concept of the political, and theorizes it in terms of a non-coincidence of, first, those phenomena on the stage of politics that I introduced as formal political activities and, second, the operating principle of politics. Given that this post-foundational 'political difference' was itself established in starkly divergent ways (Arditi 2003: 308–10, Marchart 2007), it should be made transparent that this study finds orientation in the Schmittian rather than the Arendtian tradition.

The basic idea informing the 'political difference' in the Schmittian tradition of post-foundational political theory quickly becomes clear when considering Carl Schmitt's seminal essay *The Concept of the Political*. In the opening paragraphs, Schmitt (1996: 19–20) rejects his contemporaries' understandings on account of their equation of politics and the state. The modern nation-state, he affirms, is just one form of organizing the political space. Like the principality in early modernity or the polis in ancient Greece, the nation-state is just a historical attempt to capture and institutionalize politics. Each of these historical forms of organizing the political space sets the stage of politics in a specific way, determining which 'plays' are performed. Therefore, each set-up portrays different practices as being political and points to a contingent reality of official politics, yet none transcends its contingency or is able to describe the 'essence' of the political.

The political space mutates over time. Today, the political space already diverges from the Westphalian nation-state in that it includes the political activities of subnational and transnational governance regimes in addition to those of government and citizens. To come to terms with this contingency of the political space and officially-designated politics, post-foundationalism proposes relating the function of politics to the 'becoming-other' (Arditi 2003) of social spaces. In the final instance, accordingly, politics goes beyond a kind of interaction that occurs within a pre-established order and concerns the process of ordering itself. Michael Walzer (1984: 315), as noted earlier, characterizes this process as the 'compartmentalization' of society through the 'liberal art of separation'. Following Ernesto Laclau (1999: 146), Claude Lefort (1988: 3, 11), and Oliver Marchart (2007: 155), one may also speak of the process of reinstituting society.

The difference between (this substantial conception of) politics and (the formal understanding of) political activity can thus be summarized as follows: politics is the process of setting up and restructuring the stage of politics as well as other social spaces such as the marketplace; and it is the process by which society is formed and given meaning (in Lefort's [1988: 11–12] terminology 'mise–en–forme' and 'mise–en–sens'). Political activities, in contrast, are the forms by which politics are officially represented within a given social order ('mise–en–scène'). And while practices of formal political activity on the stage of politics may often serve the political function of influencing the process of reinstituting society, they are primarily a symbolic representation of this process and an attempt—and perhaps even a normative claim—to dominate it. The process of reinstituting society may nevertheless be co-enacted in other forums besides the stage of politics—everywhere in fact, which is why marketplace-based activities, such as work, consumption, production, and entrepreneurship, may also take on political functions.[3]

3.3 Politics in the Marketplace

Relating politics to the process of reinstituting society does not answer the question of whether intentions or consequences should be given priority in its study. Instead, intentions-based and consequences-based accounts serve different kinds of studies of the political, namely studies that are interested primarily either in forms of and possibilities for political thinking or in forms of and possibilities for political conduct. After all, sometimes an agent's plans cause a political intervention to fizzle out, while consequences need not be intended for them to occur or matter. This study focuses on the possibilities for political conduct, which means that the methodological difficulty of any attempt to 'look into the heads' of actors can be ignored, as well as the fact that actors must not be imagined to be voluntaristic individuals. However, it is much easier to imagine that actors aim at and dream of a reinstitution of society than it is to imagine that their actions could bring such a transformation about. Post-foundational political theorists frequently abet this impression by tending to reduce politics to rare moments of epochal change (Marchart 2007: 131). It therefore must be emphasized that politics is here understood as referring to the ways in which human conduct contributes to the process of reinstituting society, not the final result of a significant transformation. Accordingly, some clarification is needed about what conceivable contributions to the process of reinstituting society might look like.

To orient ourselves in regard to this 'horizontal' axis of the concept of the political, we can turn to Michael Freeden (2013, 34–5; see also Freeden and Vincent 2013, 1–2), who has provided a very useful assemblage of micro-components of political conduct, distinguishing six general types. Acts contribute to the process of reinstituting society if they:

A. Appropriate the locus of ultimate decision-making, including determining, parcelling out, and regulating domains and boundaries of competence among social spheres.

B. Distribute material and symbolic goods.
C. Mobilize or withdraw public support.
D. Organize the social complexities through which stability or conflict and disruption are manufactured.
E. Make policy and select options for collectivities.
F. Wield power (which cuts across the above five categories).

The first category speaks about the capacity of politics, emphasized by post-foundational political theory, to re-compartmentalize social spheres and alter the rules of the political game. Categories B–E are meant to convey what post-foundational political theorists have also emphasized against more traditional conceptions of politics, namely that political conduct does not only contest or de-contest one or another position in social conflicts and thus contribute to rendering certain collective plans authoritative at the expense of others, but additionally redefines antagonisms by reshaping collective identities (cf. Wenman 2003: 61). Schmitt (1996: 25–6) accordingly emphasized the ways in which it is publicly decided who is friend and who is enemy; Derrida's (1997: 116) revised and more moderate expression of this thought is that politics is performed through the construction of a 'we' and the simultaneous demarcation of an 'other' (Derrida 1997: 116; see also Beckstein 2011, 41–3). The last component, the wielding of power, is obviously a residual category. While categories A–E include a number of ways in which power is wielded, these categories cannot be reduced to the wielding of power. At the same time, not all manifestations of power, relevant in politics, are captured by categories A–E. Freeden points, among other things, in particular to the exercise of control over future social time or influence on audiences through verbal and non-verbal forms of communication.

This disambiguation of micro-components of political conduct reaffirms that the spectrum of activities that could qualify as political exceeds the range of activities found in the political sphere by a large amount. Many more practices than those formally (and in ordinary language) recognized as political are likely to comply with one or another of the six components. This does not mean that the organs of the state are denied a central role in politics, as many empirical practices that comply with one of the six components will either directly or indirectly feed into conventional governmental politics.[4] At the same time, this characterization of even those practices traditionally recognized as political, or as micro-components of political conduct, reminds us that, for instance, parliamentary legislation or governmental policy-making is just one intermediary (though often a very important) moment in political processes. Forms of political conduct at later moments influence how, how effectively, and whether at all governmental politics are played out. Quite generally, as Paul Ricoeur (1977) affirmed, the meaning of any (political) action is determined by its recipients in addition to its transmitters.

How do these micro-components of political conduct manifest themselves through economic activity? Which of them are irrelevant for capturing politics in the marketplace, and which are especially important? Can an economic practice influence the process of reinstitution of society only by influencing parliaments and governments? To find answers to these questions, a closer look at economic life is needed; hence the following chapters respectively focus on practices of work, consumption, production, and entrepreneurship. In so doing, the micro-components of political conduct provide an orientation as to what we must be looking for. But finding manifestations of these micro-components of political conduct can only be the first step in a discussion of the significance and implications of these findings, and such a discussion can be expected to yield insights not only about political potentials and realities in the marketplace, but also to specify, adjust, and perhaps rectify our understanding of the political more generally. Post-foundational political theory and Freeden's disambiguation of micro-components of political conduct serve the important purpose of indicating the breadth that a plausible understanding of politics must cover; besides clarifying the spectrum of possible politics on the 'horizontal' axis, they also indicate what the collective process of politics may maximally achieve, namely a fundamental transformation of the parameters of social life. Yet this definition of the logical endpoint of the 'vertical' axis of politics reveals the pressing need to develop criteria in regard to what an individual political action must minimally achieve to justify the attribution of political quality. Besides taking stock of conceivable possibilities for doing politics in the marketplace, a major task will therefore be to encourage reflection about a compelling conception of micropolitics that can adopt this function in the theoretical framework of post-foundational political theory. In discussing the politics of work, the following chapter makes a proposal for such a conception.

Notes

1. The decision to denominate the economic sphere a 'marketplace' is inspired by Karl Polanyi (1977: 123–4) who distinguishes between the 'market as a place' and the 'market as a supply–demand–price mechanism'. The purpose of this nomenclature is to relax the analytical grid, with its demanding strain on the *oikos* and *polis* family of words. In addition, it helps to insinuate the imagery of the seemingly anachronistic public sites of town squares where commercial exchange has always been saliently wedded to social connection. For studies about the social function of marketplaces, past and present, see Postles (2004) and Watson (2009).
2. In particular, Weber (1978: 65) argues that formal political activities may 'serve the interest of economic ends' and will usually, though to varying extents, be 'economically oriented with respect to provision for the necessary means'.
3. In this sense Marchart writes: 'antagonization may occur in any social subsystem, not only in the system of politics [. . .] any form of action may be

turned into political action' (Marchart 2007: 174; see also Arditi 2003: 308). It should be noted, however, that not all post-foundational theorists see an imperfect match between the political and its institutional formats. For Slavoj Žižek (2008: 194), for example, the contingently instituted political space exclusively represents the political. Lefort also considers the sites of political enunciation to be monopolized in a 'single gentrified sub-system', and the possibility of antagonisms as emerging in other social spheres does not occur to him except when he discusses the dangers of totalitarianism (Arditi 2003: 321; cf. Gould 1991: 338).

4. To repeat, this study does not rely on a state-centric conception of politics that considers practices only to be political if they are, as Sidney Verba and Norman S. Nie's (1972: 2) famous definition of political participation holds, 'more or less directly aimed at influencing the selection of governmental personnel and/or the actions they take'. The rejection of state-centrism, as most thoroughly theorized in the Schmittian post-foundational tradition, however, should not be understood as a particularly controversial claim. Thus, even Verba and Nie admit (in the paragraph following their definition) that political activism does not always need to take a detour through government: '[A]ttempts to influence the authoritative allocations of values for a society [. . .] may or may not take place through governmental decisions'.

4 Work and the World of Micropolitics

Work, Marcel Mauss once said, is a 'total social fact' (Mauss quoted from Zimmermann 2001: 16561). Work is an activity that human beings find hard to avoid: people need something to eat if they are not to starve from hunger, to clothe themselves if they are not to freeze to death, and perhaps also to find entertainment if they are not to die of boredom; and to obtain such things they usually work, which is to say, they contribute manual labour, services, or expertise to productive processes.

Nevertheless, work is situated historically and culturally, with what is considered to be work varying historically and across cultures.[1] Moreover, one might wish to distinguish a number of stages of development in the history of working life. For instance, it has been stated that working life was revolutionized in the 18th and 19th centuries by industrialization and the rise of the factory, while since the 1960s it has increasingly become characterized by automation and the 'man–machine dialogue' (Ehmer 2001: 16571). Yet both transitions are nothing compared to the Neolithic Revolution, claims Raymond Williams (2009: 335), for only with agriculture was 'real work, steady work, labor for one's livelihood [. . .] invented'.

The Neolithic Revolution may have been an important transition in the history of working life or even its dawn. At any rate, it is telling in regard to the changing nature of work that the two unsteady but nevertheless pivotal work practices of Mesolithic and Palaeolithic periods—hunting and gathering—are today often imagined as something in which people engage when they actually do not work: gathering is celebrated by avant-gardist economists as a subversive 'counter-economic' practice (see Section 5.4), while hunting often conjures a morally-controversial leisure activity or the unnerving job-seeking of the unemployed.

What counts as work has significantly varied throughout history, and so has the social meaning of work. It is interesting to note that 'work' has only been commonly aligned with the idea of value creation since the 18th century; at that time, we are told, the physiocrats successfully 'economized the concept of work' (Conze 1972a: 174). And whereas nowadays people gain access to society by having an occupation, in ancient Greece working meant being excluded from it. The Greeks saw the scourge of necessity in (manual) work (Beck 2000: 11). In Christian theology this view reverberates as the deity's curse of travail ('in the sweat of thy face shalt thou eat bread, till thou return unto the ground'; Genesis 3:19). However, the devaluation of work was never complete in Christian thought. Even very early Christian thinkers such as Benedictus of Nursia insisted that work was always also a service to God ('ministerium ex fide in Deum'), and thereafter the concept was gradually enriched by more positive connotations. In the end, the normative primacy of the *vita contemplativa* was abandoned. Engaging in work came to mean doing what is imposed by biological necessity, while simultaneously practising religious self-cultivation. Affirming this revaluation, Martin Luther seminally preached that a person's work for God is like a prayer, and thus popularized the understanding of work as a calling (Conze 1972a: 158–67, 1972b: 490–6, Weber 2002a: 39–46).

Much later, early socialists reinforced the anti-aristocratic resentment that to some extent had motivated the Christian rehabilitation of work. Henri de Saint-Simon welcomed the advancing delegitimization of aristocratic unproductiveness and celebrated the newly emerging society as 'industrial'—that is, industrious and diligent (Beck 2000: 12). Once industrial society had emerged, however, Karl Marx observed that only very few people benefitted from this general industriousness, while the majority were alienated from the act of working and the products of their work, from fellow workers, and finally from themselves (Marx 1992b: 322–34).

Given the existence of such contrasting social meanings of work, one might wish to differentiate at least between work and labour, thus gaining one term that rhymes with accomplishment and self-cultivation and another that is evocative of subjugation and the scourge of necessity. Hannah Arendt famously insisted on a distinction along these lines.[2] However, I will not follow her in this regard; instead I will understand 'work' as a technical category that is analytically delimited by the economic activities of consumption, production, and entrepreneurship, and employ the term 'labour' when referring (with no pejorative connotation) to the contribution of manual work to productive processes. Moreover, work will not be restricted to relationships of permanent and paid employment, as ordinary usage tends to denote when being 'out of work' means being unemployed and when 'being at work' is contrasted with 'being at home'. There is no compelling sociological reason to exclude domestic work, occasional jobbing, or begging from the understanding of work, as all of these practices contribute labour or services to productive processes or aim at generating a livelihood, and at any rate definitely occur in the economic sphere of the marketplace.

Whereas a macropolitical approach might direct the investigation towards the most recent developments of working life in the face of new technologies and globalization, the present micropolitical approach serves to interrogate the ways in which practices of work may serve political functions today. Section 4.1 will therefore offer an overview of the variety of forms of worker politics. A review of current scholarship on this subject reveals that worker politics are far from the verge of extinction, especially as new opportunities for individualized employee activism are identified. Occasionally, however, one might wonder whether signs of subversive behaviour are recognized a little too easily, as Section 4.2 will discuss. In Section 4.3 three conceptions of micropolitics will be differentiated that promise to give us a better orientation towards assessing the political quality of individual and individualized acts. The first conception is inspired by Antonio Gramsci, the second stands in the tradition of Michel de Certeau, and the third is constructed on the basis of recent writings by Anthony Giddens. Each conception significantly enhances our ability to theorize about politics underneath the level of great events in a meaningful way. Still, Section 4.4 will argue that we need to delve more deeply into the parameters of interaction if the notion of micropolitics is not to be squandered in the truism that everything is political.

4.1 Collective and Individualized Forms of Worker Politics

Industrial action is the classic form of worker politics. In fact, it is the classic form of politics in the marketplace. It is most widely known in the form of the strike (Hyman 1989), but includes also other forms of organized refusals to work as employers expect. Slowdowns, overtime bans, or work-to-rules are less visible but also less easily suppressible forms of industrial action. Here, trade unions ask workers to reduce productivity and efficiency, for instance by meticulously complying with management directives and therefore refraining from undertaking tasks that are customary but have not been contractually agreed, and which are thus not enforceable (Roy 1952). Occasionally, workers also collectively continue to work as before, thus ignoring management plans regarding redundancies or, in order to pre-empt lockouts, occupy their factory straight away.[3]

In the past, industrial action had various targets and was organized to exert pressure on the management of firms or more distant authorities such as the state. The action aimed at obtaining higher wages, improving labour conditions, compelling new state legislation in the face of inflation and unemployment, or pushing for reform of other social issues. The scale of industrial action stretched from intra-firm to cross-industry (general strike), with levels of impact varying massively. As is well known, the record of industrial action is one of both staggering success and abysmal failure.

Assessments of industrial action's current pertinence and predictions about its role in the future, however, stand in stark contrast to its history. Successes might have been exceptions rather than the rule, but commentators believe that in the future we may have to wait for them in vain. Pessimistic outlooks on industrial action are encountered frequently in the literature, and industrial action is reported to be dying away in the modern era. Perhaps surveillance methods and the ability to standardize workflows have improved; maybe globalization has reduced the dependency of management on the local labour force; or perhaps the segment of the labour force that has permanent employment increasingly enjoys material gratification. At any rate, the strike has become a rare occurrence, and in the past three decades membership in trade unions has dramatically declined throughout the advanced Western world. If successes alternated erratically with failures in the past, then today, observers suggest, it is 'all quiet on the workplace front' (Thompson and Ackroyd 1995: 615; see also Bélanger and Thuderoz 2010: 136–40, Kelly 2005: 283–5).

A minority of scholars objects to this conclusion. Even though the relative power of trade unions has diminished, it is argued that strikes, slowdowns, or work-to-rules have retained their capacity for promoting worker interests. In addition, unions have managed to develop new strategies to mobilize solidarity across national borders and act in concert with social movements—targeting, for instance, international agencies such as the World Trade Organization (Bircham and Charlton 2001: 340–1, Herod 2007: 29). A third group of scholars sees union action ending with the industrial era—as does the majority—but adds that new forms of worker politics have emerged:

> [R]esistance, misbehaviour, and dissent have not gone away with the decline of trade unions or organized industrial action, or the introduction of new technologies and new working practices. Unlike strikes, which were concentrated in particular industries and geographical locations, misbehaviour continues to be ubiquitous and, in many circumstances, is more difficult to control.
>
> (Ackroyd and Collinson 2005: 318)[4]

In contrast to industrial action, the new forms of worker politics are practised in the absence of central organization such as trade unions. To indicate this difference, it has been proposed that we should distinguish between collective resistance and strategies for individual misbehaviour (Ackroyd and Thompson 1999: 199). For reasons that will soon become clear, I prefer to distinguish between forms of industrial action and employee activism. At any rate, the study of these 'new' forms of worker politics reaches back to the early 20th century, and it is no coincidence that the man who laid the foundation for the study of employee activism was the same one who is known for having revolutionized management techniques for streamlining work flows and increasing workplace surveillance.

Frederick W. Taylor analysed employees' work performance on shop floors to draw up principles that would help managers increase productivity and efficiency. While conducting field studies, he observed that workers habitually worked less than they could, and was not surprised—since his study focused on the problem of inefficiency from the outset. But he was struck to discover that workers also reduced their efforts in a calculated manner and that clear behavioural patterns became evident, notwithstanding the apparent absence of collective organization. The 'natural laziness of men is serious', Taylor (2008: 12) reports in *Shop Management*, as well as in *The Principles of Scientific Management*, yet it is harmless compared to their 'systematic soldiering'. Workers arrived late, loafed about, dragged feet, took excessive breaks, and left early, in order to avoid arousing suspicion:

> So universal is soldiering for this purpose that hardly a competent workman can be found [. . .] who does not devote a considerable amount of his time to studying just how slow he can work and still convince his employer that he is going at a good pace.
>
> (Taylor 2008: 14; see also Taylor 2007: 15)

For industrial efficiency, these individualized, yet highly patterned practices constituted a grave problem, and industrial efficiency was the only criterion Taylor applied. Apparently not particularly interested in questions of shop morale or workplace struggle, he believed that it was in everybody's interest to cut the ground from under systematic soldiering by synthesizing workflows.

More recent contributions to the discourse of scientific management have extended the vocabulary for individualized worker practices that impede productivity. Extensive analyses of 'counterproductive', 'antisocial', or 'dysfunctional behaviour' have been provided as well as studies of employee 'aggression', 'retaliation', and 'revenge', with the terminology used in these studies imparting the message that recalcitrant employee behaviour needs to be managed away. Occasionally, scholars go even further and criminalize the discovered practices. To set the tone for their typology of 'employee deviance and delinquency', Sandra L. Robinson and Rebecca J. Bennett (1995: 555) employ a quotation from Virgil's *Aeneid* as an epigraph: 'Had I a hundred tongues, a hundred mouths, a voice of iron and a chest of brass, I could not tell all the forms of crime'.

By contrast, scholars with an interest in workplace struggle integrate such forms of employee recalcitrance into the repertoire of worker politics. Thus, practices of work limitation have been reconsidered as subtle political strategies to protect jobs by controlling shop-floor output. Acts of sabotaging production (e.g. by wasting resources, divesting the company of assets, lying about hours worked, restricting information from management, or quitting the job) are discussed as 'weapons of the weak' (Ackroyd and Collinson 2005: 307, Collinson 1994, Dubois 1979, Edwards and Scullion 1982, Fleming and Spicer 2007: esp. 28, Scott

2000, Thompson and Ackroyd 1995: esp. 628; see also Ambrose et al. 2002). 'Soft' forms of employee recalcitrance seem to have received the greatest attention. On the one hand, scholars observe employees escaping inwardly and mentally disengaging from their occupation. On the other hand, workers have been found to refuse to internalize the conciliatory discourse of company value statements or even to reveal hypocritical management pretensions through ironic parody and cynicism. For instance, employees rendered corporate culture absurd by over-identifying with it or, which occasionally amounts to the same thing, by following the official script to the letter (Ackroyd and Collinson 2005: 306, Bain and Taylor 2003, Bélanger and Thuderoz 2010: 138, Kunda 2006, Rodrigues and Collinson 1995).

These efforts have contributed to broadening the spectrum of worker politics beyond traditional forms of industrial action and more recent strategies of transnational mass mobilization. Nevertheless, management studies' findings tend to have been reframed and reassessed from an anti-managerial perspective, rather than thoroughly re-theorized as strategies of worker politics. The nomenclature is revealing: practices such as individualized work limitation or cynical dis-identification with company values are not subsumed under relatively impartial notions such as worker politics or employee activism. Instead, management studies' terminology is inverted. 'Systematic soldiering' and 'dysfunctional behaviour', for instance, are translated into 'dissent' or 'employee practices that have an oppositional or subversive intent or effect', or, with a tongue firmly in cheek, into 'misbehaviour' (Ackroyd and Collinson 2005: 305, 313). While nomenclature need not necessarily correspond to intended meaning, the terminological choice here reveals that individualized forms of worker politics are theorized as being inherently confrontational and reactive against corporate authorities.

Employee activism tends to be thought of as a defensive (though normatively progressive) reaction to aggressive and proactive (though normatively regressive) management power. However, the dualistic picture of an oppressive power and a pristine space of resistance is difficult to maintain. First, Jacques Bélanger and Christian Thuderoz identified management practices that nicely illustrate the blurring of oppressive and resistive power relations. What they call 'responsibilization' designates management strategies that aim to increase efficiency and control by handing over responsibilities to workers and empowering them (Bélanger and Thuderoz 2010: 144). Similarly, Hugh Willmott (1993: esp. 538; cf. Fleming and Spicer 2007: 39–40) presents a case in which workers' stultification of corporate culture simultaneously testified, in the eyes of observers, to the company's commitment to freedom of expression. Second, there is good reason to assume that the proactive and reactive, dominant and inferior sides of power relations often cut across organizational hierarchies. Management policies are likely to find partial support or even divide the labour force where workers do not share the same agenda. The promotion of gender neutrality or measures against sexual harassment, for instance, are sometimes backed by a number of employees, whereas others fear that the implementation of such policies will transform the workplace into a hyper-rationalized and de-humanized zone (Kondo 2002: 223–4; see also Ackroyd and Collinson 2005: 317, Fleming and Spicer 2007: 4, 32–5, 48–9; Thompson and Ackroyd 1995: 625).[5] Finally, workers might take the initiative and proactively influence the flow of power rather than attempting to contain it through resistance.

Scholars should therefore resist the temptation to reduce employee activism to intra-firm wage bargaining or some kind of anti-capitalist class struggle by postmodern means. Terminologically, it appears more appropriate to speak of 'employee activism'. Conceptually, one needs to add 'positive' forms of individualized worker politics to the aforementioned forms of employee recalcitrance. Positive equivalents of work limitation and sabotage might be practices such as the (re-)appropriation of time, the self-determination of one's work rhythm, and the extraction of material resources. Quitting might be interpreted in terms of an individualized worker politics of ideological career choice (see Best and Connolly 1982: 120–1, Fleming and Spicer 2007: 190, Giddens 1995: 91–2, 1997: 82). The public voicing of grievances and whistle blowing might be seen as counterparts to practices of withholding information from management. Not least, identity-related forms of worker politics should be understood more broadly as reconstructive processes of reinscribing employee identity and crafting alternative subjectivities (Ackroyd and Thompson 1999: 25, Fleming and Spicer 2007: 6, 35–8).

Table 4.1 Collective and individualized forms of worker politics

Union action	Industrial action *(e.g. strikes, slowdowns, overtime bans, work-to-rules, occupation of factories)* Mobilization of transnational worker solidarity
Employee activism	Work modulation *(e.g. work limitation, 'systematic soldiering', re-appropriation of time, self-determination of work rhythm)* Appropriation of company assets and the workplace *(e.g. sabotage, restricting information from management, extraction of material resources, humanizing the workplace, whistle-blowing)* Ideological career choice *(e.g. resignation, discriminating between occupations)* Reinscribing employee identity *(e.g. cynical dis-identification, role distancing, inward escape, crafting alternative subjectivities)*

4.2 Crafting Collective Subjectivities Individually?

There may be many forms of political activism in working life; yet does this claim not leave us in danger of 'banalizing workplace struggle' (Fleming and Spicer 2007: 186; see also Bélanger and Thuderoz 2010: 153, Kerkvliet 2005: 3, Thompson and Ackroyd 1995: 615)? An act of sabotage may simply satisfy personal revenge, 'soldiering' may just give a worker an extra break, and an act of cynical dis-identification with corporate values might just shore up one's moral high ground. How can we *not* see an inflationary use of the word 'politics' if anything less than complete compliance is taken to be an act of resistance? Moreover, the reviewed literature on individualized forms of worker politics is almost exclusively concerned with intra-firm relations, and does not consider whether the consequences of employee activism transcend companies' premises and unfold with broader societal significance. Should we not be more economical with our employment of political vocabulary?

The peril of diluting the notion of politics is most imminent in regard to identity-based forms of employee activism, such as role-distancing or the crafting of alternative subjectivities. Arguments that work has an impact on an individual's identity reach far back in the history of ideas. In the introduction to this chapter, we traced Luther's revaluation of the social meaning of work from travail to prayer. Luther suggested that an occupation is something more than an ordinary job, namely a profession to which one has a calling. On the far side of the Alps, Renaissance thinkers such as Giovanni Pico della Mirandola, Giordano Bruno, or Marsilio Ficino celebrated the creative productivity of the artist and *homo faber*. At the same time, they made clear that daily working life is neither reducible to reproduction (i.e. a striving for subsistence, which we share with animals) nor opposed to contemplation (i.e. the activity by which we surpass them and approximate divinity). Precisely because of its everyday and ritualistic character, as well as the idea of mastering a practice, they were able to detect a dimension of inward cultivation in the activity of work. Thus, Renaissance thinkers' theorization of working life testifies not only to a humanist turn but also reclaims the esoteric knowledge of gnostic, hermetic, and alchemistic traditions, which laid paramount emphasis on refinement and transmutation (Heller 1978: 394–412, 445–8; Yates 1999).

Far from being abandoned in modernity, the conceptual connection of work with self-cultivation reverberates in the thought of Karl Marx and Friedrich Engels. Work under conditions of capitalism could cause severe alienation, because work for them was inherently linked with a person's inner life:

> Labor is, in the first place, a process in which both man and Nature participate, and in which man of his own accords starts, regulates and

> controls the material re-actions between himself and Nature. [. . .] By thus acting on the external world and changing it, he at the same time changes his own nature'.
>
> (Marx 1990: 192)[6]

Due to the (identity-)transformative capacity of work, Marx thought that work would turn out to be 'not only a means of life but life's prime want' under more pleasant conditions than capitalism, namely communism (Marx 1989: [I] 87). Sigmund Freud, to mention a sceptical voice, did not look at work with such warm enthusiasm. But even though he interpreted the influence of working life on the personality structure as a neurotic denial of one's pleasure-seeking 'id', he harboured not the slightest doubt that work strongly shaped personal identities (Hardy 1990: 38–43).

The history of ideas is ripe with affirmations of the character-moulding capacity of work. However, and this is the crucial point, there is a large jump from this position to a theory of worker politics and, tellingly perhaps, the great thinkers of the past did not pursue such a path. For a theory of worker politics, at any rate, it is not enough to settle on the insight that working helps to form one's character. If politics refers to the process of reinstituting society, and if individualized forms of employee activism are to be political, there must be some link between the individual and societal levels.

Such a connection is rarely established in the literature. Bélanger and Thuderoz point to this gap in their review of scholarship on employee practices of cynical dis-identification:

> [T]hese covert forms of opposition were apparently only observed at the level of the individuals who were seeking to protect their self. The reader does not find evidence of any attempt among participants to build upon social cohesiveness (not to mention social organization, which does not seem possible at all in this context) in their search for preserving a healthy basis of social distance from the company.
>
> (Bélanger and Thuderoz 2010: 152)

To be sure, the point here is not to deny that everything has at least some political relevance for the process of reinstituting society; the commitment to a practice-based ontology in fact requires embracing this truism. What from a macro perspective presents itself as systemic structures, great events, and so forth, does not exist if it is not constituted by individual actions. Neither is the point that worker politics, identity-related or otherwise, can never be political to a significant extent. However, we need to clarify the conditions under which they are so. Hence, if we are to attribute political significance to identity-related forms of employee activism, we need to explain how an act of individual self-cultivation might contribute to the crafting of collective identities; and if we are to increase our knowledge about worker politics and other informal kinds of politics more generally, we need to explain how individualized practices can trigger broader societal consequences. What's required, in short, is a meaningful conception of micropolitics.

4.3 Three Conceptions of Micropolitics

There is no lack of scholarly reflection about the concept of micropolitics. In particular, three traditions of thought stand out and inform the present study: the theory of 'molecular politics' offered by Antonio Gramsci, the tradition of 'politics of everyday life' identified by Michel de Certeau, and the theory of 'life politics' of Anthony Giddens.

Many more conceptions of micropolitics can be distinguished. For example, Ulrich Beck's 'subpolitics', which will be discussed in Chapter 6; and James C. Scott's (1990: 183) notion of 'infra-politics'; Michel Micheletti's (2003: 25–9) theory of political shopping in terms of 'individualized collective action'—as well as the many more or less relevant considerations in philosophical and sociological scholarship that go by the name 'micropolitics' (e.g. Burns 1962, Connolly 1999, Deleuze and Guattari 1987: 229–55, Schippers 2009). Lastly, one may wish to mention those notions that political theorists have established *en passant*, as theoretical excess, or to demarcate and sharpen their understandings of the political (e.g. 'politesse', [Schmitt 1956: 149, 2002: 117, 120] or 'quasi-politics' [Hitzler 1994: 12]). However, investigating the particularities of a Gramscian, de Certeauian, and Giddensian conception of micropolitics is already a demanding task, given the salient lack of systematized analyses of the concept (and comparisons of the varying conceptions) of micropolitics.

Molecular Politics

Gramsci invokes the military experiences of World War I to understand the functioning of politics and inquire into the possibilities for overcoming capitalist society. He first reminds us that those who expected a swift victory with large territorial gains came back down to earth with a jolt. World War I unfurled as a war of position, not as war of movement, much to the surprise of the authorities and soldiers, such as those German volunteers who sprayed the slogan 'Trip to Paris' on railway wagons for their journey to the trenches in August 1914. Second, Gramsci affirms that a war of position neither takes place exclusively in the actual trenches, and nor is it won or lost there. In many ways, such a war is fought through supplies, through organizational and industrial systems at the rear of the army in the field, and by the home front (Gramsci 1971: 234). If people who want to engage in politics do not want to find themselves as unprepared as the German volunteers, Gramsci suggests that they should be aware that political life is usually closer to the paradigm of a war of position than that of a war of movement.

One insight to be gleaned from Gramsci's war-of-position metaphor is the reversibility of power structures, an insight that reinforces the aforementioned doubts on dualistic pictures of power and resistance. A marginal shift of the front line may have the ironic effect that one's own carefully constructed fortifications (institutions, discourses, practices, symbols, etc.) fall into the hands of the enemy, and are subsequently turned against oneself (Marchart 2010: 291 n. 2). Moreover, in the struggle for hegemony, just as in warfare, dazzling triumphs may only be ostensible successes, may come at a hefty price, and may ultimately be of little value. '[T]he Germans won almost all the battles brilliantly,' Gramsci (1971: 88) states in this sense, 'but lost the war'.

Of even greater importance is the lesson on the perimeters of politics. Just as the war of position does not take place in one officially declared, neatly arranged battlefield (it is not even confined to the trench system, including the main fire trenches as well as the support and the dummy trenches), so political power is not monopolized on the stage of politics. 'The state', Gramsci (1971: 238) writes, is 'only an outer ditch, behind which there [stands] a powerful system of fortresses and earthworks'. This dispersion of power, Oliver Marchart explains, challenges visions of an expeditious coup d'état that apparently clings to the daring expectation of seizing rule by rolling over the enemy at a stroke and storming the seat of government. Instead, 'the achievement of hegemony is preceded by a tedious, decades-long, if not century lasting [. . .] war of position' (Marchart 2010: 290).

Pointing out the anachronistic assumptions underlying accounts of politics as a war of movement, Gramsci primarily had in mind orthodox Marxists, who were waiting for the explosion of a worker revolution in the West. Visions of politics as macropolitical events certainly live on in sections of today's radical left, but one may simply think of the 'Obama-effect': the hopelessly inflated expectation that the electoral victory of one's favoured oppositional party or politician will prompt a sudden and complete break with the past (Marchart 2010: 295–6). Electoral victories are not meaningless, of course, and neither are charisma and the vision of authoritative personalities. However, even if such events foster change, realistic citizens must accommodate themselves to protracted political processes. Moreover, an event should be taken not only as the beginning of a political process, but as the result of on-going ones as well. In Gramsci's (1971: 57) words, '[a] social group can, and indeed must, already exercise "leadership" before winning governmental power'.

Gramsci's differentiation of the war of movement and the war of position draws attention away from heroized narratives of political struggles and towards an analysis of the concrete functioning of hegemony. Instead of romanticizing the most sensational representations of politics as singular and indivisible events, it invites us to delve into the inner life of political struggles and explore how particles of action are bonded to larger compounds, shift the front line, or procure supplies in the rear of the battlefield. In a word, it encourages rethinking politics as a 'molecular' process.[7]

Gramsci developed the concept of molecular politics with a view to shaping collective identities in the realm of cultural activity (see e.g. Gramsci 1971: 330–1). Yet one can find a straightforward and congenial theorization of politics as a molecular process applied to identity-based work practices in Aaron David Gordon's political theory of Labour Zionism (Gordon 1929, 1938a, 1959; see also Goldberg 1996). Writing in the beginning of the 20th century, Gordon considered hard manual work to be perfectly suited to the task of religious self-cultivation. Tellingly, he consistently employs the word 'עבודה' (avoda), which in Hebrew denotes work or labour and, at the same time, the temple service. Gordon occasionally even speaks of labour as a religion (Avineri 1981: 155, Yarden 1998: 323–4). In addition, Gordon was convinced that the spiritual self-cultivation of an individual worker synthetically contributed to the crafting of a collective self. In particular, he argued that work provided the solution to the preeminent problem of Jewish identity as he saw it, namely that the Jews were not a real nation. Only by performing simple, hard, manual work, rather than engaging in intellectual(ist) and commercial occupations, could the Jewish nation finally become 'normal'. The title of Gordon's German collection of essays could not be more telling in this sense: *Erlösung durch Arbeit* ('Salvation Through Labour'). Consequently, Gordon dismissed diplomacy-based attempts to create a Jewish state and instead advocated a much more hands-on approach. Jews should literally forge the nation with their own hands by taking up the plow, working the Holy Land, and erecting kibbutzim and moshavim:

> If we do not till the soil with our very own hands, the soil will not be ours—not only not ours in a social, or in a national, but not even in a political sense. The land will not be ours and we shall not be the people of the land.
>
> (Gordon 1938b: 60)

Empirically speaking, Gordon's theory of Labour Zionism is not completely outdated in terms of being a strategy for forging collective identity by engaging individually in certain kinds of work practices rather than others. The Israeli settler movement, at least, makes no secret of its aspirations and manifest attempts to sink political roots into soil and soul through labour.[8]

Politics of Everyday Life

Certeau's (1984) seminal work, *The Practice of Everyday Life*, paves the way for a diverging conception of micropolitics. Certeau recalls that Michel Foucault (1979), in *Discipline and Punish*, refrained from examining the localizable and solidified institutions of power, and instead inquired into the 'microphysics of power' (Certeau 1984: xiv). Foucault unwrapped the heterogeneous apparatus of laws, administrative measures, and educational principles, as well as scientific, philosophical, and moral statements, and other knowledge structures that endogenously constitute the disciplinary system. In a similar way, Certeau aims to study phenomena that are usually overlooked: 'the goal is to perceive and analyze the microbe-like operations proliferating within technocratic structures' (Certeau 1984: xiv). However, in contrast to Foucault, Certeau shifts the focus from the productive apparatus of government to its subjects, and the ways that they manipulate and evade the apparatus. Whereas Foucault concentrates on the minuscule mechanisms that produce repressive technologies of discipline, Certeau wants to bring to light:

> [the] popular procedures ('miniscule' and quotidian) [. . .] the clandestine forms taken by the dispersed, tactical, and make-shift creativity of groups or individuals already caught in the nets of "discipline". Pushed to their ideal limits, these procedures and ruses [. . .] compose the network of an antidiscipline.
>
> (Certeau 1984: xiv–xv)

Gramsci was of course also interested in small acts of resistance. Moreover, certain similarities in the use of physics metaphors are obvious. For instance, Certeau (1984: xiv, 201) characterizes the ruses of antidiscipline as 'infinitesimal movements, multiform activities [that] are homologous to that "boiling mass of electrons, protons, photons"'. Yet unlike Gramsci's molecular politics, Certeau's 'practice of everyday life' is not situated in the context of a cross-societal (counter-)hegemonic struggle. Certeau makes the limited reach of antidiscipline clear by distinguishing between tactics and strategies. Strategies are sets of productive acts that aim to renegotiate the constitution of the social order, which can be adopted only by 'a subject of will and power (a proprietor, an enterprise, a city, a scientific institution)'. As the agents of the 'practice of everyday life' are ordinary individuals, antidiscipline is only 'tactical in character' (Certeau 1984: xix; cf. Marchart 2010: 297–8).

Everyday life activities such as talking, reading, going about our daily business, shopping, cooking, and so forth, Certeau affirms, accommodate a rich arsenal of clever tricks for getting away with things—quotidian and impromptu ways to dodge discipline. But these are evasive manoeuvres rather than operative steps in laying an ambush, to continue the war metaphor. Whereas Gramsci's molecular politics facilitates marginal shifts in the front line and leads to real territorial gains, Certeau's tactics of everyday life only constitute a 'poaching in countless ways on the property of others' (Certeau 1984: xii). In other words, antidiscipline is unsuited for eventually becoming discipline itself: 'The place of a tactic belongs to the other. A tactic insinuates itself into the other's place, fragmentarily, without taking it over in its entirety. [. . .] Whatever it wins, it does not keep' (Certeau 1984: xix).

Due to this limited reach, Paul Ginsborg argues that Certeau's theory of a practice of everyday life cannot be regarded as a proper theory of the politics of everyday life. To develop such a theory, he continues, it would be necessary to align antidiscipline with Gramsci's molecular politics by stressing the 'powerful cumulative effects of individual actions' (Ginsborg 2005: 77–9). Thus by refining Gramsci's theory, rather than providing an alternative conception of micropolitics, Certeau's contribution consists of showing that tactics of everyday life assist Fabian strategies in a counter-hegemonic war of attrition. Ginsborg's argument is valid and there is considerable textual evidence that Certeau himself sympathizes with Gramsci's conception of micropolitics.[9] At the same time, it is possible to bend Certeau's theory in another direction, and thus acquire a conception of micropolitics in its own right. The key to doing so consists in emphasizing our capacity to reclaim the everyday, and questioning the frame of reference of the political. After all, the understanding of politics as a reinstitution of society provides no definite answer to the question of what exactly is meant by 'society', where its boundaries lie, and therefore what reach an action must obtain to be of political significance.

According to Gramsci's theory, molecular processes acquire a political quality insofar as they contribute to the struggle for hegemony between capitalist and communist forces. The ultimate frame of reference is the world order, even though the war of position happens to be fought in a multiplicity of local sites. As is quite common in political science literature, local sites, regions, nation-states, and the world order are thought of as hierarchically-ordered levels of analysis. The political significance of molecular interventions accordingly depends upon alignment with others until they reach higher and higher levels, ultimately touching the global order. Hence, for Gramsci, the political raison d'être of the local lies in its particularity, that is, in its being an incomplete part of an encompassing, more or less global totality. Without this nexus, local struggle has no political raison d'être.[10]

Certeau's theory invites reflection on whether the category of the local could itself be considered a 'whole' in its own right, in the following sense. Everyday life, after all, does not only refer to a range of quotidian practices; it also alludes to the limited nature of those realms that are of greatest existential relevance from the perspectives of individuals. Alfred Schütz's phenomenological–constructivist notion of a 'lifeworld' is the cue for conceiving of the local as a frame of reference for a meaningful theory of politics of everyday life.[11] Lifeworld comprises those territorial and virtual, material and mental realms that constitute an individual's experienced reality. In contrast to the notion of the local as a parcel of an objective global totality, the term lifeworld denotes a locality that defies complete subordination because, from the individual's point of view, it is a whole, namely the individual's tactile zone of operation. The zone itself is permanently in flux, yet the intersection of the lifeworld's coordinate system is firmly drawn around the individual. Events outside of an individual's lifeworld may, objectively, impact upon his or her life. However, in order to be palpable an event needs to impact upon his or her 'Lebenslage' (life situation), that is, the subjective experience of material and immaterial conditions of the person's life (Schütz and Luckmann 1973: 36–44, 51; Kraus 2006: 123).[12]

Understanding Certeau's theory of the practice of everyday life against the backdrop of the notion of a lifeworld reveals its distinctiveness as a conception of micropolitics. An individual act can be plausibly attributed a political quality even if it does not contribute to transforming society-as-objective-totality. By managing to evade or manipulate exogenetic discipline, individual practices contribute to the reinstitution of society-as-lifeworld. This Certeauian conception of micropolitics brings glocalization efforts and locally-confined interventions such as attempts to humanize the workplace to the table of political scholarship. And while the concept of the politics of everyday life cannot substitute other theories of macro- and micropolitics, we should think twice before dismissing it. Sometimes, after all, a revolution is not enough to substantially modify one's subjectively experienced life situation—in spite of radical changes in the political system and other landslide effects that objectively affect society as a whole. Those who insist on the exclusive validity of conceptions that focus on the global order rather than on individual lifeworlds might well be criticized for disregarding the fact that politics is ultimately a practical affair of the here and now; one that matters for real people and their very real lives.

Life Politics

A third conception of micropolitics, life politics, is sketched by Anthony Giddens. Giddens's starting point is his diagnosis that the end of the second millennium can be characterized by a trend towards individualization and the augmentation of reflexivity. Late-modern society, he argues, is characterized by a decline of belief in a pre-given order of things, with social norms that were advocated by authorities such as the church or parents no longer uncritically adopted by individuals, who instead increasingly question tradition. Thus, individualization and augmented reflectivity on the part of individuals has engendered a novel field of policy whose subject consists in personal and group identities. Questions arise about the legitimacy and desirability of concrete lifestyles where 'the self has become a 'reflexive project'" (Giddens 1997: 32):

> The political outlook of the left—and therefore, in counter-reaction, the right—has always centred on a notion of emancipation. Emancipation means freedom, or rather freedoms of various kinds: freedom from tradition, from the shackles of the past; freedom from arbitrary power; and freedom from the constraints of material poverty or deprivation. [. . .] Emancipatory politics obviously remains important to any radical political programme. It is joined today, however, by a series of concerns coming [. . .] from detraditionalization plus the disappearance of nature. These concerns raise issues of life politics. Life politics, and the disputes and struggles connected with it, are about how we should live in a world where everything that used to be natural (or traditional) now has in some sense to be chosen, or decided about.
>
> (Giddens 1995: 90–1)

Put in concrete terms, this means, for instance, that women increasingly question the allocation of subordinate roles in households and partnerships, recasting their private lives and, together with their partners, pioneering new kinds of domestic partnerships. More importantly for the present context, they also recast their professional lives. Women—but also male workers, apprentices, and students—rethink the importance they attach to working life and think about desirable careers (Giddens 1995: 91–2, 1997: 82).

According to Giddens, reflexivization has given a political twist to the question 'how should I live?' At the same time, he claims, new processes have been set in motion where the formation of personal and group identities are intersubjectively negotiated. The 'reflexively mobilised order [. . .] on an individual and collective level has radically altered the existential parameters of social activity' (Giddens 1997: 214). In general, 'the national polity has become only one among other points of reference for an individual's life', and people have 'many more options than they had before' (Giddens 1995: 15, 92). In particular, the reflexive rewriting of individual biographies is not a self-referential or solipsistic endeavour: 'Life politics is not, or not only, a politics of the personal' (Giddens 1995: 91). Instead, the individual development of personal lifestyles stands in a mutually-causal relationship with broader societal structures. Remaining faithful to structuration theory, Giddens argues that the reflexive rewriting of individual biographies readjusts authoritative role models, social norms, intersubjective identities, and, hence, collective biographies:

> The experimental character of daily life, it is important to see, is constitutive. How we tackle the decisions that have to be made in

> the course of our actions helps structure the very institutions we are reacting to.
>
> (Giddens 1995: 83)

In contrast to the Certeauian politics of everyday life, Giddens does not readjust his frame of reference of the political. Life politics is not geared to one's lifeworld but to society at large, even more so than in earlier times because, under reflexive modernization, 'more or less the whole population lives in the same '"discursive space"' (Giddens 1995: 15, see also 94). With respect to Gramsci's micropolitical conception, life politics takes a rather different form. In the Gramscian model, the molecular particles of action are added to compounds that constitute two sides of a hegemonic antagonism. In Giddens's model, by contrast, individual (life-)political conflicts are self-sufficient, even though they find themselves in a mutually-dependent relationship with others. Life politics is issue-based, cause-oriented, and evolves around fragmented policy issues. Agents, instead of sharing general party-ideological commitments, 'have a project identity' (Bang 2009: 119). The negotiation of biographies takes a form that cannot be grasped in traditional (binary) oppositional terms because life politics—as the title of Giddens's book on this subject proclaims—is *Beyond Left and Right*.

In their respective way, all three conceptions indicate plausible explanations as to how practices can acquire a political significance even if they are identity-related and individually enacted. The Gramscian theory of molecular politics counters romantic expectations that envision the struggle for hegemony in terms of collective agents and sudden eruptions of power. It invites us to descend from the macro mode of narrative (e.g. a great event, a collective will) to the micro mode of minute analysis (i.e. the complicated netting of small acts and individual wills). Molecular politics underlines the particularistic importance of individual acts. The Certeauian politics of everyday life puts emphasis on the fact that objectively global events are not always subjectively relevant for an individual. It scales down, contextualizes, and subjectivizes the frame of reference of the political and draws attention to those quotidian practices through which individuals meaningfully intervene in their respective tactile zone of operation. The politics of everyday life is a 'post-hegemonic' conception of micropolitics by virtue of its tendency to pluralize the process of reinstituting in society a multiplicity of (overlapping and mutually influencing) struggles towards restructuring individual lifeworlds. Giddens's life politics is 'post-hegemonic', too, but in a different way. It grasps the process of reinstituting society as thematically fragmented. It does not claim that work practices are of relevance for any particular political issue, but it holds that certain norms, role models, and subjectivities are renegotiated in work places rather than in other social spheres.

These three conceptions supply important theoretical support for making micropolitical sense of individual work acts and individualized practices of employee activism. However, while they effectively challenge the 'rarification' of politics, little effort is made to defend micropolitics against conceptual overstretch—what, if anything, is not political? This neglect is problematic because, whereas conceptions of macropolitics may consider the singularity and global reach of great events to be indicative of their political quality, micropolitics is located in a plurality of particular or quotidian interactions. It needs to be made clear when an act is of political quality to an interesting extent and when it is not; that is, we need to learn to better differentiate between the *presque rien* and *pas encore* of politics (Marchart 2010: 301). For this task, we must delve more deeply into the mechanics of micropolitics and reflect on the ways in which particles of action interact and link together.

4.4 The Mechanics of Micropolitics

The political quality of an individual act is obviously not determined by an intrinsic property. Politics is constitutively interactive and denotes acts that assume functions in complex webs of social interaction. Criteria that are occasionally suggested in discussions of micropolitics, such as whether an act is overt or behavioural (as opposed to merely cognitive), are not by themselves plausible indicators as to whether an act will significantly have an impact on political processes. Neither is knowledge about whether an act is intended or politically motivated particularly relevant.

A criterion for assessing political quality that is sensitive to this interactive character of politics is what we can call the adverse polarity of action. It is often implicitly suggested that a politically meaningful act should be at odds with dominant norms or established social institutions. Giddens, for instance, ties his conception of micropolitics to the causation of transformative effects. Individuals engage in life politics if (and only if) they question tradition and alter behavioural routines. In a similar way, Gramsci occasionally insinuates that molecular politics exists only if an act contributes to the destabilization of hegemony (e.g. Gramsci 1971: 172–3). Conditioning politics on change and the modification of the status quo, it should be added, is not specific to accounts of micropolitics, since theories of macropolitics also identify the political with global transitions or revolutions. Not infrequently, or so it seems, in political science literature change is used as a synonym for politics.

Perhaps the continuing popularity of the adverse-polarity criterion is due to past scholarly attempts to wrest a place for agency from structuralist theorizing; perhaps it also stems from a reified understanding of structure as constituted by stable entities rather than dynamic processes; it could also be due to the prevalence of emancipatory interests among scholars. At any rate, it is not clear why the attribution of political quality should be withheld from acts that prevent change. Take, for instance, Benedict J. Kerkvliet's (2005) study about the work practices of

Vietnamese farmers in the second half of the 20th century. The farmers caused considerable political effect precisely by not altering their conduct. By systematically playing the fool and showing reluctance to alter their habits, they ultimately prevented the implementation of collectivist agricultural policy. As a second example, recall those workers who struggled against the promotion of gender neutrality or measures against sexual harassment (see Section 4.1). Certeau's emphasis on antidiscipline might capture such cases and is thus to some extent helpful in protecting the conceptualization of micropolitics from an exclusive focus on change. However, antidiscipline is still tied to counter-hegemonic activism, whereas the conception should also capture hegemonic interventions that aim to stabilize the status quo. Conservative thinkers have always had a clear idea of the politics of consolidation and perpetuation. In fact, believing that desirable institutions, once established, are all too easily swept away by the tides of time, they have stressed that politics is not only about changing an unpleasant present, but also about averting a worse future. In short, adverse polarity is not a compelling criterion either; the study of the mechanics of micropolitics is incomplete if it includes kinetics but excludes statics.

Instead of concentrating on the phase of initiation of social interaction, attention should be directed to the phase of propagation, the dynamics proper. Little seems to have been written about this, and what has been offered in theorizations of micropolitics are mostly vague references to causal aggregation effects (see e.g. Giddens 1995: 79, 151; 1997: 214), Hobson and Seabrooke 2007: 15, Swanson 2005: 105).

Gramsci is slightly more explicit, but also attributes political value to particles of action only on account of their capacity to accumulate: 'an endless quantity of books, pamphlets, review and newspaper articles', where 'conversations and oral debates repeated countless times [. . .] in their gigantic aggregation [. . .] give birth to a collective will' (Gramsci 1971: 194). Elsewhere (Gramsci 1971: 109) he states that 'molecular changes progressively modify the pre-existing composition of forces'. It hence appears as if individual actions represent more or less even addends of a sum. This impression is reaffirmed when he suggests that only the actions of individuals occupying posts high up in hierarchies can unleash exceptional powers. Machiavelli, he argues, was just:

> a "private individual", a writer, and not the leader of a State or an army; the latter too is a single individual, but has at his disposal the forces of his State or army and not merely armies of words.
>
> (Gramsci 1971: 173)

The actions of politicians in offices are obviously privileged given their authoritative command over material and human resources, and also because their actions are staged as politics from the outset. But does the impact of the behaviour of an ordinary individual, writer or worker on societal processes necessarily equal that of every other ordinary individual? If it did, the idea of micropolitics could be reduced to the claim that everything is political: every person would always and with the same quality act politically, whatever he or she did. Any behaviour would be either discipline or antidiscipline, would perpetuate or challenge the prevailing hegemony, and would not be worth mentioning individually. This analytical impasse elicits the idea that a necessary criterion for (micro) political quality consists in the capacity of an act to break with the additive arithmetic of quotidian practice by exerting disproportional influence and driving forward a new set of dynamics.

Gramsci's imagery of physics and extremely minute particles such as molecules—despite its apparent ineptness for integrating ethological aspects such as interpretation, socialization, learning, decision-making, and so forth—articulates the difference that individual acts might make. From the physics metaphor Gramsci takes the insight that social change consist of an accumulation of countless particles of action. The water we can drink or swim in, one may say, is a compound (mostly) formed of water molecules. Of course, it is true that a single water molecule makes up exactly the same amount of a water drop as any other water molecule within that aggregate. However, it is also true that there is an incredible variety of molecules that fulfil entirely different functions within larger components. For example, a very small amount of hydrogen sulphide in a glass of water unleashes the foul odour of rotten eggs; an even smaller amount of plutonium makes a drink of water lethal. Within molecules, matter is even more complex, as compounds with the same number of atoms (i.e. compounds with the same molecular formula and weight) do not necessarily share the same properties because they can be joined together in different ways ('isomers'). The chemical formula C3H8O may refer to n-propyl alcohol, isopropyl alcohol, or methoxyethane, depending on the configuration of the atoms. Whereas the first and second isomer will have properties of alcohols, the third will have properties of ethers. Macromolecules, finally, raise further questions, as the molecule's folding in space becomes important (Massumi and Manning 2008: 2). Put simply, the whole point about nanotechnology—no matter whether physical, chemical, or political—is not to add or subtract particles at the scale of 10^{-9}m in order to incrementally alter the constitution of a larger structure. Instead, the point is to manipulate the structure in the right place and the right way. The quantity of interventions is not the key to reconfiguring the matrix of a subsequent series of processes, but the where and how of a targeted intervention.

The arithmetic that underlies nanotechnological interventions, we may say for simplicity's sake, is multiplicative, not additive. A straightforward example that illustrates the working of this arithmetic in political action is provided by 'Operation Payback'. In December 2010, denial-of-service (DDOS) attacks were launched against MasterCard, PayPal, PostFinance, and other companies that had withdrawn banking facilities from WikiLeaks in reaction to the releasing of US diplomatic cables (which itself is a rather good example of a micropolitical intervention that unfolded with expansive effect). Supporters of 'Operation Payback' downloaded a tool (predominantly the Low Orbit Ion Cannon) that multiplied website requests, or connected their computers with a botnet (a network of computers that can be centrally controlled by the bot herder), which allowed the organizers of the operation to draw from additional hardware resources and flood those companies websites with requests. Unable to cope with the demand for services, the websites of these multinational companies temporarily collapsed, with comparably few activists bringing about consequences that otherwise only masses of people could have achieved.

Whether an additive or multiplicative arithmetic underlies any empirical act in societal processes will, even if it is a matter of fact, be often very difficult to evaluate. However, we can access theoretical guidance for empirical analysis by distinguishing two sets of modalities of action. First, we can imagine the difference between an additive and a multiplicative arithmetic by considering whether an actor comments on an issue or frames it. Commenting on it, the actor backs up a position by adding another opinion or argument; whereas by framing the issue, the actor redefines the initial problem, pre-structures the range of possible solutions, and channels thought in respect to practicable means of implementation. Given its capacity to prescribe whether a problem exists at all, the art of issue-framing has been described as 'the supreme instrument of power' (Schattschneider 1975: 68; cf. Rochefort and Cobb 1994). Without being 'in power' themselves, issue-framers predetermine the options for which actors in authoritative positions, such as policy-makers, can utilize their power resources. As we will see in greater detail in Chapter 6, the employees of the Human Genome Project, for instance, effectively pre-structured policy-making about the scope and limits of genetic diagnostics and therapy.[13]

Second, multiplicative arithmetic can be discerned where a collective practice is prefigured, instead of simply reiterated. Though Giddens does not spell out this difference, it is implicit in the practices he generally conceptualizes as life politics. The choice of a lifestyle, role model, or career, on some occasions, may serve primarily inward functions such as self-cultivation, yet contribute little to the dissemination of the respective lifestyle, role model, or career. On other occasions, however, it may have a demonstrative appeal. Self-artistry, then, may mean comporting oneself 'as the universal standard to which everyone else must conform' (Connolly 1999: 146; see also Kogl 2009: 534). Such life politics might be interpreted as a deformalized and popularized remake of the 'politics of exemplarity' that medieval and Renaissance thinkers requested from political leaders on the stage of politics (Thumfart and Waschkuhn 2005: 68). The genre of mirrors for princes, after all, was based upon the assumption that more influence could be exerted on the masses by princes displaying virtues and leading by example than by the passing of laws and penalization.

Unlike mere reiteration, leading by example can transcend additive arithmetic because it means both adopting a practice and setting a standard. In addition, the politics of exemplarity may also put multiplicative dynamics in operation without realistic hopes or aspirations of ever rendering a practice dominant. As a case in point, Marchart reports from a weekly demonstration in Vienna against the inclusion of Jörg Haider's right-wing party, the FPÖ, in government. From about three hundred thousand protesters at the first meeting, the number of participants gradually decreased to the point of marginality. Nevertheless, Marchart argues, one would be mistaken to take the evanescence of protesters as evidence of political failure: even a handful of protesters was enough to prevent complete normalization and effectively testified to the absence of a consensus (Marchart 2010: 296–7). Thus, exemplary activism may serve as a symptom of repressed antagonism. It may also keep opposition to a public policy alive, or it may just publicly prove that the issue is contestable and not just a technical problem waiting to be solved.[14]

4.5 One Man, 3.312 Votes

Studying the relative power of individual voters, political scientists have found that the probability that a vote will affect the outcome of an election varies considerably. Political scientists have revealed that voters in large jurisdictions in the United States have greater influence on the presidential election than voters in smaller states. In proportion to the square root of the relative ratio in population, a voter in California enjoys about twice the voting power of a voter in Virginia. From a strictly mathematical point of view, it has even been discovered that the democratic formula of 'one person, one vote' for New Yorkers was effectively 'one man, 3.312 votes' (Banzhaf 1968: 317; cf. Margolis 1983). Regardless of whether these findings have interesting empirical implications or are flawed due to overly artificial assumptions, practices other than voting embody the real possibility that one individual can wield much greater political power than others.

So far, scholars of micropolitics have not paid sufficient attention to the different arithmetics that may underlie small-scale interventions. As a result, their conceptions primarily help to amend macro theories by showing that individual behaviour matters because, in the aggregative, it is the reiteration of practices undertaken day after day by countless numbers of people that confers structurality on systems and institutions. These conceptions are unsatisfying when used to establish a scholarly approach that does not subordinate individual acts to the bigger picture but rather looks at the former with a view to the latter. They ultimately fail to show us how we can identify the difference between politically relevant and political irrelevant individual actions. The arithmetic criterion proposed in this chapter, which requires individual acts to unfold with expansive effect, is one such tool. It allows us to discriminate between interventions that do and do not significantly stabilize the social machinery, catalyse or decelerate its dynamics, realign its course, or set novel processes in operation.

Concerning the subject of worker politics, the arithmetic criterion may serve as a warning that individualized forms of employee activism should neither be silently assumed nor vociferously asserted to be general substitutes for industrial action, even if it is unclear whether centrally-organized strikes and slowdowns will play an important role in 21st century politics. But the arithmetic criterion also suggests that a single case of employee activism may occasionally achieve as much as trade unions did in the early 20th century.

Notes

1. For conceptual histories of 'work', see Conze (1972a), Ehmer (2001), Williams (2009: 334–6), and Zimmermann (2001).
2. It seems that Hannah Arendt was the first to systematically distinguish between work and labour. She stresses that in contrast to 'work', 'labour' has always had markedly negative connotations, and is inherently linked with toil. The Latin *laborare* (in contrast to *facere*) has its etymological root in the imagery of a slave staggering under a heavy burden. The German *Arbeit* (in contrast to *Werk*) refers to violent effort; the French *travailler* (in contrast to *ouvrer*) received its meaning from an instrument of torture (Arendt 1998: 80). Note, however, that sometimes the term 'work' also has had a strong sense of toil, and that even though labour etymologically tends to have more pejorative meanings, some have prized labour over work precisely because of its simplicity, severity, and connectedness with the soil (Williams 2009: 335).
3. For a history of workplace struggles, see Kittner (2005).
4. For similar arguments see Bélanger and Thuderoz (2010: 136) as well as Fleming and Spicer (2007: 4). Stephen Ackroyd and David Collinson (2005: esp. 318) provide a useful survey of studies of workplace-centred forms of employee activism.
5. For a literary exploration of the ambiguities of corporate measures against sexual harassment, see the chapter 'Accountancy' in Alain de Botton's (2009: 225–66) photo-novel *The Pleasures and Sorrows of Work*.
6. Although I maintain that Marx and Engels did not carve out a theory of worker politics, it should be noted that Engels at least attributed effects of societal, and in fact evolutionary, significance to the activity of work. See in particular Engels's (1972: 251–64) unfinished essay 'The Part Played by Labour in the Transition From Ape to Man'.
7. Gramsci (1971: 194) writes accordingly: 'It would be possible to study concretely the formation of a collective historical movement, analysing it in all its molecular phases. [. . .] Instead, currents of opinion are normally taken as already constituted around a group or a dominant personality. This is the problem which in modern times is expressed in terms of the party, or coalition of related parties: how a party is first set up, how its organizational

strength and social influence are developed, etc. It requires an extremely minute, molecular process of exhaustive analysis in every detail, the documentation of which is made up of an endless quantity of books, pamphlets, review and newspaper articles, conversations and oral debates repeated countless times, and which in their gigantic aggregation represent this long labour which gives birth to a collective will'.

8. Gordon's romantic-nationalist notion of 'national labor' was not unfamiliar to that of his contemporaries in the late 19th and early 20th centuries. Karl Thomas Richter (1875: 12–13), for instance, described work as an activity that 'puts its stamp on the human character, makes the nation'. Wilhelm Heinrich Riehl (1862: 108) maintained that work allows for 'developing the personality of the People'. See also Conze (1972a: 210).
9. Desisting from speaking of politics, de Certeau (1984: xvii) attributes only a 'political dimension' to the tactics of everyday life. In other passages, he insinuates that these can acquire positively productive qualities akin to Gramsci's molecular politics. For instance, he describes the mass of seemingly defensive everyday practices as 'illusory inertia', as 'ways of reappropriating the product-system', or else integrates them into 'the mute processes that organize the establishment of socioeconomic order' (Certeau 1984: xxii–xxiv, 201).
10. The logical model underlying such accounts, which subordinate local multiplicities to a territorial One, can be characterized, following Gilles Deleuze and Félix Guattari (2009: 503–10), as 'arboreal assemblage'. Local political struggles can accordingly be imagined as secondary (or tertiary, etc.) levels on a hierarchical tree-structure, where a number of nodes are child to a parent node, which itself merges together with its siblings into an ancestor of a still higher level up to the root node. See also Khan (2008).
11. Edmund Husserl introduced the term 'lifeworld' into phenomenology as the primordial setting that pre-structures an individual's experience of the world (1984: Part III). The concept bears similarities with Martin Heidegger's 'being-in-the-world' and Wittgenstein's 'forms of life'. Jürgen Habermas (2005: Chapter VI: 'Lifeworld and system'), among others, has replenished Husserl's egological conception by giving it a social and communicative dimension, with the result that the lifeworld appears as that which embeds consciousness in a subjectively perceived, yet intersubjectively negotiated, experience. Alfred Schütz relied upon the concept in working towards a theory whose primary concern consisted in the theorization of subjectively-meaningful action (Schütz and Luckmann 1973). For an interpretation of Schütz's conception of lifeworld, see Eberle (1984). For a conceptual history of lifeworld, see Bermes (2002).
12. The concept of lifeworld constitutes one possible way of liberating the local from subordination under a global totality. For a comparative overview of alternative deconstructions of the local/global dualism, see Gibson-Graham (2002).
13. Ironic or not, the emergence of nanotechnology as the latest research priority in physics and chemistry has itself been criticized as hype created by strategies of issue-framing and problem definition (Glimmel 2005).
14. At one point Gramsci also refers to a case of exemplary politics. Notably, in this case the function of exemplarity is not one of obtaining the majority. Anarchism, says Gramsci, is a political movement that largely relies upon means of exemplarity. Anarchists would even conceive of terrorist acts as 'propaganda by example', where the specificity of their exemplary politics is the absence of direct hegemonic aspirations. The anarchist movement, Gramsci (1971: 149) writes, exists only 'on the margin of the other parties, "to educate them"'.

5 Shopping for Change?

Consumption, formally understood in terms of a microeconomic activity, refers to practices of appropriating, possessing, accumulating, and distributing—in a word, utilizing—physical goods and intangible services. The consumption of goods and services meets basic needs and fulfils desires; as such, we all necessarily engage in practices of consumption. Consumption is inevitable, even if people consume different products, different quantities and qualities thereof, and obtain them from different providers and economies.[1] Given the centrality of consumption in daily life, recent commentators have found it striking that scholars of politics have had little to say about it for so long. For some time, when scholars of politics addressed consumption, they appear to have instantaneously thought of it as a pathological phenomenon of late modernity (Humphery 2010: 16, Prinz 2003: 13). In the more recent literature, by contrast, consumption activities are not infrequently considered a potent source of politics. In fact, some believe that it might turn out to be the main form of political mass participation of the 21st century.

In this chapter I will first give a brief summary of these two contrasting positions on consumption, in the form of simplified narratives (Section 5.1), though I do acknowledge that more positions could be distinguished. Tim Edwards (2000: 11), for instance, identifies five ways of characterizing the consumer; Yiannis Gabriel and Tim Lang (2006) even depict ten different consumer-types.

However, rather than overcomplicating the debate, the goal of the following discussion is to demarcate the main poles of scholarship on consumption. In a second step, some specific arguments offered by consumption 'pessimists' are considered more closely, in order to probe the claim of 'optimists' that consumption activity serves as an alternative means of engaging in politics (Sections 5.2 and 5.3). While the optimists' claims will be affirmed, albeit with reservations, I argue in a third step that scholarship needs to take the vast diversity of consumption practices more seriously if a clearer understanding of the political possibilities of consumption activity is to be achieved (Sections 5.4 and 5.5).

5.1 Narratives of Consumption

The history of ideas has more than one story to tell regarding the political significance of consumption. Yet perhaps, one of the most interesting stories is that there is no story to tell at all: that is, a number of recent commentators report a deafening silence on consumption in politics-related academic writing. They argue that consumption has been 'neglected, under-theorized, treated as an exogenous, structural category, and granted "agency" or transformative power, only in the atomistic abstract terms of demand' (Goodman 2002: 272; see also Bauman 2007: 53–4, Edwards 2000: 16, 128; Ritzer et al. 2007: 425 n. 1). Karl Marx certainly considered consumption to be crucial to economic life, if only because 'without consumption there can be no production' (Marx 1992b: 362). Yet neither Marx nor his followers deemed consumption to be as worthy of consideration as production, to say the least. The question of what consumption actually means for the individual and society more generally took a back seat as theorizing about the conditions for seizing control of the means of production came to the fore. Hopes of transforming the relationship between capitalist and worker were pinned on immediate labour processes; possibilities for carrying out political struggles were sought on the shop floor, not the shopping floor. Economically speaking, the 19th and early 20th centuries were defined by changes in the modes of production; it is thus understandable that Marx and his followers, as well as many others, devoted most of their attention to this dimension of economic processes. Nevertheless, it is far from excessive to speak of a 'producerist bias' (Ritzer et al. 2007: 411).[2]

To some extent, this perceived neglect of consumption analysis is due to the fact that the utilization of goods and services has only recently been examined under the term 'consumption'. Historically, 'consumption' was popularly applied to a 'wasting away', the '[w]asteful expenditure (of time, money, etc.)', or synonymously used to mean 'destruction'. In medicine, moreover, the term served to denote diseases that cause a wasting of the body, specifically tuberculosis ('thou most fatal of Pandora's train, Consumption!' Henry Kirke White versified). Based on the association with destruction and decay, 'consumption' was introduced as a technical term in economics to signify that by utilizing goods consumers withdraw assets from the general economic process. Reasonably considered, of course, the utilization of goods is the goal of economic processes, but, economically speaking, it puts an end to them.[3]

The first narrative concerning the political significance of economic consumption activity draws its inspiration from the etymology of the term. Unlike in economics, however, the meaning of the terms destruction and decay is taken in a much less technical sense. In particular, the historical meanings that developed from its use in the medical field are recalled in order to indicate the societal effects invoked by consumption activity. Thus, rather than an individual activity, consumption is thought of as a collective pathology of capitalist mass society, as over-consumption or (hyper-)consumerism: at its root it is 'a painful, contagious, socially-transmitted condition of overload, debt, anxiety and waste resulting from the dogged pursuit of more' (Graaf et al. 2005: 2).

In this narrative, people fall prey to the lures of advertising as well as the attractions of packaging, and are 'infected by consumerism' (Carlo Petrini quoted from Grefe 2011: 18); they are enticed, ensnared, seduced, and debouched by blatant or surreptitious, but invariably fraudulent and extraneous, pressures (Bauman 2007: 1, Slater 2005: 33). The preoccupation with commodities turns shoppers into 'shopaholics' who want to return to the 'consumer temples' the very moment they leave, even if they realize that they have purchased things they do not need. True, says Benjamin Barber (2007: 4), people have a choice about whether to seek satisfaction through material gratification; but he adds that 'pathologies of liberty' can be as perilous as 'pathologies of tyranny', such that through consuming, consumers eventually consume themselves. To the degree that inhibitions against materialism, individualism, and hedonism are lost, the motivation for civic engagement drains away: the citizen in people is 'used up' (Hobsbawm 2009: 104). Thus, there is an obvious social significance to consumption, but it does not give rise to optimism. Consumption as pathological consumerism is 'regarded as the cause of, rather than the cure for, society's ills' (Hilton 2007: 121); rather than empowering people, it 'tranquilizes' them.[4]

In the second narrative, the consumer is not a helpless victim and cultural dupe but, in contrast, a reflective, self-asserting individual. Advertisers are not 'hidden persuaders' (Packard 2007) who induce desires through subliminal stimuli; rather they fulfil the function of historians of their times who seek to grasp the mentality and desires of their contemporaries (Lears 1994: 229, Marchand 2008). And if the conception of consumption as a pathology is inextricably linked to the collective phenomenon of consumerism, the second position stands out against the backdrop of another macro-category, namely the idea of 'consumer sovereignty'.

When William Hutt (1940: 70) coined the term 'consumer sovereignty', he wanted to express the idea that consumers ultimately rule the (market) economy, and therefore can be seen as analogous to members of a democratic polity. Entrepreneurs may steer the economy, yet they take orders from consumers, who unmistakably express, through the language of money, what is to be produced. Insofar as demand actually determines supply, there is some sense in comparing consumers—more precisely, the collective consumer—of a market economy to the people of a democratic polity. Advocates of the second narrative on the political significance of consumption activity, however, assume that the analogy also applies at the individual level. The individual consumer is characterized as a citizen, namely a 'citizen-consumer' (Scammel 2000: 354), and acts of consumption are portrayed as an alternative to going to the polls:

> [T]here is a remarkable structural homology between democratic elections and consumptions choices [. . .] the act of shopping allows for the timely expression of highly specialized and individualized preferences—including aesthetic, religious and political ones. For the individual consumer, political consumerism comes close to a 'very immediate democratic process'.
>
> (Holzer 2006: 413, quoting Nava 1991: 168)

Noreena Hertz goes a step further, claiming that shopping is actually the better alternative, and that it would be a replacement for voting: 'Shop, don't vote!', she recommends to her readers. 'Politics has gone on sale; consumer politics is the real new politics' (Hertz 1999, 2002: 141).[5]

As in studies of worker politics, the additive arithmetic implicit in judgments about the relevance of individual shopping activity is not recognized as a methodological flaw. To remedy this flaw and show that consumer politics is the real new politics, or at least some kind of politics, one would have to specify the conditions under which individual shopping acts cause multiplicative effects, as argued in the last chapter. In addition, the notion of shopping in these works notably contains no allusion to materialistic self-gratification and the obsessive shopping sprees with which it is commonly associated. Perhaps it is a less traditionally gendered category than previously thought (Edwards 2000: 10). At any rate, the shopper-citizen displays many of the virtues modernity worships, such as self-assertion and autonomy. The consumer rationally chooses, after having investigated the social and normative contexts in which material products are embedded. When it comes to the traditional economics actor, there is only one difference between him and the shopper, according to advocates of this view: the 'ideal-type Egoistic Economic Man [is] modified to an ideal-type Responsibility-Taking Political Consumer' (Micheletti et al. 2006a: xiv).

5.2 Supermarket Activism and What Else?

As striking as this enthusiasm about the empowering capacity of consumption is the unhesitating reduction of consumption to shopping in the second narrative just reviewed. In fact, the delimitation of consumption to shopping is a highly pervasive feature in those strands of scholarship that assert that consumption activity offers opportunities for political agency. The titles of prominent books, book chapters, and articles on this subject are telling: *Supermarket Activism* (Hertz 2002: 145–58), *Political Virtue and Shopping* (Micheletti 2003), *Politics in the Supermarket* (Stolle et al. 2005), *Politik mit dem Einkaufswagen* ('Politics with the shopping trolley' [Baringhorst et al. 2007]), and *Radical Consumption: Shopping for Change* (Littler 2009), for example. In each of these cases, shopping is used *pars pro toto* and intended to stand for consumption activity in general. The terminological constriction is deliberate and employed as a figure of speech, which can be inferred from the fact that examples of other consumption practices are commonly included in the discussion. Nevertheless, there is a problematic tendency here: not only are other practices of consumption discussed under the title of shopping, but their political significance is investigated according to the conditions of shopping practices. In other words, employing a rhetorical device that uses a part to stand for the whole faces the danger of eventually thinking the whole through the part.

No doubt buying food in the supermarket and clothes on the high street are acts of consumption, which should therefore be examined in the context of scholarship on the political dimensions of this economic activity. Yet the context in which shopping takes place is peculiar, and differs significantly from other consumption practices in which people engage. By thinking of consumption through shopping we curtail ourselves to long-term routine behaviours. Moreover, shopping is acted out in one register (by the use of money, not by symbolical means), takes place in one kind of economy (the official economy, not grey markets or the black market), and concerns one kind of economic sector (the sector of manufactured goods, not the sector of services). Shopping addresses only some targets (entrepreneur and producer practices, rather than consumer practices or products and brands), can be better instrumentalized by certain segments of society (the economically secure—less so by the poor), and, finally, serves a limited range of ideological causes (namely, only those that accept the currently established official economy). In short, refraining from investigating consumption activity only via shopping requires a rethinking in terms of both breadth and depth. If we are to obtain greater clarity about the ability of consumption to take on political functions (in short: political consumption), we need to take into account the variety of consumer activities.

For instance, boycotts (and buycotts) are forms of political consumption that are more short-term and event-like than supermarket activism (Friedman 1999). A modification of consumption behaviour is undertaken only temporarily; habits are suspended rather than altered. Instead of directly coercing a change in supply, the goal is social ostracism. While less demanding in a behavioural sense, a boycott is more demanding in terms of organization. The window of opportunity for boycotts is short and only occurs in special conditions; it must be exploited as long as the public's attention span can be stretched. Moreover, because boycotts are not necessarily related to a real change in shopping behaviour but instead require a temporary, though concerted, suspension (be it for single day) of a consumption habit, they are more likely than shopping activism to be utilized by the poor.

Monetary rewards or refusals to purchase specific products are a straightforward way of signalling support or rejection of producers; however, approval or dissent can also be expressed by semiotic rather than material means, or in Hirschman's terms 'voice' rather than 'exit' (Hirschman, 1981: 4; see also Fiske 2009: 566).[6] Web 2.0 commerce, for instance, provides platforms for individual consumers to voice their disappointment, appreciation, or demands to manufacturers or providers of services. In addition, consumers can address other consumers directly, and there is potential power in the fact that many firms rely upon their reputation at least as much as they do on the quality of their products, whereas they have much less control over the former than the latter. Consumers can thus exploit this potential to co-market products and co-create brands (Certeau 1984: esp. xiii, Nava 1991: 163–6, Ritzer et al. 2007: 415–17, Simons 2005: 158–61). Marketers have always known that consumers, when flaunting their brand-name clothes in school, on the street, or other social settings, influence the social attributes of these products. They have also always known that this is done for 'better or worse', depending on who flaunts them, where, and how. In recent years, they have also been forced to face the fact that they might not have exclusive control over the representation of their products in advertisements. 'Culture jammers' and online 'hacktivists' have devised new strategies and rediscovered practices already common in the first half of the 20th century that aim to alter product messages by parodying or distorting advertisements, brand names, or logos (Lasn 2000).

In distorting advertisements, activists hope that slight modifications in the symbolic representations of products will drastically alter the reputation of the associated firms. As such, culture jammers take up Saul Alinsky's theory of 'political jujitsu', which holds that activists without hard power can still forcefully intervene in the process of reinstituting society by 'utilizing the power of one part of the power structure against another part' (Alinsky 1989: 148; cf. Klein 2010: 281). In the knowledge of their relative weakness, culture jammers attempt to use the momentum of producers' iconocentrism against themselves.

A good example of political consumer jujitsu is the case of the Nike sweatshop email (Peretti 2006). In 2000, Nike aimed to strengthen its image by linking Nike products to liberty and individuality. The corporation launched the NIKEiD campaign, an online service that provides personalized shoes. The programme was advertised as being 'about freedom to choose and freedom to express who you are', where customers were invited to select styles and colours, and to have their names or other messages written on the sides of their shoes. However, a student challenged Nike and requested a pair of shoes customized with the word 'sweatshop'. Nike, unsurprisingly, refused. However, eventually the firm had to resort to rather tenuous arguments ('material [. . .] we simply do not want to place on our products') after a number of previous justifications of their decision were shown to contradict the guidelines of their own campaign. The email correspondence, which sheds light on Nike's stance on the limits of the freedom of expression, made its way around the world.

The last form of consumer politics we should briefly mention at this point differs from shopping in another respect, namely in that the target of this activism is financial services. Shareholder meeting activism deserves to be highlighted, especially given the relative importance of financial markets in today's economy. It can be acted out in the semiotic register, as when activists gain entrance to annual meetings and make their voices heard make their voices heard. While the chances of getting a resolution passed are usually modest at best (activists seldom represent the majority of shareholders or immediately garner sufficient numbers of sympathizers), the tactic aims to generate publicity, to shame the company, and to pressure it into action—which is apparently enough to trouble chief executive officers. In a 1996 survey of Canada's top 100 CEOs, 'unpredictable questions top the list of "worst nightmares" at annual meetings' (Hertz 2002: 162).

If shareholder activism is acted out in the material register, it is analogous to supermarket activism insofar as stocks and equity funds that comply with selective normative beliefs are chosen. Divestment or negative screening works by banning stocks from portfolios that are believed to further adverse values. Currently popular 'sin-stocks' include purveyors of alcohol, tobacco, and arms, the nuclear power industry, and firms that use pesticides in farming, disregard human rights, or support oppressive regimes. Positive investing (also called 'socially responsible investing') involves selecting stocks to reward good performance on corporate behaviour issues such as labour conditions and environmental sustainability, as well as directing investments in institutionalized projects that further favoured values (e.g. community investment). Since investment in 'virtue stocks' is a booming business in Europe and the United States, investors can take normative considerations into account without sacrificing portfolio diversification. Shareholder activism by material means might therefore be a real option, even if having recourse to normative considerations when selecting stocks is deemed justifiable only as long as financial performance is not negatively affected (Lane 2005).

A comparative analysis of different practices of consumption would contribute help to clarify their political potential, but would go far beyond the scope of this chapter. Nevertheless, it would be a mistake to make general claims about the political potentials of consumption and ignore the recommendation made above to think about political consumption through a variety of consumption practices. The following two sections will therefore discuss major objections that have been raised against the idea of a politics of consumption by making recourse to different practices of consumption. This strategy promises more specific

Table 5.1 Forms of political consumption

Target of action	*Material means*	*Semiotic means*
Product or brand	Utility adaptation *(i.e. re-determining what need the product serves)*	Symbolic repossession *(i.e. re-determining what the product stands for)*
Entrepreneur or producer practice	Supermarket activism Buycott/boycott Positive investing/divestment	Web 2.0 platforms, labelling Hacktivism Shareholder meeting activism
Consumer practice	Downshifting, saving, stealing Recycling, bartering, gleaning	Culture jam Anti-commercial iconoclasm

and nuanced conclusions with regard to the political potentials that may reside in consumption practices, and to reveal that generalized objections apply to certain consumption practices only.

5.3 Consumer Activism and the Theme Park of Radical Action

Empirical investigations were conducted in order to confirm the narrative of the consumer as citizen, with surveys in Europe and the United States showing that people increasingly claim to have brought their consumption behaviour in line with normative commitments since the mid-1980s (Cowe and Williams 2000; Littler 2009: 29, 76, Pattie et al. 2003: 446; Pattie et al. 2004: 78). Statistics also indicate that markets are booming with 'ethically responsible' products, services, and funds (Celent 2007, Fairtrade International 2011, Hertz 2002: 159; Langley 2007, Lee and Vihinen 2005: 4, Social Investment Forum Foundation 2007), while anecdotal and case-study evidence suggests that corporations respond when targeted by consumer activism (Friedman 2006, Hertz 2002: Ch. 6, Jensen 2005). Confirming this narrative, though with little enthusiasm, a business journalist from the *Financial Times* (Kellaway 2010) was recently even compelled to warn managers against consumers gaining too much influence over brands. However, in reaction to the view of optimists, critical objections have been raised that question whether consumption activity can really contribute to active citizenship. I consider three of these objections in the following section.

Acting as Watchdog or Scapegoating the Most Visible Corporation?

Advocates of the citizen-consumer narrative claim that consumption allows individuals to combine private interests directly and spontaneously with broader policy questions: consumers can 'think politically privately' (Micheletti 2003: 2, 11–12). Because of this, they argue, the politics of consumption is more appealing to today's citizens than elections and party membership (Dalton et al. 2003: 2, Micheletti 2003: 24–34). These alleged advantages are a fundamental problem for the first set of objections: it is argued that consumption practices lack consistency and coordination, and therefore cannot be a real alternative to traditional forms of politics.

If consumers are likened to jujitsu fighters, there is a slight sense of romanticization at work when it comes to the way in which political struggles are decided in late modern societies. Jujitsu may offer surprisingly efficient techniques to outmanoeuvre a stronger and better-armed opponent; but what if the opponent operates from a distance or does not provide the fighter with a target? Firms that do not directly sell to the public are difficult to boycott; firms that do not bear a famous name are hard to shame.[7] In these cases, political consumer jujitsu devolves into shadow-boxing, and 'semiotic robin hoodism' (Klein 2010: 280) turns outs to be Don Quixote's fighting of windmills. But even if the opponent is tangible, how promising can it be in the first place to fight against single corporations? Naomi Klein (2010: 422–4) warns that directing the public eye on a single corporation runs the danger of letting others off the hook. Consumer activists may claim to question entire industries when pestering a corporate unit, or, as Ulrich Beck (1996: 129) envisions, they may hope to serve as 'permanent forced father confessor for a sinful business sector'. In actual fact, however, they might just scapegoat one individual, particularly visible, and therefore vulnerable provider. Moreover, even if a company can be forced to comply, amendments are likely to be adopted only where the political consumers' spotlight was last focused. The production site that aroused indignation might be closed down while business everywhere else goes on as usual. Targeting single corporations therefore runs the risk of 'missing the forest for the biggest tree' (Ortega quoted from Klein 2010: 423). Consumers might be too on-edge and too myopic to serve as an attentive business-practice watchdog.

Institutionalized political consumer initiatives have wider coverage. Various labelling schemes and organized audit practices have been established over the course of the past twenty years to monitor and rank products and services, and to increase control and transparency (e.g. EU Eco-Label, Fairtrade Labelling Organizations International, Forest Stewardship Council, Ethical Investment Research Service). However, these initiatives seldom go beyond a liberal and defensive insistence on consumer rights. In addition, they often pull in different directions and are at odds with other consumer initiatives. To cite just one blatantly contradictory incoherence of today's ethical consumerism, in 2000 Levi Strauss was accepted as a member of the Ethical Trading Initiative and therefore recommended to 'ethically responsible' shoppers while, at the same time, it was also being boycotted for its continued failure to compensate its workers for previous harms perpetrated (Hilton and Daunton 2001: 2; for a detailed case study see Domask 2003). The point here is that the general impediment for consumption in terms of its being a useful political tool, according to this first line of criticism, is that it is marred by a particularism and a privatism that undermines any attempt to act in concert:

> None of these politics of consumption [. . .] represents a coherent ideological movement mobilizing a unified consumer interest in the same sense that socialism or communism was perceived to act as the potential mobilizing force of a labour interest.
>
> (Hilton and Daunton 2001: 2; see also Streeck 2012: 36, 44–6)

The comparison of consumers with workers, as in this quotation, brings out the heart of the critique quite clearly. The point is not so much that consumers lack a common concern; after all, they can be seen as being exploited in a similar way to workers. Whereas workers are underpaid, one might say, consumers are 'overcharged' (Bauman 1999, Humphreys and Grayson 2008, Ritzer and Jurgenson 2010: 20). Moreover, consumers are turned into 'prosumers' by being asked to scan and pay at the self-checkout counter and to bag their own purchases in the supermarket. Although their 'consumer labour' creates surplus value, this neo-Marxist argument states, it is not fairly compensated (e.g. through price cuts). However, the point of the critique is rather that whereas the exploitation of workers leads to solidarity, consumers are dissociated by their individualized tastes and tokenistic form of action. Unlike the proletariat, the 'consumtariat' (Bard and Söderqvist 2002: 114; cf. Žižek 2010: 236) is not even theoretically a viable candidate for fostering societal transformation. Characterized by a particularism and spontaneity that systematically pre-empts acting in concert, political consumption might simply peter out in impulsive and aimless actionism with ever-changing agendas and contradictory single-issue campaigns. In the absence of central party organization, Slavoj Žižek summarizes, such activism will never be more than a 'marginal disturbance' (Žižek 2002: 558).[8]

The Co-optation of (Counter-)Culture

Perhaps, however, political consumption is not just an ineffective instrument for effectuating change; it may actually be actively counterproductive. A second strand of criticism argues this point, revolving around the argument that consumer politics ultimately feeds the consolidation of mainstream (hyper-)consumerist culture.

Benjamin Barber argues that culture jammers risk something when playing a game the rules of which they want to subvert: by making use of the attention-snatching techniques of advertisers, they run the danger of eventually being 'out-jammed' themselves (Barber 2007: 290; cf. Humphery 2010: 53). Subversive messages and signs of rebellion, intended to distort a firm's advertisement and air a grievance, quickly come to broaden an advertiser's vocabulary. Once authentic counter-cultural slogans are reflected in catchphrases such as Apple's 'Think different' or Burger King's 'Sometimes you gotta break the rules'.

The fashion label Diesel has repeatedly drawn inspiration from culture jammers in recent years. In the 1998 'For Successful Living' campaign, the boundaries between advertisement and jam were blurred to the point that jamming and advertisement were indistinguishable. One poster ('Lucky Ice-Cream: For a Better Tomorrow') bears a close resemblance to a famous photograph by Margaret Bourke-White that shows a destitute group of Afro-Americans during the Great Depression, queuing for bread in front of a cheerful billboard celebrating the American way of life. Diesel's poster differs from Bourke-White's photograph primarily in that the crowd now is a group of supposedly North Korean workers, with the billboard in the background depicting Diesel models. In fact, the whole advertisement series alludes to Bourke-White's questioning of the American way of life by contrasting the idyllic world of abundance promised by corporate advertisements with real-world inequalities and misery. Thus, a second poster ('Lucky Star: The Only Magazine') from Diesel's advertisement series depicts (again, supposedly) a North Korean worker on a bus. On the back page of the newspaper the worker is reading one can see a Diesel model praying, on his knees, under the motto 'Our way—the only way'. Diesel's 2010 'Be Stupid' campaign alludes to radicals rioting against the state ('Be Stupid: Governments Will Hate You'), and ridicules social criticism ('Be Stupid: Smart Critiques, Stupid Creates').[9]

It is not far-fetched to believe that the culture jammers' critique sometimes inspires advertisers because it can help them to put their finger on the pulse of a particular moment and learn which representation is best suited to catching a potential customer's eye. 'The danger for the jammers', Barber says, 'is that they lose even when they win'. By participating in the branding game they 'add luster to the image of marketing rather than undermine its culture' (Barber 2007: 290).

An alternative view might state that counter-culture is not being saturated and co-opted—but only because it was a part of the mainstream culture from the outset. Kalle Lasn and the activists who gather around the Adbusters Media Foundation vociferously call for economic change by politically engaging in the marketplace in order to reverse the 'suicidal consumer binge' (Lasn 2000). To that purpose they have created a magazine with technical and ideological advice for anti-corporate and anti-consumerist activism and have instigated a 'Buy Nothing Day' (under the motto: 'participate by not participating').[10] Despite such sanguine tones, one may doubt how radical Adbusters really are. It is not quite clear how their 'antipreneurial' (Quittner 2008), anti-corporate, anti-consumerist agenda diverges from mainstream entrepreneurial, corporate, consumerist culture in any significant way. For instance, in order to prepare properly for the first Buy Nothing Day in 2003, Adbusters invited 'anticonsumers' to purchase T-shirts with the name and motto of the event printed on them. While the T-shirts have been removed from Adbusters's shelves, other 'tools for activists' are still available. The 'antitrademark Blackspot sneaker' (75$) and the 'high-top Unswoosher' (99$) are today sold online and in over 100 retail outlets worldwide.[11] The blackspot may look like a blotted-out logo; nevertheless, a logo it inevitably is, and it is not entirely clear how a designed black spot could be the 'swift kick in the brand' that Adbusters sensationally claims it to be. '[C]ultural rebellion of the type epitomized by Adbusters magazine', Joseph Heath and Andrew Potter conclude, 'is not a threat to the system—it is the system' (Heath and Potter 2006: 3).

If those who are widely considered the most radical exponents of consumer politics fail to stand in real opposition, considerable doubts arise against the view that consumption practices can be political in any meaningful way, let alone be radical. And if Adbusters's blackspot constitutes just another brand, does this then not apply to the various fair-trade, organic, locavore, and other labels too? Labelling has basically the same purpose as branding: it attaches a certain message to the product in order to make it more attractive to consumers by claiming to take their desires into consideration. The product may promise to have some sort of special quality, and advertisement may tap into more pretentious concerns, appealing to the cosmopolitan, the radical, the non-conformist, the ecologically-spirited, or humanitarian-minded; but the function of a label is to persuade potential customers to buy some specific products rather than rival ones. Labelled products may well be comparatively green, fair-trade, or open-source, but what a label implies might be circumstantial to the greenwashing, sweatwashing, or—as in the case of the blackspot sneaker—blackwashing of the product. In the final analysis, the primary concern might just be about grabbing or extending market shares—that is, if it is not just another marketing trick for talking consumers into buying allegedly new products (Göran 1988, Micheletti 2003: 161).

Feeling Good, Not Doing Good?

Following these objections, we may doubt whether consumers can really be 'likened to resistance fighters', as Michele Micheletti (2003: 16–17) claims, who rebel against market rather than state actors. Rather, one might agree with another of her claims, namely that 'privately politically thinking' consumers 'can feel themselves to be authors of global political acts' (Micheletti 2003: 2). Consumers may indeed feel that their choices in the marketplace are politically relevant, yet there is a critical difference between self-perception and publicly palpable deeds. Consumer power might be more of a vain illusion than a real force that impinges on markets.

For Patrick West, illusion is the decisive characteristic of the whole field of new non-conventional forms of activism: 'It is about feeling good, not doing good' (West 2004: 1; see also Touraine 2000: 93; cf. Edwards 2000: 6). Civil activism has shrunk into insignificance in political reality, he claims, but exorbitantly grown in appeal. In contrast to the social movements of the 1968 generation, today's forms of non-conventional political articulation have 'little to do with changing the world'. Self-proclaimed activists are busy with informing others how eager they are to take responsibility and how hard they work towards creating a better world. To experience a warm glow of self-satisfaction they engage in 'conspicuous compassion', 'ostentatious caring', or 'recreational grief'—yet they do not engage in serious politics (West 2004: 1–11, 44).

Perhaps having an 'activist–political' self-conception is more important than actually challenging the prevailing order, so that the goal becomes feeling radical while nevertheless leaving everything in its place. The essence of such a self-conception, Ingolfur Blühdorn accordingly claims, is:

> [N]o longer the political alternative, but alterity, i.e. the desire of individuals to be different from the system and experience themselves as autonomous subjects. [. . .] [Such] kinds of non-conventional political articulation can thus be interpreted as offering a supplementary form of identity construction which helps to compensate for the shortcomings of consumption-centred identity formation. They provide late-modern individuals with an opportunity to experience themselves both within (compliant with) and at the same time outside of (in opposition to, i.e. autonomous from) the system. Exactly this is required to escape the late-modern dilemma. [. . .] [T]he demonstration of autonomy, identity and political agency inside the theme park of radical action allows for full complicity with the status quo outside this arena, it may be described as a post-political and itself consumptive form of political articulation.
>
> (Blühdorn 2006: 36)

According to the pessimists, either the politics of consumption is politically irrelevant or it further degenerates the democratic culture of liberal societies because it offers no way out of the advertising industry, nourishes a 'vote-with-your-dollar' mentality, and eventually leads to the 'commodification of dissent' (Humphery 2010: 56). In addition, it entices citizens away from established political theatres that are less suited to demonstrating one's virtuousness (just think of the secret act of voting). Citizens who look for channels of political articulation should not bank on consumption, but conversely attempt to relativize the social significance of consumption by conventional democratic means. Proper democrats should 'civilize—that is to say "civicize"—markets', affirms

Barber, and 'restor[e] the sovereignty of citizens *over* consumption' (Barber 2007: 293, 295, emphasis added).[12]

5.4 Opportunities for Political Consumption

In some respect, both optimists and pessimists about political consumption are right in their own ways. Optimists breathe fresh air into our understanding of consumption by emphasizing the co-productive qualities of consumption activity and the change it can induce in consumers' self-understanding. Pessimists rightly warn against cultivating the hope of renewing active citizenship by placing too much emphasis on a self-encouraging narrative that runs the danger of wasting energy. In another respect, the disagreement is less important than it appears because differences in opinion turn out to be differences in the perspective taken and the audience addressed—at least on closer inspection. Pessimists take a step back from economic life in order to bring the broader picture of society's ills into focus, while optimists examine the role of individual consumers and report from the front. The patronizing undertones of pessimists are not entirely rejected, but rather complemented by the moralizing ones of optimists. Accordingly, the pessimist Barber declares that Cornelia, the dedicatee of his book *Consumed*, 'knows how to shop', namely how to satisfy 'real needs'; but she also 'knows why shopping isn't enough' (Barber 2007: dedication). The optimists Dietlind Stolle and Marc Hooghe similarly reserve the term 'political consumer' for people who make 'conscientious' choices based on sufficient knowledge of labelling schemes, while excluding those that 'purchase labelled products based purely on private motivations, such as lifestyle issues' (Stolle and Hooghe 2006: 280–2; see also Micheletti 2003: 19, Micheletti et al. 2006b: xii–xvii, 2006c: 295).

In yet another respect, optimists and pessimists are equally wrong. Both underline the complicity of political consumption with (hyper-)consumerism, globalization, and capitalism. For the pessimists, as we saw in the previous section, this complicity means the bankrupting of political consumption. Optimists do not generally write off consumption as a tool for activists on this basis, yet they admit that political consumption is useless for anti-consumerist, anti-globalist, and anti-capitalist causes. Micheletti et al., for instance, conclude that:

> [M]ost political consumers accept globalization and consumer society as a fact of life. They accept the structural foundation of global capitalism and the enticements of material consumer society. What they want to do is modify their negative side effects. This makes political consumerism less satisfactory as a political tool for many anti-globalists and people highly critical of market capitalism in general.
> (Micheletti et al. 2006b: 297)

The shared mistake is twofold: on the one hand, both camps overlook the economic diversity of practices of consumption that offers consumers the possibility of discriminating not only between different products on supermarket shelves, but also between different kinds of providers and even economies. On the other hand, they neglect to confront the fact that acts may achieve the opposite effect, despite being complicit with the very practice they seek to challenge.

Acknowledging Economic Diversity

Both pessimists and optimists consider practices of consumption incapable of renouncing capitalism and (hyper-)consumerist culture. For the pessimists, the political utility of consumption practices is therefore largely undermined. Barber (2007: 286) writes in this sense: 'Taking over capitalism with "good commodities" is not the same thing as subverting commodification'. Optimists hang on to the idea of political consumption because commodification, capitalism and (hyper-)consumerist culture does not occur to many people as major problem.

The example of The Body Shop illustrates that the view of optimists is reasonable. The Body Shop stands out for its firm stance on animal rights, as well as being known for being unwilling to abjure the privatization of profits. The persistent demand for Body Shop products since 1976 has done nothing to challenge the world of multinational capitalism, yet it has significantly contributed to the delegitimization of animal testing. If, as it seems, protecting animal rights is of greater concern to people than challenging capitalism and commodification, it would be problematic to paint the effects of this demand for Body Shop products as politically meaningless. A justification of this picture might be possible, though not particularly attractive, by reviving paternalistic distinctions such as those between true and false consciousness or needs.[13] If we agree, in contrast, to what Richard Rorty, echoing John Dewey, calls the priority of democracy to philosophy, we must refrain from theoretically delimiting the possible range of politically meaningful issues, because scholars are not granted a privileged position in identifying the most pressing political causes (Rorty 1988; see also Walzer 1981: 397).

There are two additional reasons to question whether practices of consumption could allow a modification of capitalism and (hyper-)consumerist culture. Firstly, downshifting and anti-consumerist iconoclasm (for instance, Adbusters's TV anti-commercials) are arguably modest 'means to achieve a more moderate and equitable level of consumption' and 'hasten the demise of consumerism itself' (Humphery 2010: xiii, 53). Second, practising abstinence from purchasing capitalist commodities might present considerable difficulties, but it does not require a categorical 'ascetic withdrawal', as Barber (2007: 257) claims.

Barber's claim that self-denial to the point of self-sacrifice is inevitable if we want to escape consumerist and capitalist practices leads back to our discussion of the nature of the economy (see Chapter 2); as such, I will refrain from repeating the arguments made there. Suffice it to say that if the economy were understood as a social institution that is maintained by the conduct of its members, instead of a capitalist systemic singularity, we would be less likely to assume that all of today's practices of consumption reinforce (hyper-)consumerism and capitalism. J.K. Gibson-Graham (2006a: 56) calls this assumption a peculiarity of today's 'capitalocentric discourse', where 'economic difference is condensed by fusing the variety of noncapitalist economic activities into a unity in which meaning is anchored to capitalist identity'. To escape 'capitalocentrism', Gibson-Graham and other scholars from post-Marxist and feminist traditions urge us to acknowledge the diversity of economic practices and reflect on the consequences of this heterogeneity, in order to shape the economic order. Many of today's economic practices, they say, are linked to the supply-demand-price mechanism of the market, and are capitalist in their capacity to generate profits that are unfairly distributed. Other practices, however, are capitalist but not market-based, while others still are not even capitalist. Engaging in non-market-based and non-capitalist practices, they underline, is politically important because the status of capitalism will be attenuated if alternative economic processes are perpetuated at the expense of conventional practices (Gibson-Graham 2006a: 53–78, Swanson n.d., 2002, 2007b, Watkins 1998).

While these scholars abstain from applying the logic of economic diversity to consumption activity, the implications for the present context are nevertheless apparent. Consumer choice is not exclusively confined to products from different providers in the supermarket or even different supermarkets and other businesses within one all-embracing capitalist market-economy. Instead, choice concerns the products and services of different economies. Practically speaking, consumers will not always have the ability to avoid shopping centres, supermarkets, or high street shops if they want to enjoy amenities or simply satisfy basic needs. But sometimes they will, and they might be able to acquire products and services from non-capitalist or non-market-based sources: from neighbourhood markets, household or community economies, from grey or black markets, or the multifarious economy of leftovers, where the appropriation of products goes under such names as aggressive recycling or gleaning.[14] Some processes in these economies might generate surplus and be exploitive too, but the point is that, contrary to claims that consumption necessarily perpetuates capitalism, there is a ready availability of choice between capitalist and non-capitalist practices of consumption. If the latter are reiterated over the former, the economic order de facto changes, though gradually rather than all of a sudden.

The Potentials of Complicity and Compromise

The existence of alternative practices of consumption casts doubts on the idea that consumption cannot serve as a vehicle for anti-capitalist/anti-consumerist activism. In addition, there are good reasons to question why opposition to the practices one seeks to challenge should only be considered possible in the form of uncontaminated resistance. Becoming complicit with the practices one seeks to challenge might entail the risk of complete co-optation; however, it also offers an opportunity to alter the opposed practice by paying the price of partial co-optation, which is to say, to compromise it. Naomi Klein's *No Logo* is one example of an argument for the potential of complicity and compromise.

Previous attempts at political consumption activism have been ineffective and largely co-opted by the corporate world, Klein says, because of a strategic error. Activism was directed against specific products, individual firms, or the persuasive powers of advertisers, whereas the real problem lies in the overall economization of politics—'the effects of marketing on public space, cultural freedom and democracy' (Klein 2010: 303). If consumer activism in its material and semiotic forms is to exert a meaningful political impact, she affirms, it must prove its utility as 'a tool—one among many—that is being used, loaned and borrowed in a much broader political movement against the branded life' (Klein 2010: 309).

Klein makes clear that political consumption can be a useful tool and that her book is intended to contribute to the movement against branded life. She leaves us in no doubt about this aspiration, even though her challenge exists as a markedly commercial product itself. *No Logo*—the 'bible for anti-corporate militancy' (*The Independent*, quoted from Klein 2010: front matter)—was published and marketed, amongst others, by Rupert Murdoch's media conglomerate News Corporation. Just like Abbie Hoffman's bestseller, *Steal This Book*, or Michael Moore's documentary, *Capitalism: A Love Story*, it is a perfectly judged product and promising investment for corporate actors despite, or perhaps because of, its anti-corporate message. In *No Logo*, we 'see the world of multinational capitalism speaking to itself', as Timothy Bewes puts it. Yet rather than tarnishing Klein's message and authenticity, the opportunistic complicity of her criticism with the practices she opposes secures the conditions for its potential success. *No Logo* could not have acquired the wide discursive reach and 'catalysed what is arguably the largest, certainly the most visible radical political movement in the Western world in recent years', had it been published by an independent publisher instead of making use of the manifold resources of a global publishing operation (Bewes 2002: 260–1; see also Littler 2009: 76). To return to the metaphor of martial arts, rather than relying on her own energy and mounting an attack on a vastly superior enemy, Klein tried and arguably managed, to some extent, to turn the momentum of the branded world against itself.

As well as being complicit with their means, *No Logo* is also complicit with the practices it opposes in terms of their nature. 'No Logo', after all, is a logo itself—just like Adbusters's blackspot. Klein is perfectly aware of this fact and plays with the seeming contradiction. For instance, a photograph showing a boy wearing a jumper with a 'No Logo' label is reproduced in the book, and the title on the book cover is completed by a (fake) registered trademark symbol. Klein can do this because opposing the branded world was never, for her, about summoning a logo-phobic movement: *No Logo* is not the negation of the logo as such, but a challenge to the currently predominant status and function of logos. The alternative to the branded world of logos is for Klein not an unbranded world, but a branded world that is different and, in some sense, better. It is one in which the product has regained importance vis-à-vis the brand, because unless the 'commercial cacophony' (Klein 2010: 284) is quietened, the normative tones that ring out of certain producer practices will be drowned out.[15]

This readiness to choose means that are complicit with opposed practices and to accept compromised results allows seemingly corrupt forms of political consumption to find unexpected justification. The frustration with consumption practices that promote greenwashed, sweat-washed, or blackwashed products, rather than products that actually are green, fair-trade, or open-source, is understandable. However, hypocrisy can still contribute to providing grounds for making authentic results possible. Demanding codes of conduct, to which producers sanctimoniously conceded for image-related reasons, add to the resources available to political consumers. Corporate lip-service allows consumers to highlight a company's failure to comply with its own standards—a violation that often has an impact on the company's reputation and the loyalty of its labour force and shareholders, and often more than a failure to comply with standards imposed by third parties (Klein 2010: 434). Companies may 'become hoist by their own discursive petard', or 'rhetorically entrapped' (Hobson and Seabrooke 2007: 17, Schimmelfennig 2001: 48).

By the same token, consumers may promote norms that they only pretend to affirm; discursively standardizing what previously counted as an eccentric departure from the norm, they reaffirm the promise of social recognition. By engaging in the muddied waters of the consumerist paradigm and hazarding complicity and compromise, the counter-culture can become mainstream; and indeed it must be willing to become mainstream because activism will remain void of subversive potential as long as it sees itself as a form of counter-culture and backs away from becoming majoritarian itself (Marchart 2010: 301–6).

5.5 Political Consumption and the Variety of Ideological Causes

Concerning consumption activity, there is little reason to object to the proposal to integrate political consumption into the repertoire of non-conventional forms of political participation, even though a number of reservations are surely necessary. Implicit in the discussion of micropolitics in the previous chapter is that a conceptual distinction is required between the macro-trend of ethical consumerism and the micro-practices of political consumer activism. While analyses of the former may legitimately presume that an aggregative arithmetic is at work, investigations of the latter must look for the multiplicative effects of individual action. Calling for a boycott is accordingly more likely to qualify as politics than participating in one; contesting or de-contesting products, brands, or producer and consumer practices in publicly noticeable ways such as culture-jamming is more promising than changing one's private shopping habits. Taking into account the multiplicative criterion for the study of micro-practices of political consumer activism forces scholars to set a higher benchmark for attributing political quality to individual acts of consumption. In another regard, as this chapter has made explicit, a broadening of the view is in order. The political significance of political consumer activism is easily missed if we disregard the diversity of consumption practices. Consumption is instantiated in the possibility of exploiting diversity, which is to say, through choice. Choice not only concerns a selection of products, but also discrimination between products of different providers and different economies. Furthermore, consumer choice concerns how products are used, along with their social meaning, as well as the role that consumption materially and symbolically plays in one's life.

There is one particularly striking consequence of failing to think the political significance of consumption through the diversity of consumption practices. This consists in seeing only a limited range of ideological causes to which political consumption can be applicable. Not only is consumption reduced to shopping, as we saw above, but the *terminus technicus* that I propose we call 'political consumption' or 'political consumer activism' is often qualified by adjectives that evoke ideological connotations. Designations such as 'civic consumerism', 'responsible shopping', 'ethical', 'responsible', 'conscious', 'socially conscious', 'conscientious', or even 'cosmopolitan caring consumption' (Barber 2007: 293, Humphery 2010: 56–7, Littler 2009: 3–7) might not allude to one clearly demarcated ideological stance. However, they do not seem particularly suited to the anti-globalist anti-capitalist calls to opt out of capitalist markets by turning to alternative economies and consumption practices, or to anarcho-libertarian calls to overthrow the established order by engaging in 'counter-economics'.[16] We cannot necessarily assume that these labels include the downshifting and anti-corporate activism so entertainingly preached by the (fake) Reverend Billy of the 'Church of Stop Shopping', who conducts exorcist rituals in strip malls to cast out the demons of (hyper-)consumerism and warn people against the 'shopocalypse'.[17] Apparently similarly little attention has been paid to the (real) Bishop of Reading's idea of political consumption. Only 'the highly educated or suited and booted', he says, stroll through the aisles of Marks & Spencer and buy fair-trade and organic products. 'Jesus', by contrast, 'would probably have shopped at Aldi and Asda' (Right Reverend Stephen Cottrell, quoted from Gledhill 2009). Moreover, the liberal moralizing cosmopolitanism that is implied in many of the aforementioned designations scarcely leave room for conservative suggestions that we buy regional and national products, or, even more unlikely, patriotic ideas such as those of George W. Bush and Dick Cheney offered in the aftermath of 9/11. American citizens, they suggested, should 'stick their thumbs in the eye of terrorists' by going on with Western-style consumerism and shopping-as-usual.[18]

Investigating political consumption, we need to take into account this ideological diversity and further explore the connection between different practices of political consumption and particular ideological causes. It is not sufficient to warn against 'illegitimate' and 'biased' forms of political consumption, or to voice concerns that 'political consumerism can go wrong' (Micheletti et al. 2006c: 295).

Notes

1. This definition of consumption is informed by the *Oxford English Dictionary* online edition (www.oed.com, accessed 24 September 2013). There are of course much narrower definitions. Mary Douglas and Baron Isherwood (1996: 37), for instance, are in favour of a privatistic notion of the concept that excludes the moment of acquisition and distribution (exchange, transfer), as well as illegal uses, and 'define[s] consumption as a use of material possessions that is beyond commerce and free within the law'. At the same time, broader definitions exist. A notion of consumption is embraced in cultural studies that is not restricted to economic practices, but in fact applies to whatever kind of external thing or utterance with which an individual happens to be confronted.
2. Despite the emphasis they place on issues related to production, Marxist contributions have not entirely dismissed consumption (Edwards 2000: 15–18, Ritzer et al. 2007: 411–12). In addition, consumption was a (modestly controversial) issue amongst early socialist thinkers (Thompson 2001).
3. For the use and etymology of the term 'consumption', see the entry in the *Oxford English Dictionary* online edition (www.oed.com, accessed 20 October 2012). See also Bauman (2007: 53–4).
4. This picture of consumption was drawn by members of the Frankfurt School, such as Theodor W. Adorno, Max Horkheimer (1997), and Herbert Marcuse (2007). For more detailed discussion see Edwards (2000: 18–28), Nava (1991: 158–63), Ritzer et al. (2007: 411–14), and Simons (2005: 154–8).
5. Similar claims are made by Dalton et al. (2003), Micheletti (2003: 16), and Scammel (2000: 352). I will criticize the comparison between consumer and citizen power in Chapter 8. See also Beckstein (2014).
6. Cultural studies laid the foundation for widening the spectrum of a potential politics of consumption. First, reference was made to the ways in which the tangible, physical characteristics of products are altered by consumptive acts of (mis-)appropriation. For instance, a bottle of wine may be transformed into a petrol bomb. Second, emphasis was placed on the symbolic repossession of products. The crucial thesis, in this respect, is that 'the apparent

one-way technological flow of the mediation of culture is resisted by the active interpretation of messages by the people' (Simons 2005: 158).

7. The strategy of secondary boycott was proposed in order to hold the 'unbrandables' accountable. Because direct action against the culprits is not a feasible option, boycotts and shaming manoeuvres are organized or threatened against those firms that finally turn resources and products into a brand (Klein 2010: 425–7).
8. See also Nava (1991: 170) and Prinz's (2003: 13) discussion of Habermas's stance on consumption. Despite admitting the absence of a coherent ideological movement, Matthew Hilton and Martin J. Daunton argue that, collectively, heterogeneous consumer struggles can still be grasped as a 'transnational movement': 'The link that will continue to bind these different groups [. . .] is the common realization of the economic structures behind commodity culture. The politics of consumption is no longer about shopping for identity, but about the global institutions that shape and determine the markets we are forced to operate within' (Hilton and Daunton 2001: 3; see also Hilton 2007: 123).
9. The print ads of Diesel's 'For Successful Living' and 'Be Stupid' campaigns can be found at: www.coloribus.com/adsarchive/search/?x=0&y=0&q=diesel+lucky and http://pool.mediashow.ro/popular?g2_albumId=398914, both accessed 24 November 2014. The difficulty of distinguishing between a jamming of culture and advertisement is exemplified by the fact that even Naomi Klein gets caught up in confusion. Characterizing the aforementioned advertisement as a direct replica of Bourke-White's photograph, she addresses the Diesel campaign as 'Brand O' instead of using its proper name, 'Successful Living' (Klein 2010: 307). 'Brand O' is not a part of Diesel's advertisement series, but a spoof ad by Adbusters that shows the Diesel advertisement in the deserted and deprived area of a (presumably) Western city, and is subtitled 'Successful Advertising'. Adbusters's spoof ad can be found at https://www.adbusters.org/content/diesel-brand-o, accessed 28 October 2014.
10. In issue number 91 Adbusters called for revolution and indeed fixed a date: 'Carnivalesque Rebellion: Nov 22–28 2010 we shut the world down for a week [. . .]. We create a sudden, unexpected moment of truth—a mass reversal of perspective; a global mindshift—from which the corporate/consumerist forces will never fully recover' (Lasn 2010).
11. Information is provided on the Adbusters website (https://www.adbusters.org/campaigns/ blackspot, accessed 12 July 2012).
12. It should be noted that Barber occasionally considers the idea that consumption is a viable tool for politics. He writes, for instance, that '[i]f dialectic means anything, it means that consumers themselves harbour the secrets that can release them from consumerism' (Barber 2007: 260). However, his general message is that (hyper-)consumerism can ultimately only be defeated on the stage of politics, not in the marketplace.
13. Although distinctions such as that between true and false consciousness or true and false needs have lost much of their attractiveness, they often reverberate implicitly in contemporary scholarship on consumption. For an explicit reaffirmation of these ideas, see Barber (2007: 293).
14. Jacinda Swanson (n.d.) discusses the political potential of the market of leftovers in a commentary written about Agnés Varda's 2000 documentary *The Gleaners and I*. An example of a community economy is the English market town Todmorden, where there are initiatives to grow vegetables in public spaces and share them with the whole town. For a report, see Fowler (2010).
15. A world without brands is difficult to imagine, especially if the conception of branding is broad enough to include Barrack Obama as a 'superbrand'.

Obama's image, Klein argues in the preface of the 10th anniversary edition of *No Logo*, was 'the most successful rebranding campaign of all time'. Regardless of how successful Obama was in improving the deficient product that was the American government, Klein is convinced that he managed to solve the branding problem that was so patent under the Bush administration (Klein 2010: xix–xxiii).

16. 'Counter-economics' denotes the acquisition of all kinds of illicit goods and services (e.g. gambling, illegal drugs, weaponry), as well as the acquisition of goods and services in illegal ways (e.g. unlicensed transportation, untaxed products from illegal immigrant workers or children, pirated material), as long as no physical harm is involved (Zimmermann 2001).
17. To get an idea of Reverend Billy's activism, visit www.revbilly.com/ or watch the 2007 documentary produced by Morgan Spurlock and directed by Rob VanAlkemade entitled *What Would Jesus Buy?*
18. Bush is said to have claimed: 'We can't let the terrorists stop us from shopping' (quoted from Norris 2005). As concerns Cheney, Peter G. Gosselin and Warren Vieth (2001) write in the *Los Angeles Times*: 'In a remark that captured policymakers' peculiar bind—trying to revive economic ebullience even as they say they are preparing for military action—Cheney called on Americans to do their patriotic duty by continuing to shop. "I would hope the American people would, in effect, stick their thumbs in the eye of the terrorists and say that they've got great confidence in the country, great confidence in our economy, and not let what's happened here in any way throw off their normal level of economic activity," he said'.

6 Political (By-)Products of Economic Production

It is well known that corporations are politically active entities. Sometimes corporations are even regarded as a fifth branch of government because through lobbying they exert significant influence at all levels of governance. This chapter, however, does not investigate how corporate actors are politically engaged through lobbying (on the stage of politics), but how, and whether, they contribute to the process of reinstituting society through their production activity (in the marketplace). By production I understand the economic activity of organizing and undertaking the conversion of resources into usable products, which may be either goods or services. Production activity therefore includes instances of the economic process that temporally precede the actual moment of resource-conversion, such as the acquisition of resources required for production, as well as the steps which follow it, such as the marketing of goods and services. As distinguished from the economic activity of work, production does not primarily refer to the practices of lower-ranking employees who perform the work of production, but rather to those who control and direct the production process—that is, those who run a business.

One concern of this chapter is examining the modalities by which the production activity of economic actors such as businesses might bring about broader societal effects and thus contribute to reinstituting society. For this purpose, producer politics is differentiated into three categories: the politics of, behind, and beyond the product. However, only a cursory overview of conceivable forms of producer politics will be provided. Furthermore, this chapter will leave largely untouched what many, especially Marxist, theorists consider the most important political aspect of production activity, namely the various ways in which workers are controlled, disciplined, alienated, and exploited on the shop floor. The focus will be on the outward effects of production rather than intra-firm relations.

The main concern of this chapter, however, is a seemingly fundamental objection to the idea that such a thing as producer politics actually does exist. This objection can be encountered in more overt or more covert forms, in scholarship as well as textbooks and newspaper articles. Analytically considered, the objection stands on two feet: on the one hand, there is the view that individual producers are not involved in politics because the societal effects resulting from production activity are caused by other (collective) agents and (structural or systemic) forces. On the other hand, it is frequently suggested that the societal effects resulting from production activity should not be approached as a form of politics in its own right, because they come about as mere by-products of the main, essentially economic, operation. In engaging in practices of (economic) production, producers do not intend to participate in politics, and if production activity accrues to social objectives, this is a marginal, secondary, accidental, indirect, collateral effect.

Whoever accepts the arguments presented in the preceding chapters of this study might see no need to refute this twofold objection. Chapter 2 justified in general terms a micro-political focus on the concrete interactions of economic life against macro perspectives that, by their very nature, can capture only patterned behaviour and systemic structures. Chapters 3 and 4 clarified the understanding of (micro)politics informing this study, which holds that an act is to be attributed a political quality if it causes multiplicative effects on the process of reinstituting society, regardless of whether the actor intended to trigger these effects. The presence (or absence) of political intentions is not a criterion for the presence (or absence) of politics. However, regarding the former, we should pay attention to the specific discursive manoeuvres by which political producer power is theoretically denied. And regarding the latter, it is important to note that the question of intentionality is of crucial practical relevance here, because strategies for intervening in the process of the reinstitution of society are available only if political intentions are present in producers—or at least, if they are not generally absent.

After providing a rough overview of conceivable forms of producer politics and sketching a framework for studying them (Section 6.1), the objection against the existence of producer politics will be analysed in detail. First, claims stating the absence of producer power as it springs from macropolitical approaches will be specified (Section 6.2). Then the question of intentionality will be discussed against the backdrop of Ulrich Beck's theory of subpolitics, which provides additional reasons for believing that producer power is becoming increasingly important for the process of the reinstitution of society, but presupposes that producers do not (authentically) pursue non-economic goals (Section 6.3). Rejecting this presupposition, the final section indicates why generalized guesses about producer intentions are particularly detrimental to activist strategizing in the marketplace (6.4).

6.1 The Politics of, Behind, and Beyond the Product

When production is not taking place, economists speak about the stabilization or destabilization of prices, or the regulation of supply. But the non-event of (non-)production may also be accompanied by effects of broader societal significance. The OPEC cartel's limitations, and their creation of shortages of supply, as evidenced by the 1973 oil embargo against the United States and Western Europe, is a straightforward case in point. Yet a particularly illustrative exploration of the political relevance of non-production is given in Ayn Rand's novel *Atlas Shrugged*. Published in 1957, *Atlas Shrugged* draws a picture of the United States as it becomes ever more statist and collectivist. Rand introduces the reader to the burdensome task of the novel's heroine, Dagny Taggart, to keep her grandfather's railroad company running despite the aggravating anti-business climate. Meanwhile, important business leaders, bright innovators, and industrialists of great integrity keep disappearing under mysterious circumstances. The search for the economic elite initiated by government functionaries proceeds without success. However, Taggart finally unravels the mystery: John Galt, who had absconded from his business when the company guideline was altered to 'each according to his need' instead of 'each according to his ability' (Rand 1999: 323), secretly organizes a producer strike to instigate regime change. In a sweeping speech (that runs to some seventy pages), Galt compares producers with the primordial titan Atlas, of Greek mythology, who bears the world upon his shoulders, and calls for producers to 'shrug' (Rand 1999: 455): by collectively refusing to lend industriousness and genius to the society, the collectivist regime will be brought to its knees. Soon afterwards, the established order starts to crumble and Galt emerges to begin building a society on the grounds of laissez-faire principles and rational selfishness.

Atlas Shrugged—'the capitalist manifesto' (Kelley 2007)—is a piece of fiction, and it remains so even after the financial crisis of 2007–2008, when the fiscal stimulus packages and more restrictive economic regulations launched by the Obama administration prompted the rescue of the screenplay of the novel from developmental hell. Thus, Hollywood's first anti-bailout film was released on the 15th of April, 2011. However, the farmers' holiday during the Great Depression (Shover 1965), and the closing down of business by some ten thousand Belarusian shop-keepers in 2003 as part of the campaign 'For Better Life!' serve as evidence that large-scale producer strikes are not entirely absent from actual history.[1]

Turning to production rather than the refusal to produce, a three-tier model helps to show how the effects of production activity may acquire political significance: the *politics of the product*, the *politics behind the product*, and the *politics beyond the product*. The politics of the product concern decisions about why a certain product or service is provided rather than another. The decision may be reached, of course, in a multiplicity of ways, ranging from the unquestioned adoption of social norms to intra-firm deliberation, or disagreement between the producer and government or other businesses. The politics of the product may be discerned when discussions arise about the quality of products or when normative criteria are used to discriminate among clients. The marketing agency Spread the Word, for instance, provides its services to producers of charitable products only (Jackisch 2009). Besides the material output—how producers envision 'furnish[ing] the world' (as Ingvar Kamprad puts it in the 2004 biographical documentary *Mr IKEA*)—the politics of the product also concerns the semiotic output of production: how producers inform potential buyers, create or modify wants, and fabricate desire (cf. Caruana and Crane 2008; Littler 2009: 51).[2]

The politics of the product also exhibits itself in illegal practices. The provision of illicit goods and services is arguably the main business of criminal organizations.[3] In addition to affecting the lives of individual persons, as well as the conditions and outcomes of 'white' markets, criminal organizations are also a direct political source, and not only because they cause the loss of fiscal revenues within states. Criminal organizations whose business strategy is to operate in the shadow of the state have a manifest interest in preventing political change, and legal deregulation in particular, as the stability of the established order—including its legal prohibition of certain goods and services—is a core factor in their business models.

Other businesses that offer illicit services may, however, actually aim at political change. The Sicilian Mafia, in its beginnings, may be a case in point (Gambetta 1996: 261). According to legend, the Sicilian Mafia was in fact born during the Sicilian Vespers in 1282 as an expression of resistance against the Frenchman Charles of Anjou, who was at the time occupying Sicily. 'Mafia' allegedly served as acronym for 'Morte alla Francia, Italia anela' (Death to France, Italy desires!). However, there is more empirical evidence of recent cases in which criminal business organizations had an explicitly political agenda. A prominent example includes the Jane Collective's underground abortion service, which operated in Chicago from 1969 until abortion was legalized in the United States in 1973 (Kaplan 1997).[4] In cases such as this, the provision of illicit products and services was undertaken as 'an experiment aimed at eventual policy development or as compensation for services that, providers believe, should be offered or allowed by government' (Sapiro 2000: 11). Finally, one might include practices of 'managerial misbehaviour' and 'white collar crime' (Ackroyd and Collinson 2005: 307, Geis et al. 1995, Holcomb and Sethi 1992, Punch 1996) as well as 'dirty tricks' in the financial sector that have aroused public interest, particularly in recent years, such as stock dumping, insider trading, and (naked) short selling (see e.g. Braunberger 2011).

The second subcategory, the politics behind the product, refers to the complex social and normative contexts in which production is embedded, and in particular the input of production: the kind of resources and capital on which producers rely. When it comes to human capital and the selection of employees, for instance, various criteria spring to mind that determine how choices are made: from qualification and appearance, sex, racial background, religious belief, and even national or social background. Furthermore, the politics behind the product refers to the throughput of production, the procedural quality and methods by which inputs are turned into outputs, such as the techniques of resource extraction or labour conditions. Think, for instance, of the controversy over methods of keeping and slaughtering animals for food production. Different cultural and normative viewpoints appear to favour different methods. In 2010 a chorus of outrage was sparked in the United Kingdom, along with a boycott, when it was discovered that most meat sold in British supermarkets is halal. The main reason for the boycott (Liddle 2010) was opposition to the way that animals are killed in order for their meat to be considered halal. That is, the animal must be conscious while being killed (though in practice, animals slaughtered according to the halal method in the United Kingdom are often stunned first by being dipped in electrified water). Defenders of halal retorted that the prayer recited during the slaughtering procedure is an expression of real respect for the animals (though in practice, the prayer was sometimes played on a tape).

The third subcategory, politics beyond the product, refers to political effects emanating from production activity that are, it seems, part of it in a logically subordinate sense.[5] Production activity usually generates more than one output. Besides the main product (or joint products, e.g. gasoline and kerosene as resulting from the processing of crude oil), secondary outputs accrue from production activity that affect third parties. In economics, these secondary out-puts are termed externalities. Externalities may be positive. For instance, the fireproofing of a person's home improves the safety of neighbours' homes. Or they can be negative. Industrial discharge, waste, residues, air, water, soil, and visual pollution are costs that—to a large extent—are not reflected in prices and yet will usually be borne by people who have not chosen to incur such costs.

Economists have made considerable progress not only in identifying such market failures but also in developing ways to mitigate them by restructuring tax incentives; however, many by-products of economic production cannot be captured in terms of economic costs and benefits. Production practices may, for instance, distribute certain symbolic goods besides the economic product and externalities; they may mobilize or withdraw public support, or wield power in some other way. The subcategory of politics beyond the product is meant to capture this potential political relevance of economic production activity.

Moreover, practices fall into this third subcategory that take place both in the marketplace and on the stage of politics, or that are wedged somewhere in between. Besides corporate 'political strategies' such as public relations activism (Holtzhausen 2000) and astroturfing—the corporate financing and coordination of (fake) grassroots activism, as allegedly undertaken by

Table 6.1 Dimensions of producer politics

Politics of non-production	Delayed provision or destruction of products Refusal to provide specific products, producer strike
Politics of the product	Material output ('furnishing the world') Semiotic output ('fabrication of desire')
Politics behind the product	Input (discriminatory acquisition and employment of resources) Throughput (quality of production procedures)
Politics beyond the product	Residues ('secondary outputs', 'externalities) Social initiatives ('political strategies')

the Koch brothers with the Tea Party movement (Antle III 2010)—it is fair to characterize corporate social responsibility initiatives and the corporate philanthropy industry more generally as a kind of politics beyond the product.

Having sketched the three subcategories of producer politics individually, the differentiation can be illustrated by a brief example. Adbusters is primarily known for its anti-consumerism and anti-globalization magazine. However, in the last chapter we saw that it is also a shoe producer. In this capacity, Adbusters engages in the politics of the product by producing and selling (and advertising as such) high-quality shoes that are made of recycled and sustainable materials, comply with vegan standards, and are unencumbered by private trademarks (the blackspot, while being a definite logo, is open-source). As for the politics behind the product, Adbusters appears not to rely upon sweatshops or child labour, and markets its shoes via independent retailers only. Finally, the politics beyond the product concerns the utilization of the profits to finance anti-corporate, anti-commercial, and alter-globalization campaigns.[6]

6.2 The Denial of Producer Power

An analysis of producer politics must rest upon the assumption that individual producers actually control the effects of their activities even though the legal system and the behaviour of others create an incentive structure that can influence their decisions. Yet for producers, this incentive might be particularly strong, so strong that there might be little room for manoeuvre. That is, producer politics might turn out to be a chimera. One factor frequently considered to pre-structure producer agency is the rules of market capitalism; another is consumer power; and a third is the regulatory force of the state. The problematic implication of the denial of producer power is obvious enough: producers are exempted from political accountability. 'Nothing is so important in the defense of the modern corporation', J. Kenneth Galbraith (1983: 119–20) affirms accordingly, 'as the argument that its power does not exist'. More precisely, however, producers are let off the hook where people are affected negatively and not given credit where societal effects have a positive impact; and more generally, they are not grasped as political agents. All parties concerned, including third parties as well as policy-makers, are discouraged from analysing the political role that individual producers play in democratic societies.

Karl Marx's argument regarding the lack of producer power references the structural forces of capitalism. The oppression and exploitation of workers, Marx writes, do not come down to the actions of individual producers; rather, producers themselves are pawns in the hands of capitalism. Not the capitalist, but:

> capital employs labour [. . .] the capitalist does not rule the worker in any kind of personal capacity, but only in so far as he is 'capital'; his rule is only that of objectified labour over living labour; the rule of the worker's product over the worker himself.
>
> (Marx 1994: [3/k] 122)

To properly capture Marx's thoughts about the structural limitations of producer agency requires greater attention than space allows at this point, but we have already raised concerns in Chapter 2 about the way in which agency vanishes before our eyes in macropolitical approaches to the economy. With regard to producer agency, however, a particularly appealing objection can be made. In companies, checks and balances are established to delimit the range of behavioural options open to people operating within them. These checks and balances aim to increase the likelihood that management decisions will improve the firm's financial performance. Normative commitments among managers are accordingly blocked from influencing the company's course of action if they come along with a willingness to take a loss. This means that two or more courses of action never lead to the same financial performance. Maximum profit is not achievable in multiple ways, and as long as companies are modelled with profit maximization as the primary operating function, the determination of management decisions is not a matter of deliberation and choice but calculation (Jensen 2002: 239). Evoking the idea of consumer sovereignty, which suggests that supply is an echo of demand, additionally backs up this objection against the existence of producer politics.

We have already disputed the plausibility of the idea of consumer sovereignty in the preceding chapter; however, the argument concerning the institutionalized imperative of profit maximization suffers from two problems not yet addressed. The first is that company-internal checks and balances only decrease the likelihood, but do not rule out the possibility, of normative considerations other than profit-maximization influencing the decisions of corporate decision-makers. The second problem is the empirically unwarranted generalization that profit maximization is the primary operating function according to which all businesses are modelled.

To marginalize the relevance of producer politics in a different way, the role of the state can be invoked. Consumer demand may determine what, when, and how something should be produced, but the state determines what, when, and how something cannot be produced. The state prohibits and criminalizes certain economic practices (e.g. the cultivation of certain drugs) and implements regulation to internalize certain effects that result from production activity (e.g. with carbon emissions trading) or to compensate for others (e.g. by imposing Pigovian taxes). The state regulates production activity to control the societal effects resulting from production, and where it does not regulate—in the silence of law—it tolerates them. Sometimes the state even welcomes them. Remember that Adam Smith's idea of an invisible hand articulates the hypothesis of prosperity as a complete collateral effect. It predicts that the safest route to economic growth and welfare consists in allowing people to follow their rational self-interest and, for that matter, to rationally ignore whatever goes beyond it.[7] In consequence, the state really is in charge of most societal effects that emanate from production activity. Producers neither author nor control these effects in the last instance; they only execute them. It is the government's responsibility to speak up if the state tolerates the wrong kind of side effects. According to John Dewey, in fact, being in charge of side effects is the very definition of the state: 'When indirect consequences are recognized and there is effort to regulate them, something having the traits of a state comes into existence' (Dewey 1999: 12).[8]

Here, Ulrich Beck's theory of 'subpolitics' has something to say. Regardless of whether at one point in time the nation-state could control corporate activity's side effects, this does not hold true anymore today. With economic globalization unfolding, the information and telecommunications revolution, and the increasing pace of technological innovations, the indirect effects of production activity (and other forms of 'subpolitics') encroach ever more deeply on the structuration of living conditions. The state has ceased to be at the helm of social change, and hence it can no longer shoulder responsibility for the side effects of production activity. The (by-)production of societal consequences, of course, is unlikely to have soared in all fields of business, but it is difficult to deny that there is something in Beck's observation, once we visualize the destabilizing potential of algorithmic trading, through which apparently more than half of all orders on exchange markets are placed (Buchanan 2011).

If it is true that production activity impinges on the reinstitution of society to a greater extent today than in earlier periods, and that the state is increasingly incapable of exercising control (which I do not question at this point), then we need to rethink the traditional status attributed to producer power. The problem, for Beck, however, is that the shift of political power towards business actors does not change their nature.

There is still no place for political causes on their agenda, he claims: they don't and won't do politics deliberately. Only social movements and non-governmental organizations might manage to mitigate the loss of regulatory power, in his view.

This diagnosis has a certain appeal and alludes, I am inclined to believe, to a feeling that many people share regardless of educational background, social position, or party-political affiliation: companies will participate in the regulation of undesirable side effects of their production activity only if it serves their narrow economic interests, and hence will not participate very often. The following section questions the plausibility of this view, and relatedly, Beck's theory of subpolitics.

6.3 Economism-in-Disguise?

Before we proceed, recall that we applied the proposed framework for the analysis of producer politics to Adbusters as a shoe manufacturer, to indicate that it can be seen to engage in politics of, behind, and beyond the product. Unsurprisingly, Adbusters' publicly stated philosophy invites us to understand their shoe business as being expedient to a political agenda:

> We are a global network of culture jammers and creatives working to change the way information flows, the way corporations wield power, and the way meaning is produced in our society. [. . .] For too long we've ignored the market, written it off as enemy territory. Yet, what do mega-corps like Walmart and Coke fear most? Competition. We're talking about a new breed of bottom-up enterprise that does things differently: promotes ethics over profit, values over image, idealism over hype. A brand of grassroots capitalism that deals in products we actually need—and believe in. No sweatshops. [. . .] Just sustainable, accountable companies. Run by us.[9]

The Islamic, anti-imperialist, cosmopolitan company Mecca Cola, to give a second example, is equally insistent in its claim of instrumentalizing business for political causes. The fundamental idea of Mecca Cola, the company's website underlines, was to 'create a profit-making business which would help to relieve human suffering' and thus 'pu[t] the economy to work in the interest of ideology.' A suffering that cries out to be alleviated in Mecca Cola's view, then, is that of the Palestinian people, who are experiencing 'the most wretched and the most contemptible acts of apartheid and Zionist fascism'.[10]

Producers like Adbusters and Mecca Cola claim to do politics by economic means. Yet are such ideological agendas credible? Hardly any company refrains from informing the public about its 'ethical mission'. The 'promise of a humanitarian surplus' (Žižek 2010: 357) is common courtesy nowadays, and Adbusters's and Mecca Cola's activist statements might just be another marketing ploy. Economically, it seems after all, the communication of political ambition pays off rather well in times where post-material values are held in high esteem: Adbusters has sold more than 25,000 pairs of shoes, while Mecca Cola has become the official drink of the Organization of the Islamic Conference, sells over two million bottles per month in the United Kingdom, and has grabbed a market share of approximately 25% in the Middle East states and a respectable 1.7% in France (Usunier and Lee 2009, 214; Viboonchart 2008).

Readers might remember situations in which they have not hesitated to claim that producers happily jump on whatever bandwagon they like for profit's sake, but do not authentically pursue philanthropic or other political purposes. If so, their view would be in line with that of current scholarship, as corporate commitments to ideological goals other than profit-making tend to be considered as simply economism-in-disguise: 'recent literature suggests that the fact that corporations use zealous lobbying and political strategies to foster their economic ends does not change them into political actors' (Néron 2010: 347). The hypothesis that there is a total absence of political intentions among producers is also built into Beck's theory of subpolitics, as can be seen from the distinction between the (active) subpolitics of civil society agents and the (passive) subpolitics of producers:

> They [social movements and non-governmental organizations] 'aim to' do politics. In contrast [. . .] corporations [. . .] are non-political sources of power in modern society. [. . . They] are not interested in gaining political power or 'doing' politics per se. Rather, they happen to do politics as it were as a side-effect.
>
> (Holzer and Sørensen 2001: 11; see also Holzer and Sørensen 2003: 8)

To illustrate how passive subpolitics works, Beck (and subsequently Holzer and Sørensen) gives the example of research on human genetics, and in particular the Human Genome Project (Beck 2009: 204–12, Holzer and Sørensen 2003: 83–4). The Human Genome Project develops new possibilities for genetic diagnostics and therapy. Its successes are scientific innovations, yet along with scientific innovation, the Human Genome Project creates highly problematic precedents that parliaments are forced to accept as unalterable premises for legislation. Knowledge about genetic diagnostics and therapy, once acquired, cannot be ignored, and its use can hardly be prevented, whether or not this therapy is desirable for the population at large. And as a result, political regulation concerning the permissible range of genetic diagnostics and therapy systematically lags behind the work of the project. Thus, the theorists of subpolitics argue, the staff of the Human Genome Project exert political power. And as scientists strive for scientific progress, they exert political power unintentionally. But this last conclusion does not quite follow. It is true that the Human Genome Project's factual impact upon social life 'does not mean that scientists purposely try to make politics' (Holzer and Sørensen 2003: 84). But neither does it mean that they do not try. The fact that the medical innovations of the Human Genome Project pre-structure legal regulation does not tell us anything about the actual intentions of the scientists involved. Empirical evidence would be a means to justify this claim, but the theorists of subpolitics do not provide this. And what is more, however intuitively plausible an example of scientific innovation might appear (is it not true that scientists strive for unbiased knowledge about the world?), the Human Genome Project is actually a much harder empirical case than the theorists of subpolitics would have us believe. Even among medical scientists, the project has been criticized as politically biased. Shortly after the research project was launched, Alfred Tauber and Sahotra Sarkar (1993) published an article exposing 'The Ideology of the Human Genome Project' (and how often have we heard medical scientists speaking of ideology?).

The idea of passive subpolitics is unable to account for this political complexity because it is conceptualized as an intervening variable in the political process, not as politics itself (see esp. Holzer and Sørensen 2003: 91). In what is emerging as the 'age of side effects', society is being reinstituted as a 'risk society' (Beck 1996: 11; Beck 2009: 57, 80; see also Giddens 2002: 35), the backdrop of potential struggles between for instance risk takers and risk bearers (those who are happy to speculate for gain and those who have too much to lose to take the chance) goes unnoticed. Once again, or so it appears, humankind is overshadowed by its creations. And to a large extent the diagnosis rests upon the unproblematized supposition that producers (and other subpoliticians, such as the scientists of the Human Genome Project) do not pursue political goals.

But perhaps Max Weber's ideas on the potential for political intentions among producers add plausibility to the hypothesis. In his famous discussion *Politics as a Vocation*, Weber (2002c: 318) reflects on the 'availability' of different social groups to 'live for' politics. Property is an important factor, in his view. Nobles and medieval patricians were economically available, since they either held sufficient financial assets or acquired them from occasional gainful occupation. Modern professional politicians are also economically available because they 'live from' politics. Other social groups such as industrial workers, Weber claims, in contrast cannot devote time to politics since they have to work in order to assure a livelihood. Producers are in a better economic position. Nevertheless, Weber says, the producer 'is, of all the representatives of the propertied strata, the type who is least able to make himself available for politics'. First of all, producers lack time. They are 'tied [. . .] outwardly by the demands of the work inherent in running and making profits in a bourgeois-capitalist business'. Their business is unremitting, intense, and exhausting. Much more decisive than time pressure and work strain, however, is another factor. The 'modern manufacturer', Weber argues, is also 'tied inwardly'. Apart from the time he or she lacks:

> something else, something more important, which one might call inner availability, distance from the everyday conflicts of interest in the private economic sphere. [. . . He or she] is an interested party who is too directly involved in this struggle to be politically useful.
> (Weber 2002b: 111)

According to Weber, producers' minds are too absorbed in their business to engage in causes that go beyond the optimization of financial performance. If societal effects result from production activity, which is something Weber does not consider, they must take the form of unintended side effects.

Yet, tellingly, Weber does not stop at the argument concerning the temporally and mentally absorbing business of producers. In *The Protestant Ethic and the Spirit of Capitalism*, he (2002a) argues that, in addition to actual intentions, a subjacent layer of motivation must be taken into account. The this-worldly ('diesseitsbezogenes') goal of profit-maximization is often sought because it is a means for achieving (or being assured of) the otherworldly ('jenseitsbezogenes') goal of salvation. Protestant ethics fuels producers' pursuit of wealth, and the spirit of capitalism is, as it were, itself an unintended side effect. Whether Weber's protestantism–capitalism thesis is correct or not, the differentiation between intentions and motivations indicates that the pursuit of ends is a multi-layered issue, making it very difficult to say what an actor really strives after. Jo Littler (2009: 53), for instance, wonders accordingly whether the popular frame of corporate social responsibility discourse claiming to 'give something back' is a subliminal expression of guilty conscience among producers, for 'having taken something away' previously.

Moreover, the teleological action model underlying the assumption that producers and political goals do not go together is problematic, as there is little empirical evidence that actors always pursue clearly predetermined goals. Accounts that grasp goal-determination as an ongoing process that accompanies acting, and acknowledge the possibility of continuous goal-modification (Beckert 2003, Joas 1996), appear much more plausible. Yet the identification of economic goals as the exclusively conscious plans of producers is highly questionable even if we disregard unconscious or semi-conscious motivations and arguments about the processual and creative nature of goal-determination procedures. Even economists that deploy models of a purely economic character without bothering to integrate considerations of bounded rationality or patterns of reciprocity underline the persistence of non-economic intentions in rational agents. *Homo oeconomicus* is a model of rational action that might be analytically useful for thought experiments despite being utterly simplifying in some regards and too demanding in others (Kirchgässner 2010). But this model has little to say about the alleged prevalence of economic intentions in the human psyche and less still about whether the marketplace is populated by people with an economistic mindset.[11]

These reflections raise considerable doubts about whether the hypothesis of an absence of political intentions among producers could be verified. There is no way around empirical assessment of concrete cases, and practical judgment will sometimes lead to the conclusion that a producer pursued social ends in addition to economic ones. (Tellingly, Milton Friedman (1970) castigated business people, in his famous 1970 speech, for forgetting that the sole responsibility of business is to make profits.) Occasionally, in fact, the conclusion will be reached that a producer pursued a course of action with specific societal consequences regardless of compelling economic reasoning not to do so. In *Paramount Communications Inc. v. Time Inc.* (1989), for instance, the Time Inc.'s management was charged with failing to comply with its shareholders' interests. The Delaware Supreme Court dismissed the case, but affirmed the correctness of the claim presented against Time Inc., namely that it had willingly rejected a tender offer that was highly lucrative from an economic point of view (Margolis and Walsh 2003: 270–85). And, more generally, one must ask 'why a profit-maximizing corporation would spend millions of dollars on a high-risk project (political campaigns) with minuscule, if any, tangible particularistic rewards to distribute to individual shareholders' (Clark Muntean 2006: 2).

6.4 Intentions and Activist Strategy

The hypothesis of an absence of political intentions among producers implies the same exemption from accountability as the idea that producers' actions are ultimately determined by the state or by consumer demand and the laws of the market. The categorical rationalization of broader societal consequences of production activity in terms of unintended side effects, as Zygmunt Bauman, following Stanley Cohen, explains, belongs:

> to the linguistic arsenal of 'states of denial': denial of responsibility—moral as well as legal. [. . .] what the invoking of the 'unintentionality' argument intends to deny or exonerate is ethical blindness, conditioned or deliberate.
>
> (Bauman 2007: 117–18)

In moral philosophy as well as legal theory such generalizing states of denial are frequently challenged. One way to challenge them is to break up the dualism of intended effects and unintended side effects by differentiating on a spectrum between degrees of intentionality, negligence, *dolus eventualis* (i.e. hazarding the consequences), and recklessness between intent and the lack thereof.[12] Sometimes, unintended consequences are not impossible to anticipate or intentionally avoid (Bastiat 2006: 1, Bauman 2007: 118). And if an 'imperious immediacy of interest' (Merton 1936: 901) has actually blinded producers to recognizing the foreseeable likely consequences of their actions, a harsher verdict might be justified than if the unintended consequence results from a simple error of judgment.

Morally and legally, challenging the denial of room for manoeuvre as well as the presence of political intentions among producers is an important task if we want to counter the immunization of producers against attempts to hold them accountable for the political by-products of their economic production activity. Yet in the acknowledgment of producers as political and not merely economic actors something else is at stake, and this deserves consideration. The recognition of producers as political actors is practically relevant not only retrospectively but also prospectively: whether producers are grasped as political actors or not matters for activist strategizing.

By assuming that individual producers do not have political aspirations, scholars constrict activists' range of potential alliances with producers to strategic partnerships, that is, partnerships into which producers only enter because they find a certain 'political strategy' conducive to the achievement of their economic goals. Forging strategic alliances should of course be high on the activist agenda. Activists can surely become brothers in arms with producers in situations in which the implementation of better working conditions, the internalization of externalities, or the support of philanthropic projects, can be an effective tool for companies to shore up their reputation and gain an edge over competitors, all of which pays off economically. But activists that take seriously the possibility that individual producers might actually be available for politics will also be aware that producers are potential *ideological* partners in the pursuit of political causes. Political consumers can factor in that companies might occasionally be more easily motivated to pursue social ends in addition to economic ends through 'voice' than through shaming or 'exit' (see Section 5.2). Employee activists may realize that they can find support for the implementation of norms (e.g. against sexual harassment; see Section 4.1) among management members just as they can among their workmates.

In choosing their alliances, activists are well advised to cast their net wide and remain open to strategic as well as ideological partnerships. Sometimes, after all, and contrary to what Kofi Annan once claimed, there is no 'happy convergence between what [. . .] shareholders want and what is best for millions of people the world over' (Annan, quoted from Margolis and Walsh 2003: 273); governments are not always capable or willing to implement laws to regulate the negative externalities of production activity; and one might not wish to bet exclusively on the 'active' subpoliticians' ability to mitigate the challenge posed by 'passive' subpolitics.

The choosing of ideological alliances requires activists to assess the availability of individual producers (respectively the authenticity of corporate philosophies) for joint political projects, rather than allowing themselves to become engrossed in generalizing speculations about the presence or absence of normative commitments among producers. And in assessing the availability of producers for politics, they should take the so-called Knobe effect into account, which might also be at work in the academic literature on the political role of producers. The Knobe effect tells us that the ascription of intentionality is not independent from one's judgement about the praiseworthiness or blameworthiness of an action. Whether financial interests are found to prevail, concur, or collide with ecological, philanthropic, or social ones, or are superseded by them in a producer's decision, is not independent of our stance on whether we welcome or reject the societal effects brought about:

> [A] person's intuitions as to whether or not a given side-effect was produced 'intentionally' can be influenced by that person's attitude toward the specific side-effect in question. Thus, it would be a mistake to ask for a general answer to the question as to whether people will think that an agent intentionally brought about 'some side-effect *x*'. People's judgements will depend in a crucial way on what *x* happens to be. In particular, it will make a great deal of difference whether they think that *x* is something good or something bad.
> (Knobe 2003: 191; see also Jones 2009)

If side effects are negative, we appear to be inclined to assume that they have been brought about deliberately, whereas we tend to think that positive side effects were not foreseen. When interviewees in experiments validating the Knobe effect considered a first vignette, in which the vice president of a company tells the CEO that a new project will help to increase profits, but also harm the environment, and the CEO responds that she does not care about harming the environment and just wants to make profits, more than 80% said that the CEO intentionally harms the environment. Considering a second vignette, in which the only difference is that the new project will also help (instead of harm) the environment, and the CEO equally declares her wish to make profits and be indifferent in regard to environmental outcomes, only slightly more than 20% inferred intent.

Notes

1. A producers strike was a central strategy of the campaign, 'For Better Life!', which aimed, among other things, to increase pensions, to ensure that the

opposition had access to radio and television, and to bar Alexander Lukashenko from prolonging his presidential term. Visit the campaign's website (http://charter97.org/index.phtml?sid=4&did=NM_2003&lang=3, 'Belarusians will get better life', accessed 13 January 2013). Cristina Xalma (in Figueroa 2007: 213) also reports on a lasting producers' strike organized by the Venezuelan opposition that significantly contributed to preparing the coup d'état against Hugo Chávez on 11 April 2002.

2. The expression 'fabrication of desire' traditionally carries markedly negative connotations. In the works of Herbert Marcuse (2007: 9), Theodor W. Adorno and Max Horkheimer (1997: 38), Vance Packard (2007), Wilson B. Key (1974), and Pierre Bourdieu (1984: 230–43), it refers to social control and the creation of an endless series of insatiable needs. However, producer movements such as Slow Food or advertisements that raise awareness of high quality, local, fair-trade, or eco-friendly products cannot be dismissed so easily.
3. Interestingly, illegal economic activity has sometimes been considered the defining criterion of organized crime: 'The view that OC [organized crime] is involved in attempts to monopolize markets or territories coexists in the 1960s with another characterization, namely that the essence of OC is to provide illegal goods and services' (Varese 2010: 10).
4. The history of underground abortion services stretches far back, of course, and we know little about the political implications of its practice. Interestingly, though, midwifery might have become a target for persecution in the late Middle Ages under the charge of witchcraft because midwives' skills and knowledge regarding contraception and abortion effectively impeded efforts to repopulate the European continent after one-third of the population had been consumed by the Black Death. See Heinsohn and Steiger (1999).
5. In this sense, Neva R. Goodwin et al. (2006) state: '[w]e consider only useful outputs to be economic goods and services'.
6. Given the absence of evidence to the contrary, I assume that Adbusters's own portrayal is correct. Visit www.Adbusters.org/campaigns/blackspot, accessed 13 October 2014.
7. Though I attribute the invisible hand to Smith, I do not claim that the cornerstone for a justification of a laissez-faire economy is to be attributed to Smith rather than to a selective neoclassical reading of his work. Nevertheless, the passage in *The Wealth of Nations* that contains the expression 'invisible hand' nicely spells out the logic of the by-product hypothesis: 'every individual necessarily labours to render the annual revenue of the society as great as he can. He generally, indeed, neither intends to promote the public interest, nor knows how much he is promoting it. By preferring the support of domestic to that of foreign industry, he intends only his own security; and by directing that industry in such a manner as its produce may be of the greatest value, he intends only his own gain; and he is in this, as in many other cases, led by an invisible hand to promote an end which was no part of his intention. Nor is it always the worse for the society that it was no part of it. By pursuing his own interest, he frequently promotes that of the society more effectually than when he really intends to promote it' (Smith 2009: IV, Ch. 2).
8. Ironically, the silent displacement of power away from producers to the state (and indirectly, to the people) is missing in C. Wright Mills's book *The Power Elite*. Mills alarmingly warns against the existence of a power elite in the United States—with one constituent of this being producers—that would determine the community's fate. Though well argued, a certain confusion arises because on several occasions Mills suggests that the power of members

of the elite is not really theirs but resides in their position; that it is institutional, and in the case of managers, market-driven: 'Whether they do or not take such decisions is less important than the fact that they do occupy such pivotal positions' (Mills 2000: 4). Furthermore, neither compatible with the imagery of a power elite nor with that of a power gone systemic, the conclusion claims that, ultimately, the elite's power is theirs only by virtue of the indulgence of the people, who are invited to pay greater attention to holding those at the institutional apexes accountable (Pitkin 1998: 256).

9. Source of quotation: *Adbusters Magazine*, "The Big Ideas of 2006" issue.
10. This quotation is no longer on Mecca Cola's website (www.mecca-cola.com) but can still be found on the archived website as of 28 September 2007 (http://web.archive.org/web/20070928041147/www.mecca-cola.com/en/index.php, accessed 28 September 2014). Littler (2009: 39, cf. also Murphy 2003) characterizes the spirit underlying Mecca Cola as 'Islamic anti-imperialist cosmopolitanism'.
11. For a remarkably honest acknowledgement, see Downs (1957: 5–6).
12. Drawing on Alexander of Aphrodisia's theodicy, Agamben (2007: 6; see also 2011: 118) proposes eliminating of the dualism between main effects and side effects of actions: 'Alexander argues [. . .] that collateral effects are not accidental but define the very structure of the act of governance. Neither general nor particular, neither intentional nor casual, neither foreseen nor unforeseen, neither reign nor government; the collateral effect is the way in which the divine government becomes effective, in which providence realises itself. And only therefore can the governmental machine, [. . .] only through its side-effects, the machine can become operative'.

7 Entrepreneurial Space Production

Entrepreneurship and production activity overlap in many regards; nevertheless, it is worth distinguishing between them as they usually take place at different stages in the economic process. Whereas production activity concerns the logistical, technical, operational, and remunerative execution of business, entrepreneurship concerns the moment of economic founding: the setting up of a business.

Just as the formal political founding act defines the basic framework for future interaction within a polity, so the economic founding act prestructures interactions within an enterprise. First of all, entrepreneurship institutes production and work processes, establishes checks and balances as well as other forms of organizational control, and institutionalizes the channels through which intra-firm struggles take place. Michael Walzer, as we have seen (see Chapter 2), in his discussion of the Pullman case calls for a legal norm of industrial democracy: employees should not have to go on strike to have a say in corporate decision-making. Yet, while industrial democracy is required neither by law nor prevailing custom, entrepreneurs are free to install participatory managerial structures—as for instance, has been implemented at the Mondragón Corporación Cooperativa.

J.K. Gibson-Graham (2006a: 65–6) argues that entrepreneurial founding acts not only affect employees and other immediate stakeholders, but also legitimize and normalize one or another managerial structure design, and, more generally, one or another business model. An enterprise may be established as 'capitalist' (e.g. a family firm, a private unincorporated firm, a multi-national company); 'alternative capitalist' (e.g. a state enterprise, a green firm, a non-profit firm, producer and consumer cooperatives); or 'non-capitalist' (e.g. communal, independent, feudal, slave). Surplus may be distributed to owners, shareholders, co-operators, put towards expansion, distributed according to communal (e.g. environmental) concerns, or in yet other ways. Through the normalization of different business models, entrepreneurial founding acts not only impact the lives of employees and residents but also modify the face of the economic order. Therefore, Gibson-Graham argues, it really matters, politically speaking, how businesses are set up. The ever-inventive Kalle Lasn from Adbusters, who apparently shares this conviction, accordingly states that his shoe company intends to promote a new kind of 'grassroots capitalism'; and to signify the difference between his business model and prevailing models, he calls himself an 'antipreneur' (Quittner 2008).

'Antipreneurial' politics can also be imagined in a literal sense. The undoing of entrepreneurial founding acts, Virginia Sapiro (2000: 19–20) argues, used to be an important strategy in political struggles. During the early-modern period, for instance, hegemonic forces destroyed printing presses and press offices to prevent the dissemination of unwanted propaganda. Many more entrepreneurial practices could be mentioned whose consequences transcend the premises of companies, not least the outsourcing of segments of a company's production or its entire relocation, the threat thereof, or the invisible decisions of entrepreneurs to refuse the exit-option despite unattractive tax rates and wage costs. However, rather than mapping different forms of entrepreneurial politics, the focus of this chapter falls on one kind of entrepreneurial act by which entrepreneurs non-verbally communicate with their environment and intervene in larger societal conflicts: practices of de-signing a company domicile, that is, the entrepreneurial politics of producing space.

As we shall see, macropolitical approaches to economic matters provide fairly elaborate theories of entrepreneurial space production. Again, these theories concern the global, homogenous, and unambiguous macro-trends of late modern capitalism. Though I do not aim to rule out or refute macro approaches, the goal of this chapter is to illustrate the difference that a micropolitical approach can make to our perception of practices of entrepreneurial space production.

For this task, the theoretical framework I have developed in previous chapters will be used to discuss a concrete example: the construction of a Burger King restaurant in Nuremberg, Germany. The case is particularly fitting, because macro theories of entrepreneurial space production in fact make frequent reference to fast-food multinationals to corroborate their claims. Indeed, one popular theory is even named after a company (the 'McDonaldization of society'). Before turning to the case in detail, I will spell out some implications of the 'spatial turn' for political theory and briefly review the political significance that macro theories attribute to late-modern entrepreneurial space production.

7.1 The Politics of Space Production

Questions about the relationship between politics and space obviously arise in analyses of the nature of the state. Sovereignty, after all, is commonly understood as the supreme authority over people within a territory. When it comes to enterprises, this connection is less clear, since entrepreneurial authority over employees within the premises of a company is not supreme. Contrary to Walzer's claim—set out in Chapter 2—, firms are only metaphorically comparable to polities with regard to territorial control. Pullman's company town was a quasi-state within the sovereign state, not a real state amongst others. Though not sovereign, it is still true that company founders control people by controlling territory to some extent, for instance by laying down rules, determining what can be done on company premises, or restricting access (Sack 1986: 2, 87, Ch. 6). In the Pullman case, the spatial scope of power extended well beyond the factory gates and effectively stretched over the whole town (Smith 2000: 65).

To some extent, entrepreneurs exercise control over workers and residents in a way that is comparable to the control that the three branches of government supposedly exercise over inhabitants of a nation-state. Yet entrepreneurs wield power not only within a certain territory, but also through spatialization when they set up their business. The control thus exercised over a geographical area is not legal authority, but rather authority through configuration of the physical environment. That the control exercised through spatialization is control proper, and thus can be said to impinge on people's thoughts and deeds, is the central claim of the spatial turn. To understand more precisely how spatialization relates to the process of reinstituting society (and how, in particular, entrepreneurial space production may align with the articulation and enactment of collective identity), it is necessary to briefly summarize its basic tenets.[1]

Since the 1970s, scholars have increasingly emphasized that '[g]eography matters, not for the simplistic and overly used reason that everything happens in space, but because where things happen is critical to knowing how and why they happen' (Warf and Arias 2009: 1). Their analyses have led to an understanding of spatiality that conceives of space not as a vessel that might or might not contain events, but such that the places we inhabit always carry meaning, that they are differentiated and expressive, produced and active; that they are, as it were, events themselves. Landscape features such as mountains, forests, or rivers leave their imprints on regional identities. People draw links between such features and their local community's characteristics; they extrapolate from them to life on earth more generally, and sometimes go even further and extrapolate to the supernatural.

Features of the physical environment insert themselves into a culture to an even greater extent once that culture has begun to influence the environment. The deeds of great women and men—but also the daily rounds of ordinary people—leave tangible markers of memory across landscapes, and register themselves in material cultural heritage. Footpaths, cairns, fences, monuments, and buildings such as churches, but also seemingly empty squares differentiate space and make it emerge in the form of definite places. Such places provide 'mnemonic clues and memorials to a shared past' (Kogl 2008: 14), reminding us of who 'we' are, and offering sets of prescriptions to remind us of how we ought to behave. In addition to the hierarchy of values that places communicate, sometimes the physical organization of places literally makes room for one kind of activity while leaving no space for others. Hence, if we have spoken as if space were an undifferentiated, passive physical substrate, this was because we did not consider the mutual enmeshing of the material environment and social life.

As soon as we take into account this enmeshing and acknowledge that space is a socially- and culturally superimposed construction—that space is active and not passive, produced and not given, power-laden and not neutral, hierarchical and not evenly balanced—we are able to investigate entrepreneurs' space-producing activities with a view to the formation of collective identity as one aspect of the process of reinstituting society. Put simply, we can distinguish between two basal, analytically separable, aspects of the political significance of a place. On the one hand, places are imbued with meaning and act upon those who enter their terrain in powerful ways; they tell us who 'we' are, what we may and may not do, and sometimes even structure what we can and cannot do. On the other hand, there must be ways in which human practices reconfigure the texture of a place, ascribe and attach meaning to the environment, leave, transform, or erase marks—in short, produce space. If so, people are shaped by the places in which they live and shape them in turn.

Michel Foucault (1986) pioneered this geographical enrichment of our philosophical vocabulary. Henri Lefebvre (2009) and Michel de Certeau (1984), among others, took Foucault's ideas further and urged us to improve our spatial sensibility in order to better understand power relations and their concatenation with concrete places, as well as the opportunities for transforming them. That an intensification of geographical dimensions has finally taken root in political thought might be inferred from the apparent normality that terms such as 'displacement', 'spheres', 'flows', or 'subject positions' have acquired in contemporary efforts to rethink politics (Farrar 2008: 4).

Sometimes, however, the idea of place-based politics has been considered anachronistic. Geographers have argued that meanings and worldviews, once actually embodied in the built environment, are now almost exclusively expressed in the written word (Tuan 2008: 113–15). There is indeed some evidence that the alignment of politics and identity with place became outdated the very moment spatial dynamics most flagrantly obtruded themselves upon political thinking; moreover, under a term that at the same time both absolutizes and annihilates the notion of spatial practice: does 'globalization' not indicate an era in which space is no longer particular and differentiated (e.g. bordered in nation-states), but general and undifferentiated (namely global)? Does globalization not point to an era where geographies shift from the space of place to the space of flows? Is it not that today '[s]pace is, as it were, "ironed out" in order to speed things up' (Smethurst 2000: 37)?

To be sure, there is little reason to think that places are becoming entirely irrelevant, even if globalization was an all-pervasive, linear development. Nevertheless, one must take those contributions diligently arguing that the conditions for place-based politics have significantly changed in late modernity seriously. Alexandra Kogl explains the concern as follows:

> [L]ate modern, capitalist places do not seem to be places at all. Unlike spaces that ring with a tumult of meanings, expressed in everything from a whisper to a shout, late modern, capitalist spaces seem not to express meaning at all. They seem to be merely rational, practical, and functional. They do not speak of the glory of God, as a cathedral does, or of the actual routes taken by real people, as a dirt footpath does, or of a nation's history and political ideals, as a monument does. They do not seem to speak at all.
>
> (Kogl 2008: 14)

Late modern sites such as airports, motorways, or shopping centres apparently lack the local meaning and specificity that defines traditional places. The point is not that late modern sites do not shape and are not shaped by human beings. From the fact that these sites lack a sense of place and do not seem to embody meaning it cannot be concluded that they are less ideologically imbued and powerful than traditional places. Meanings and the operation of power might be less obvious here, yet late modern sites are nevertheless marked by clear prohibitions and exhortations. Shopping centres and motorways 'mak[e] room for some kinds of activities (e.g. shopping, driving) and not for others (e.g. loafing, walking)' (Kogl 2008: 3). They forcefully assert meaning and channel the behaviour of those who enter their territory. The central characteristic of late modern places is not that they are not places at all, but that they are instances of essentially inauthentic 'abstract space' instead of 'lived space':

> Abstract space simplifies and reduces human functions and desires, organizing space into cells, each linked to production or reproduction, narrowly understood. [. . .] Excluded are such uncapitalist values as state power (other than that the market requires), pleasure and abundance (other than those of the commodity), laziness, wonder (other than that at human technical capacities), sociability and friendship (other than that represented to sell consumer goods).
>
> (Kogl 2008: 25; order of the argument reversed)

Abstract space is produced so that people will move through it according to primarily individual desires and purposes. It is imbued with 'capitalist values', it is 'economistic', and 'masculine', if not 'white' (Kogl 2008:

23–4, 31 n. 35; see also Merrifield 1993: 523). The greatest problem with abstract space, of course, is that it is being created exponentially—and entrepreneurs have been identified as major agents in the production of this abstract space. Kogl accordingly writes that the empirical difference between abstract space and lived space is that the latter is 'experienced and shaped by ordinary people over the course of their daily round', whereas the former is 'imagined and shaped by the state and influential economic actors (including real estate developers and large retailers)' (Kogl 2008: 22).[2]

In the following sections I will argue that the differentiation between abstract and lived space, as well as the identification of its agents, as presented by Kogl and other scholars who rely on macropolitical approaches, obstructs rather than helps our understanding of entrepreneurial practices of spatialization. The problem is not that these theories search only for similarities between particular entrepreneurial productions of space, while disregarding the dissimilarities, to reveal a pattern. Rather, they fail to take into account that the particular (geographical and historical) context of an entrepreneurial space-production co-determines its political meaning.

It is tempting to go about this task by taking up the Pullman case again.[3] Model towns—company-owned or otherwise—should, after all, be good examples of abstract space because they are conceived and created for inhabitants, not by them, and are therefore somewhat inauthentic by their very nature. Given that model towns represent a cleaned up, perfected, and homogenized social order, one would expect theorists of abstract space to be ready to generalize what James C. Scott (2008: 126) said about the biggest state-planned city, Brasilia: instead of planning a city, its founders actually planned to prevent a city. However, Pullman cannot be legitimately subsumed under the notion of economistic abstract space. Just like other classic company towns such as Saltaire (established in 1853 by the wool industrialist Titus Salt in West Yorkshire) or Henry Ford's Fordlândia, (established in 1928 in Brazil), so Pullman's entrepreneurial founding act is a phenomenon of an earlier historical period. As such, we would need to investigate contemporary company towns such as Celebration (the unincorporated master-planned community of The Walt Disney Company, established in 1994 in Florida) or the Novartis headquarters in Basel, Switzerland.[4] However, the Burger King restaurant in Nuremberg, Germany, should be an equally qualified case, as fast-food chain outlets are seemingly not only good examples, but in fact paradigmatic instantiations of the late modern production of abstract space.

7.2 Fast-Food Chains and the Production of Space

McDonald's and Burger King outlets are everywhere in the developed world. They can be found in city centres and suburbs as well as along motorways. There is one in the Pentagon and another on the Guantanamo

Bay Naval Base. There is a ski-through on a slope in Sweden and by now Beijing and Moscow have their own outlets as well. In addition to existing everywhere, fast-food chain outlets characteristically bear many similarities to one another:

> [T]hey generally look much the same from the outside, they are structured similarly within, the same foods are served, workers act and interact in much the same way, and so on. There is little that distinguishes one outlet of a chain of fast-food restaurants from all the others.
>
> (Ritzer 2008: 171)

Notably, conformity is not a coincidence, but a systematic policy:

> [T]he whole idea is to turn out restaurants that are virtual clones of one another. To put it another way, the goal is to produce restaurants that are as alike as one another as possible.
>
> (Ritzer 2008: 171)

Fast-food operations such as McDonald's and Burger King are everywhere and are the same everywhere as well, so we are told. As a result, it does not seem particularly far-fetched to say that they are the paradigmatic offspring of the spatial dynamics of late modernity. Paul Smethurst (2000: 33, 40, 56–7) accordingly refers to McDonald's restaurants to illustrate what scholars have in mind when they speak of the diffusion of 'utterly uniform "pseudo places"' and 'economically-driven placelessness', or the 'homogenisation of space under global capitalism'. For Kogl (2008: 31 n. 35), Burger King outlets are typical examples of 'abstract space'. George Ritzer (Ritzer 2008: 48, 170) sees sites that are 'centrally conceived', 'devoid of distinctive substantive content', and 'lack a sense of history' in McDonald's and Burger King restaurants; places that are, as he puts it strongly, 'nothing'.

In Ritzer's work, in fact, multinational fast-food chains stand for a much broader trend in late modernity. The 'McDonaldization of society' is his label for the 'process by which the principles of the fast-food restaurant [namely: efficiency, calculability, predictability, and control] are coming to dominate more and more sectors of American society as well as of the rest of the world' (Ritzer 2008: 1).[5] Though denoting a broader societal trend, it goes without saying that the McDonaldization thesis applies to the production of space more generally. Roger Lewis (2002) therefore concludes that the (sub-)process by which the constructed environment is 'becoming increasingly globalized, standardized, sanitized', is the 'McDonaldization of architecture'.

To be sure, nobody goes as far as seeing perfect incarnations of 'abstractness' or 'nothingness' in existing outlets of McDonald's and Burger King.

Ritzer reminds us that 'every fast-food restaurant has at least [. . .] some elements of somethingness associated with it'. Kogl's theoretical framework also includes this proviso, affirming that 'abstract space' and 'lived space' are characterized as the two conceptual poles of a continuum. It is often taken into account that corporate architects customize the language on restaurant signs to comply with local building commissions' legal regulations, as well as the fact the corporate identities of fast-food chains are, here and there, slightly inflected in response to local traditions. These authors do not make a case for an elusive architectural determinism. Space is not considered to be a passive vessel or static entity, but a creation in flux, an ongoing production. It is acknowledged that the material and semiotic structure of space is not only be shaped by those who initially fabricate a place, but also transformed by those who use and inhabit it. In consequence, places are conceptualized as contestable and capable of being reclaimed (Ritzer 2008: 171–7, Kogl 2008: 22).

However, these qualifications modify the picture only slightly. 'Glocalization' very much appears to be a euphemistic (and misleading) description of what is going on in the outlets of fast-food chains. Grave doubts remain about whether McDonald's and Burger King restaurants in, for instance, East Asia and Russia have really been transformed into 'local institutions' (Watson 2000: 6; see also Yan 2000: 55) and 'something that is authentically indigenous'; it is claimed that this is so because customers 'have accepted McDonald's as a local and personally meaningful experience', or 'tak[e] aspects of McDonald's into their homes' (Caldwell 2004: 16, 20) very much appears to mistake the globalization of the local for the localization of the global. It is also hard to believe that Luca Zaia, Minister of Agriculture in the Berlusconi administration, was not crossing his fingers behind his back when he assured his fellow Italians that the government-supported 'McDonald's speaks Italian' campaign 'defend[s] our identity and the "Made in Italy" trademark'. Even less plausible is his claim that the promotion of 'McItaly' burgers could help educate European teenagers 'to forget about junk food and choose a healthier and better quality food'.[6]

Ritzer rightly warns against being deceived by strategies of controlled niche marketing and fake customization. The CEOs of Burger King and McDonald's may suggest that their companies are actually 'multilocal' rather than 'multinational' (see the quotes from interviews with Jeff Campbell and James Cantalupo in Watson 2000: 12 and Zoglin 2005). However, such public relations statements might be perfectly consistent with the in-house strategy (as articulated by one of the two companies) 'to look for new, innovative ways to create an experience that is exactly the same no matter what McDonald's you walk into, no matter where it is in the world' (Herman M. Rosenthal quoted from Leidner [2006: 82]). A moment's critical reflection, affirms Ritzer, reveals that fast-food restaurants are far from testifying to the mutual and balanced interpenetration of the global and the local (i.e. glocalization). Rather, the global is unidirectionally, if imperfectly, imposed upon the local: 'Grobalization'[7], not glocalization, is what is going on. Because of their lack of 'distinctive substantive content', Ritzer claims, McDonald's and Burger King restaurants are far from the 'something' end of the continuum: The proliferation of 'McDonald's (and other fast-food chains) is therefore a near-perfect example', in fact 'the epitome of the grobalization of nothing' (Ritzer 2008: 174, 182).[8]

7.3 Burger King, Nuremberg, Germany

To a large extent, the Burger King outlet on 336 Regensburger Straße Nuremberg, Germany, precisely affirms the aforementioned type of experience.[9] In most regards, it appears to be just another clone of the thousands upon thousands of McDonald's or Burger King restaurants in the world. However, the building happens to be the transformer station of the former Nazi Party rally grounds, Hitler's largest ensemble of monumental buildings and parade fields.

Completed in 1936, the transformer station housed the generators that provided electricity for the annual propaganda events of the National Socialist German Worker Party ('Nuremberg rallies'). Notably, the generators supplied electricity for the 130 searchlights that turned the Zeppelin Field into a cathedral of light, and the Zeppelin Grandstand (from which Hitler spoke and which was fashioned after the Pergamon Altar) into a proper 'altar'. The building was already full of symbolism because of this function. In addition, Albert Speer, its architect, designed the transformer station in a style corresponding to the other representative buildings of the rally grounds. In accordance with the basic thought guiding Nazi architecture, constructions would serve both a functional and a larger purpose. On the one hand, the buildings and complexes of the Nazi Party rally grounds would set the stage for propaganda, while on the other hand, they would be propaganda themselves (Dietzfelbinger and Liedtke 2004: 62, Doosry 2002: 138).

The 'violation of human scale' (Speer 1995: 204) of the urban neoclassical buildings should communicate the rigidity of the Führer's will, overawe the spectator, and instil in each German a sense of the insignificance of the individual. (The corresponding verbal expression was the rally slogan: 'you are nothing, your people are everything'.) Speer, the ingenious official architect of the Third Reich, had no doubts about the symbolic potency of the colossal buildings (Speer 1995), and Hitler, the would-be artist, enthusiastically agreed with him. In fact, Hitler was convinced that the ideological message of his regime was most efficiently imparted through architecture. The message transmitted by material forms of expression, he lectured, is 'more compelling than the spoken word. It is the word made manifest in stone'. As such, it should 'speak as eternal witness'.[10]

The transformer station largely escaped the air raids of the Second World War, and thereafter was neither torn down nor significantly altered. Until it was sold in 2006, it was the property of the public energy company N-Ergie and sporadically used for storage (Möller 2006a). In the main, however, it served as a warning monument ('Mahnmal')—a status officially bestowed in 1973. A new Bavarian state law declared that the buildings on the Nazi Party rally ground, including the transformer station, were worthy of preservation for their significance as 'witnesses to the past' (Macdonald 2006a: 17). Set slightly apart from the main Third Reich sites in Nuremberg, the transformer station was perhaps not of central historical interest to foreign visitors. Yet, for locals it always had an eerie presence because it preserves the memory of the Nazi past in a unique way. Although the Allies had abraded all National Socialist emblems from buildings in 1945, Nazi symbolism can still be clearly identified at the transformer station: the black shadow of a stone imperial eagle holding the swastika in its claws stands out against the white granite.

In 2006, N-Ergie sold the building to an investor, who subsequently opened a Burger King restaurant. Communal construction regulations complicated the architectural conversion of the historic building, yet a sufficient number of signs and architectural features specific to the

Figure 7.1 Transformer station, Nazi Party rally grounds (1936)
Photo courtesy of Stadtarchiv Nürnberg (Signature: A 49-He-2394)

company were eventually integrated into the façade and the forecourt of the transformer station. Thus, the outward appearance could be conciliated with the standard corporate design that is implemented all over the world. The standardization of the interior was unproblematic.

It would not be unreasonable to assume that the result of this entrepreneurial act was the deprivation of a place's historical significance, such that the memorial site was turned into an economistic 'abstract space'. The political significance of the 2006 event would accordingly consist (only) in the consolidation of global capitalism. And a number of local commentators actually took this view. According to Hans-Christian Täubrich, Head of the Documentation Centre of the Nazi Party rally grounds, this is an unprecedented case of a 'Nazi-building being turned into a purely commercial site' (Täubrich quoted from Möller 2006a). Christof Popp, who had been commissioned to design a set of information boards at the Nazi Party rally grounds in the run-up to the 2006 FIFA World Cup, together with the architect Xiaotian Li, was 'shocked' to find that the historical building had been reused as if it were an 'empty shell' (Popp quoted in Möller 2006b). City councillor Joachim Thiel similarly claimed on his website that the conversion of the transformer station has deprived a historical site of its national significance, and amounted to the 'historically insensitive trivialization' of National Socialism (Thiel n.d.; for similar statements, see also Heyer 2006). This economization thesis also seems to be corroborated by the statements of the actors actively involved in the conversion process. Herbert Dombrowsky, a member of the executive board of N-Ergie, pointed out that his company had decided to sell the transformer station to the investor with the highest bid because they did not consider the building to be a site of National Socialist self-representation (Möller 2006a). The winning investor (CT Projektentwicklungsgesellschaft Bochum) stated that the management had acted out of mere economic interest (Möller 2006c).[11] More surprisingly, the municipal authorities apparently did not have any historical qualms about the development. The building directorate of the city of Nuremberg raised no objections to the project apart from imposing building regulations, and made its decision without conferring with other (and arguably more cautious) parties such as the mayor or the advisory board to the city council, which in 2004 had been established for the explicit purpose of deliberating issues concerning the preservation of the Nazi Party rally grounds as 'witnesses to the past' (Möller 2006b).

Quite obviously, the actors involved were more concerned with making business than commemorative politics. But this fact must not lead us to jump to two conclusions—one concerning intentions, the other concerning consequences—that nourish the economization thesis. On the one hand, it would be premature to conclude that the entrepreneurs were unaware that the conversion of the building would shape German memorial culture. Deliberations about the historical legacy of the

Figure 7.2 The erstwhile transformer station turned into a Burger King restaurant in 2006

Photo by the author, 2011

building must have already taken place among the decision-makers at Burger King, given that the restaurant staff have been advised to refer customers to the information board some twenty metres in front of the building when asked about the site's history. And while most employees carry out this instruction, some are happy to give their assessment of the conversion privately. Two employees thus argued independently of one another that the conversion constitutes a win–win situation: the historical legacy makes the Burger King special and the Burger King draws attention to the historical legacy. It is likely that their bosses factored in the history of the site, too, since they cannot reasonably have expected to generate positive publicity. Entrepreneurs may plausibly hope to shore up a fast-food chain's reputation by setting up outlets in prestigious historical structures (e.g. in Oxford, a half-timbered residence that dates back to the 15th century has been let by Jesus College to Pret A Manger, making it a somewhat more upmarket sandwich bar than usual); but it is unlikely that a structure that is unmistakably National Socialist in origin, and which helped turn Hitler's inflammatory speeches into moments of messianic epiphany, could have the same effect. Tellingly, bloggers soon established connections between the swastika and Burger

King's logo as 'two symbols of imperialism', and the derisive nickname 'Hitler King' took root among locals. Not least, the entrepreneurs could draw on earlier experiences of fast-food giants encountering Germany's material heritage of National Socialism. During a 1996 advertising campaign by McDonald's in Dachau, flyers were circulated in the car park next to the Dachau Concentration Camp Memorial site addressing the 'concentration camp tourist'. After sharp protest, the outlet franchisee offered a formal apology, admitting that he had ignored certain historical sensibilities (Ryback 1999: 28; cf. Schlosser 2002: 234). On the face of it, there is every reason to believe that the economic actors involved in the conversion of the erstwhile transformer station gave careful thought to the historical circumstances of their chosen site. Perhaps the decision-makers at Burger King calculated that this time the negative publicity would not jeopardize the project's economic success, or maybe they hoped to increase brand awareness through some kind of shock advertising. At any rate, it is likely that they willingly allowed commemorative politics to happen.

On the other hand, the fact that economic interests probably overruled historic qualms does not mean that the historical site was, in effect, transformed into a purely economistic space. While the move to place a Burger King restaurant in the erstwhile transformer station certainly undermined much of the building's symbolic potency as a 'witness to the past', it would be hasty to conclude that it undermined the building's symbolic potency in the context of the German material culture of remembrance as such. As I will argue in the next section, the political significance of the conversion of the erstwhile transformer station reveals itself only against the backdrop of the role that the memorialization of National Socialism has come to play—both for the construction of identity in the city of Nuremberg in particular, and in Germany more generally.[12]

7.4 The Discourse on German Nationhood

Memorial Culture and the Construction of National Identity

To properly understand the political significance of Burger King's act of entrepreneurship in Nuremberg, let us recall that, according to post-foundational thought, the construction of collective identity is a crucial aspect in the process of reinstituting society. Before political groups can defend their interests and struggle over the allocation of resources, they must establish themselves as groups in the first place. Perceptive of the contingency of collective identities, Carl Schmitt concluded that the articulation of collective identity constitutes the essence of the political. Apart from the political importance of the contingency of collective identities, Schmitt's crucial insight was that identities form relationally: the political consists in the distinction between friend and enemy (Schmitt 1996: 25–6). Contemporary post-foundational thought still considers Schmitt's insights highly pertinent, but believes that two qualifications need to be made. First, friend and enemy are not so much distinguished or identified, but constructed and continuously modified. Second, the construction of collective identities concerns empirically specifiable groups of actually existing individuals less than the demarcation of somewhat phantasmagorical projections. 'Self' and 'other' replace Schmitt's friend and enemy, and are formed in a contested process of continuous, relationally dependent reconstruction.[13]

National identity is one contested field of identity construction among many others in the political consciousness of individuals and groups. National identity overlaps with other political identities, and draws from them for its own construction as well as from factors such as language, culture, or religion. History—more precisely, historical consciousness—is another particularly important factor for the construction of national identity. Through shared beliefs in a common past, history becomes a legacy for the present that indicates the contours of a common fate. By drawing on the power of the past, people are brought into supposedly old or supposedly new forms of sociality (Fairclough et al. 2008; Fulbrook 1999: 17). As different answers may be given as to what this common past actually is and through which parts of the material and intangible heritage the common past is preserved, the ongoing process of national identity formation and reformation can be understood as a contested discourse. And a rich diversity of textual sources feeds this discourse. Apart from written and oral textual resources (e.g. public speeches, history textbooks, and oral narratives), material heritage in particular may also have an 'identity-conferring status' (McLean 2006: 3; Simon and Ashley 2010: 247; Urry 1996: 61).[14]

In Germany, the mutual enmeshing of the material environment and social life has been somewhat special since 1945 (Fulbrook 1999: 25–47; Gregor 2008; Macdonald 2009: 8–13; Niven and Paver 2010; Young 1992). While parts of the population still hoped to rehabilitate the German nation in the aftermath of World War Two by reasserting traditions from pre-fascist times, German memorial culture found itself in a quandary: first, most historical traditions were manifestly discredited (e.g. Prussian militarism) or under suspicion of having been accessories to what had happened (e.g. German idealism). Second, other traditional sources of nationalism could not be reclaimed either. The new state could not tell the story of a glorious victory over evil enemies and recall the martyrdom of those who gave their lives so that the nation could live. Instead, Germany had to exercise restraint in expressing national pride and enmities. Third, it was confronted with the undesirable, but also indelible, heritage of National Socialism, which one could not simply forget, but had to come to terms with. Thus, German memorial culture could not easily fulfil what David Miller regards as an essential feature of national identity, namely that national identity 'embodies historical continuity' (Miller 2000: 28). Instead, the state was compelled to stress the discontinuity with its own past to regain legitimacy, even if sometimes this meant only to portray the Third Reich as a terrible accident that had *happened to* the German people. At any rate, to a considerable extent post-World War II Germany re-established its 'self' through temporal differentiation by positing Nazi Germany as its 'other'.

To some extent, of course, processes of identity reconstruction can always be characterized through descriptions of what they are not. The 'other', according to poststructuralism, is not just something 'else', something that is unrelated and marginal. Rather, it is decisive and constitutive; the 'other', in the words of Henry Staten (1986: 16), is the 'constitutive outside' of the 'self'. 'Self' and 'other' are both formed in a contested process of continuous, relationally dependent reconstruction. However, in post-World War II Germany, the construction of identity against an outside exhibits itself in particularly unambiguous terms: the 'othering' of National Socialism had been the leitmotif of memorial culture in both the German Federal Republic and the German Democratic Republic, even though it is also true that the 'othering' was undertaken in different ways in East and West Germany (Fulbrook 1999: 28–35; Herf 1997; Niven 2002: 39–59; Reichel 1999). Moreover, the legacy of fascism has also been a crucial point of reference since reunification in 1990. The articulation of German identity—together with its implications for the questions of who or what one is struggling against, why and by what means—is still dependent upon, and to a large extent accomplished by, the demarcating projection of National Socialism.

It is within this context that Burger King's spatializing practice acquires its political significance, as Speer's transformer station constitutes an important part of the undesired legacy that is 'othered' in the process of negotiating Germany's post-World War II identity. Even if Burger King's entrepreneurial act had simply withdrawn a non-verbal text from that discourse, we would have to attribute a political significance that goes far beyond that commonly accredited to the space-production practices of fast-food operations. As the architectural texture of the transformer station was not actually withdrawn but rewritten, the meaning of the conversion is probably more subtle. To properly understand the meaning and significance of Burger King's entrepreneurial act, it must therefore be interpreted as an intervention in the discourse on German identity.

Competing Reconstructions of National Identity in Postwar Germany

Expressing the desire to build a new and just nation on the bedrock of horrendous crime, and aiming to objectify this claim, an *anti-fascist* material culture of remembrance emerged in post-World War II Germany that revolved around self-criticism and self-indictment (Lübbe 1983; Rüsen 2005: 2001–1). The declaration of Nazi buildings as 'witnesses to the past' can be taken as the central discursive frame of this memorialization strategy. Nazi buildings are kept as warning reminders of fascist megalomania, though mostly as torsos, in parts even rendered as such through symbolic amputation, as a 'performative statement of German willingness to recognize the past and to learn from it' (Macdonald 2006a: 23). A case in point is the 360-metre long Zeppelin building on the Nazi Party rally grounds. Although the side galleries were removed in 1967 (the big stone swastika on top of the Grandstand had already been blown up by the US Army in 1945), the overall structure of the Zeppelin Grandstand is preserved, in order to remind spectators of the 'fascination and terror' of National Socialism. The transformer station, we have seen, was also accordingly declared a 'witness to the past' (in 1973), and its official status has not changed since. The modification of the appearance and function of the building carried out in 2006, however, altered the message of the building de facto.

At first glance, the conversion into a fast-food restaurant appears to be coherent with a second memorial tradition that was popular in the first two decades of the Federal Republic. This tradition did not proclaim a German identity that opposed itself by expressing a desire to bear the stigma of the past and assume responsibility. Instead, the idea was to employ the methodology of a sober-minded functionalism that allowed for the overcoming of National Socialism both as a factual reality and as a real memory (Frei 2003; Gregor 2003a; Moeller 2003: 15–9). The aspiration was de-Nazification or, to employ a term that was frequently invoked in Nuremberg City Council discussions in the late 1950s, 'amortization' (Macdonald 2006a: 25 n. 29). Instead of integrating former Nazi buildings into a chastening landscape of warning monuments, the strategy was to use them for merely 'practical' purposes—for instance, storage—or to raze them (Macdonald 2006b: 115–6, 2006b: 18–22; Niven and Paver 2010: 2–3).

In a way, this *non-ideological* position (non-ideological, because it claims to be 'above' nationalism and ideology) actually aims at the conversion of concrete places into abstract space. Nevertheless, this strategy acquires some plausibility in the context of the legacy of fascism. Advocates of the anti-fascist stance—especially the German student movement—frequently invoked psychoanalytical categories to delegitimize the non-ideological stance as a pathological inclination to repress an uncomfortable past. Affirming this interpretation, scholars speak of an 'inability to come to terms with the past' or a 'strategic amnesia' (Large 2001: 438). However, while the effacement of National Socialist monuments certainly permitted a distancing from any sense of having been accomplices of the Third Reich, this tactic is not simple effacement but ambiguous negation, and as such has a justifiable place in the politics of memory and heritage. It is certainly true that the non-ideological stance denies National Socialism; it does not stage the past as present. But more precisely, it denies the Nazi past a positive place in German identity. National Socialism is retained as absence, retained as that for which there is no room, either materially or symbolically. Why should it be ethically uncontroversial, after all, to allow the historical legacy of National Socialism to become economically burdensome? Why should scarce public funds be expended for the restoration of megalomaniacal buildings rather than for the payment of reparations to the victims of National Socialism or for economic development and public education? Furthermore, the deliberate preservation of the historical remnants additionally risks generating positive rather than oppositional identifications with National Socialism. Similarly, restoring buildings to their original shape tends to signal their extraordinary value, given that 'museumification' invokes a feeling of astonishment and wonder (Greenblatt 2006). Thus, Arno Hamburger, Chairman of the Jewish Religious Community in Nuremberg, has questioned whether preserving the decommissioned transformer station as a witness to the past instead of turning it into a fast-food restaurant would have been the better choice, as the former option would necessarily mean memorializing Speer's achievements (Möller 2006a).

Another alternative option, which would be to simply surrender the buildings to the ravages of time, is also problematic. In his apologetic monograph *Inside the Third Reich*, Speer wrote that the decay of the monuments was factored into the architectural model of the Nazi Party rally grounds from the outset. Slow decay, Speer theorized, adds to the consecration and mythologization of monuments and generates an emotive response of awe and sympathy. The German mentality, he suggested moreover, is especially sensible to the allure of the ruin (Speer 1995: 97). Reports by the Nuremberg City Council's discussions bear testimony to the awareness of Speer's 'Theory of Ruin Value'. The view was expressed that:

> Once fallen into ruin, the Congress Hall and the Zeppelin Building would come to look even more like the now-ruined classical forebears on which they were modelled [the Colosseum and the Pergamon Altar]. Rather than diminishing their ability to speak, this would only add to their allure and it would bear proper testimony to the achievements of the Third Reich.
>
> (Macdonald 2006a: 17)

Turned into a Burger King restaurant, the transformer station is neither preserved as a warning memorial, nor left to decay. It also fails to conform to the non-ideological stance. The Nazi monument was not torn down and reconstruction work has not obliterated the entire original symbolic texture. Furthermore, the particular practical economic use to which the building was put might seem to express a certain continuity with National Socialism rather than non-ideological discontinuity. The Holocaust, or so Ritzer (2008: 27) claims, is a preliminary stage to McDonaldization ('mass-produced death'). However, the discourse on German identity has yet other memorial traditions with which Burger King's entrepreneurial act could be associated.

Although the anti-fascist stance had been dominant since the late 1960s (Moeller 2003: 15), the discourse over the reconstruction of post-World War II Germany's identity by 'othering' its National Socialist past was only temporarily settled, not lastingly resolved. In fact, new conflicts emerged in the late 1980s. Historians report a new phase of 'memory contests' concerning the memorialization of National Socialism (Gregor 2003b: 590–4; Niven and Paver 2010: 4–8, Young 1992: 271). The reunification process of the two new Germanies invigorated the question of 'which kind of memory to preserve, how to do it, in whose name, and to what end' (Young 1992: 270). The continuation of the conflict concerning the German 'self' reaffirms the idea that commemorative politics can resort to a multiplicity of strategies to renegotiate national identity, even if the cultural heritage to be memorized is not a source of pride but an undesired legacy. In particular, one memorialization strategy has found expression in material culture in the aftermath of German reunification in showcasing the 'othering' of National Socialism while simultaneously challenging the perpetuation of national shame. It is fuelled by a distinct feeling among many Germans that the National Socialist past unduly burdens post-World War II Germany. Ventilating this grievance, the recipient of the 1998 Peace Prize of the German Book Trade, Martin Walser, complained that reference to Auschwitz was frequently used in politics on a domestic and the international level as a 'moral cudgel' to beat the lesson 'Do not forget!' into Germans' consciousness and hinder their pursuit of national interests. The National Socialist legacy, he sensed, had become a means to the 'exploitation of our disgrace for present purposes' (Walser 1998).

The memorial culture arising from this feeling can be described in terms of a slightly neo-nationalist attitude that understands itself as *post-fascist*. Nazi remnants are preserved, and new memorials are built that recall the perpetrators and commemorate the victims, just as the anti-fascist tradition proposes. Yet little can be detected of the humble and conscience-stricken spirit that is characteristic of warning memorials and their insistence on self-critical preoccupation, self-indictment, and merciless documentation in order to counter forgetfulness. In marked contrast, in fact, self-confident and complacent undertones define the memorialization of the alienated past, if not downright triumphalism. To conceptualize this difference, the material expressions of this regained self-confidence can be characterized, loosely following James E. Young (1992), as counter-monuments. Counter-monuments (*Gegendenkmäler*) challenge the traditional idea of national monuments (*Denkmäler*) like warning monuments (*Mahnmale*) by staging a discontinuity with the past, and also postulating a different interpretation of the historical discontinuity. The fascist legacy is invoked not to articulate the imperative of maintaining historical guilt, as warning memorials do, but to witness present accomplishments. By way of a quasi-Hegelian dialectic, or so it appears, thesis (fascist past) and antithesis (self-indictment) are superseded by a cathartic synthesis that portrays the German nation as having successfully mastered its own past.

The Berlin Memorial to the Murdered Jews of Europe, unveiled in 2005, serves to illustrate this trend. The memorial has been internationally recognized and overall positively evaluated as an outstanding warning memorial that proves Germany's honest admission of national guilt. Following this interpretation, vehement critics have therefore lambasted the memorial as a particularly blatant expression of the antifascist stance. In Walser's (1998) terms, the memorial amounts to the 'monumentalization of ignominy'. However, it really is Germany's most remarkable investment in soft power in recent years. The Memorial to the Murdered Jews of Europe consists of 2711 rectangular stelae (concrete slabs) of up to ten cubic metres high, arranged in a grid pattern to cover nearly five acres of land right in the centre of Berlin. No less colossal than Speer's architecture, it hardly invites the spectator to reflect quietly on Germany's guilt as a perpetrator nation. Rather, it overwhelms the spectator, indeed constituting what Young considers characteristic of counter-monuments, namely a 'brazen, painfully self-conscious memorial spac[e]' (Young 1992: 271). While the memorial reinstates by architectural means the perpetrator that is missing in the name of the memorial (Sion 2010: 246) and thus invokes the responsibility to state that such horrendous crimes must 'never happen again', it also draws attention to an agent that apparently spares neither cost nor effort in coming to terms with the fascist legacy. As if to testify that Germany has successfully managed to overcome the Nazi past, the 'place of information' is located underground, whereas the visible part of the Memorial to the Murdered Jews of Europe is conspicuously framed by symbols of the reunified Germany, the Reichstag Building and the Brandenburg Gate. One cannot avoid the impression that the German nation's sense of consciousness of guilt and responsibility is staged more prominently than the guilt and responsibility itself. The fascist legacy, as a point of reference for exerting moral pressure, is appropriated and put into the service of the new Germany. To some extent, perhaps, such counter-monumental architecture allows for the overcoming of a shattered masculinity, as Corinna Tomberger (2010) argues. Yet more importantly, in political terms, the open confession of the cruelties that happened in Germany's name anticipates and

Figure 7.3 Memorial to the Murdered Jews of Europe, Berlin (2005). In the background are the Reichstag and the Brandenburg Gate.
Photo courtesy of Sebastian Demuß, 2011

undercuts attempts to exploit the disgrace of the old Germany. In fact, far more effectively than the non-ideological strategy of 'drawing a line under the past', flamboyantly staging memorialization efforts in particularly prominent places allows for claiming a moral superiority—vis-à-vis the old Germany, of course, but primarily vis-à-vis domestic antagonists and rival nations in international disputes that have not similarly 'faced up' to their past, genocidal or otherwise.

Counter-monumental culture has also found material expression at the former Nazi Party rally grounds in Nuremberg. In 2001, a spear of glass and steel was thrust into the replica of the Colosseum that Hitler had created to host NSDAP party congresses. The spear 'mak[es] a deconstructive slice through the building [. . .] and so break[s] its monumentality and strong geometry' (Project description quoted from Macdonald 2006a: 20 n. 14). Thus, the inner life of National Socialism is made visible from the outside and visitors are confronted with the new Germany's willingness to learn from history even before they enter the building. The modified transformer station exemplifies another discursive challenge to the long prevailing anti-fascist tradition of memorialization in Germany. It clearly breaks with the humble and self-critical culture of preserving the physical Nazi heritage as a witness to the past. To some extent, the transformer station-turned Burger King restaurant draws upon the non-ideological position's vision of 'amortizing' the burdensome past by putting the building to practical economic use. But there is no sign that the building will be destroyed in the near future to efface the fascist legacy. Instead, the space is perfected. Moreover, in line with the post-fascist stance, an attempt is made to use the unwelcome inheritance for one's own benefit. Rather than aiming at mere 'amortization', the National Socialist past is instrumentalized for present purposes, both materially and symbolically: the new German 'self' is grounded in the constitutive outside 'National Socialism' and the remnants of fascism serve as the foundation for its reconstruction.

Exhibiting the spirit of the post-fascist stance, attention is drawn to a physical reminder of the fascist legacy so that the observer is left in no doubt about Germany's achievement in having overcome the temptations of militarist adventures, racism, and chauvinism. Of course, the match is imperfect because the installation of a mundane and commercial structure, as a fast-food outlet is, trivializes National Socialism. But it is crucial to understand that the trivialization we witness here diverges significantly from the kind of trivialization that the theorists of economization expect. It does not dilute the historical meaning of the site, rendering it trite or banal. Instead, the building's symbolic amalgamation with a fast-food restaurant subverts the original monument's meaning and compels the spectator to work out the paradox. No less thought-provoking as remembrance-through-documentation, the site now carries the signs of the strategy of *ironic trivialization* that Nuremberg's Head of Cultural Affairs Hermann Glaser propagated in the 1980s (Glaser 1989, cf. Weiß 1992: 172). One of the few examples in which this strategy was implemented is the firebowl of the Zeppelin Grandstand on the Nazi Party rally grounds. The firebowl was removed, painted in gaudy colours, and—under the motto 'where once terror ruled there shall be joy and jolliness'—re-utilized as a paddling pool for children in the area of the adjacent swimming pools (Schmidt 2002: 248).

Blame or Praise?

The opening of a fast-food outlet in Speer's transformer station throws light on the ongoing process of reconstructing German national identity through the demarcating projection of National Socialism. Given the multiple layers of meaning that coalesce in the topographical compound of the erstwhile transformer station, the case defies unambiguous categorization into any established discursive position. And while practical interventions usually exhibit shades of grey rather than being either black or white (Miller-Idriss and Rothenberg 2012: 133–4), this case might be even more prone to ambiguous interpretation than other examples of memorial culture in post-World War II Germany. Still, the unperturbed re-utilization of Nazi heritage for present purposes clearly testifies to the reclaimed self-confidence of the German nation. Attention is drawn away from the undesirable and indelible heritage itself and towards the achievement of successfully overcoming the alienated past. Thus, the conversion of the transformer station contributes to the mainstreaming of a German self-understanding that reclaims a place for national pride. At the same time, however, because the symbolic 'othering' of National Socialism is accomplished through commerce and mass culture, rather than through new architecture (as is characteristic for the Memorial to the Murdered Jews of Europe or the Documentation Centre in Nuremberg), a partly puzzling, partly moderating and arguably (self-) ironic dimension is added that distinguishes this case from other recent material manifestations of the post-fascist reconstruction of German identity.

The case certainly lends further credence to the view that the phenomenon of national identity is by no means on the decline, despite processes of political denationalization and economic globalization (Ariely 2012; Rembold and Carrier 2011). To some extent, of course, an economistic spirit was at work in the discussed case that crowded out historical sensibilities. Nevertheless, in its ability to offer resistance to the meaning and agency of the material heritage of National Socialism and provoke controversy, the conversion of the transformer station into a fast-food restaurant might not be inferior to more conscientiously critical memorialization strategies. Re-utilized as a fast-food restaurant, the physical remnant of National Socialism speaks to people's everyday lives. As one customer I talked to put it: 'I come here frequently for lunch and rarely give a thought to the building's history. But if it were another museum instead of a place to eat, I wouldn't come here at all'. Moreover, considering the overall context, the best memorial to the Nazi regime and its victims might not be a single monument at all, nor a coherent memorial culture, but rather a pluralism of memorials. Or, as Young argues, 'instead of a fixed figure for memory, the debate itself—the perpetually unresolved amid ever-changing conditions—might be enshrined' (Young 1992: 270, see also Riera 2006: 399). Finally, the commercializing profanation that characterizes the amalgamation of Speer's transformer station with a fast-food restaurant circumvents many problems that alternative ways of 'othering' National Socialism face. The Nazi past is not effaced and repressed, as the strategy of "amortization' tends to ensure. At the same time, the fascist legacy is not allowed to pocket public funds that could be used for the compensation of the victims of fascism. The building is not allowed to shine in its original splendour; it avoids the wonder of a museum as well as the allure of a ruin. The creole gets by without the need for sobering and forthright documentation—although not the outcome that the National Socialists had actually hoped for, such documentation still testifies to the impact of their undertakings, after all. On the contrary, the conversion of Hitler's 'word made of stone' into a multinational fast-food restaurant is certainly something that the architects of the Third Reich did not anticipate: the neon sign with the company name affixed to the front wall enlivens the façade's design; the blue plastic chairs and bright red sunshades outside undermine the daunting violation of the human scale that is so characteristic of Speer's architecture; the playground with its slide infantilizes the setting. The typical fast-food chain interior makes what may once have appeared sacred profane, and the place formerly occupied by generators powering the Nazi spectacle is taken over by grills and chip pans. Red flags still fly in the wind in front of the building. But the place of the swastika is taken by a symbol that stands for liberalism and capitalism, perhaps ethnic and religious tolerance, or even Western imperialism. In any case, Americana overbuilds fascist mythology. Precisely because this is so controversial, commercial profanation might facilitate critical reflection on contemporary Germany and its fascist past in a way that other memorialization strategies do not.

7.5 Text and Context of Space

Reconsidering Ritzer's McDonaldization thesis against the backdrop of the various criticisms that have been levelled against it, Douglas Kellner concludes that Ritzer was wrong in his pessimistic assessment of the phenomenon: 'a more nuanced evaluation of McDonaldization as a social phenomenon' is required. Despite troublesome aspects, he contends, the process geared at increasing efficiency, calculability, predictability, and control has brought clear positive social effects. Going on, he makes clear, however, that no such sophistication is required when it comes to the evaluation of fast-food outlets and the space they have produced:

> I would not hesitate to develop the most sharp negative critique of McDonald's itself as a corporation and junk food emporium [. . .] The McDonald's environment is a sterile and dehumanizing site of standardized and banal architecture signifying sameness, corporate homogeneity, and artificial massified space.
>
> (Kellner 1998: ix)

If it is legitimate to assume that Kellner would be ready to say the same about the environment of Burger King outlets, then the grossly oversimplifying character of such statements should have become clear in the course of this chapter. The case of the Burger King on 336 Regensburger Straße demonstrates that fast-food-chain outlets can sometimes be meaningful sites. In the manner of *détournement*, an act of entrepreneurial space production has profaned a historically contaminated and contested place in a non-banal way. Of course, the analysed case is very specific and not representative of practices of entrepreneurial space production in most regards. Yet, if an analysis of the most favourable example of abstract space leads to such unexpected results, then surely we need to rethink the approaches and conceptual apparatus by which we explore the entrepreneurial politics of space production. If we are interested in the specific political interventions of individual entrepreneurial acts rather than in global socio-cultural trends, considerable doubts arise as to whether distinctions such as those between abstract space and lived space, or nothingness and somethingness, are useful for this task. And if we are to detect political meaning behind apparent banality, it appears necessary to descend from the elevated position of grand theory and adopt more local and contextualized approaches.

The first, more specific conclusion to be drawn from the preceding discussion is that we should refrain from reducing outlets to simple instantiations of the parent company. Place-based politics is not just an unequal struggle between big companies that produce abstract space and civil residents who seek to reclaim and conserve concrete places. Bracketing out the residents' side of the simplifying opposition, the corporate side is far more complicated. Local franchisees often lack control over their own outlets, and if rebellious, can quickly be brought in line with company standards; non-franchised outlets offer even less room for inter-entrepreneurial difference (Ritzer 2008: 170–1). Still, there is a striking reason for us to be sensitive to potential conflicts that underlie the seemingly placid surface of corporate identity. By acknowledging the potential tensions between daughter and parent company, outlets and corporations, we can add grossly neglected forms of subsidiary and franchisee activism to our picture.

On that note one might speculate whether the actual existence of such windows of opportunity for subsidiary and franchisee activism is a reason why Starbucks—'the new McDonald's' (Janet Adamy quoted from Ritzer 2008: 211)—seeks to maintain maximum central control over its subsidiaries, and refuses to franchise its outlets (Ritzer 2008: 226). It seems that Starbucks tries to learn from the experience of McDonald's and Burger King, which every now and again have been confronted with the obstreperous idiosyncrasies of their franchisees. In 2009, for instance, signs were put up at dozens of Burger King stores in Tennessee and Mississippi that were franchised by The Mirabile Investment Corporation. The signs, where the meal of the day was once announced, now displayed the message 'Global Warming is Baloney'. Burger King's head office in Miami was quick to point out the statement did not reflect their opinion, and ordered that the signs be taken down. However, John McNelis, Marketing President of the Mirabile Investment Corporation, acted in defiance. He affirmed that the corporation would continue to be a 'good corporate citizen' and put up other signs, for instance, one saying 'Welcome home troops'. Patriotic business people like him, he concluded, have a responsibility to instrumentalize the means at hand to raise 'social awareness' and 'change the direction of some of the conversation out in the field there' (McNelis quoted from Hickman 2009). In this example of franchisee activism, the message is articulated in a verbal form and puts itself forward for interpretation. As entrepreneurial politics of space production are mostly non-verbal, and because of the terseness of monumental inscription, we need to learn to decipher the latent messages of places better.

The second conclusion, then, concerns our capabilities of doing just that. The preceding discussion has shown that we will understand little of the significance of spatializing practices until we know where and how they happen, and that these two aspects are intrinsically related. On the one hand, it matters where spatialization occurs. Places, while being reconfigured, are never isolated but are nested in others; they are not produced in the 'nowhere' (even if it seems to occur in the middle of it), but always 'somewhere'. We cannot understand an intervention in the corporeal register unless we acknowledge that even the complete effacement of a place (e.g. by tearing down a building) can be meaningful because it not only acts upon that place, but also occurs within a broader spatial context. As such, interpretation needs to read material modification as a discursive intervention.[15]

On the other hand, spatializing practice does not usually completely remove earlier meanings, but rather 'comments' on them. After all, meaning can be present in the absence of material bearers; sometimes (as the non-ideological stance expects) it may even be made present through absence. The Burger King in Nuremberg does not supersede the transformer station, but is both materially and semiotically grounded in it. The material elements of the site coalesce to form a topographical compound with multiple layers of meaning. As such, an interpretation of space-producing practices must take into account the semiotic stratification of concrete spaces as well as the inherent instability of this stratification: while social meaning is fixed at one level, it may come into conflict with articulations at another. In sum, it appears legitimate to say that the limits of macropolitical approaches to the economy are particularly striking when it comes to space-producing practices. Disregarding the contextuality and concreteness of places, they may hope to adumbrate general features of entrepreneurial space production. However, a long shadow of doubt falls upon the value of such universal theories as long as the spatializing practices of globally operating multinational corporations are still place-based, and for that matter, multilocal.

Notes

1. For an overview of the spatial turn in the humanities and social sciences, see Warf and Arias (2009). A lucid discussion on the politics of space production, some of whose arguments I will criticize, is Alexandra Kogl's 2008 monograph *Strange Places*.

2. In the literature, distinctions similar to that between 'abstract space' and 'lived space' have been drawn. Lefebvre (2009: 369–70) distinguishes between 'conceived space' (or 'representations of space') and 'representational space'. In Marc Augé's (2008: 78) terminology, proper 'places' are opposed to late capitalist 'non-places'. Even though Foucault's distinction between 'utopia' and 'heterotopia' does not really square with the distinctions of Augé, Kogl, and Lefebvre, it also gravitates around inauthenticity, reductionism, and abstractness: utopias are 'sites with no real place. They are sites that have a general relation of direct or inverted analogy with the real space of society. They present society itself in a perfected form, or else society turned upside down, but in any case, these utopias are fundamentally unreal spaces' (Foucault 1986: 24).
3. Regardless of whether we see an attempt at squeezing out the maximum labour power of workers, an example of paternalistic arrogance, or a well-intentioned project of ethically responsible entrepreneurship in the Pullman case, it is clear that the structuring of space played a crucial role in the entrepreneur's endeavour. George Pullman created a small world that bore the signature of industrialization without urbanization, and which unambiguously expressed bourgeois meaning. Moreover, as indicated earlier (see p. 22), Pullman himself expected the environment he created to have an influence on the inhabitants of the town. In addition, this case bears evidence of a variety of strategies employed by residents to reclaim the space of the town (Reiff 2000).
4. Celebration, Florida, matches classic company towns in its attempts to discipline inhabitants. For the official representation of the town, visit Celebration's website (www.celebration.fl.us/, accessed 30 July 2014). Cf. also Kogl (2008: 140). The difference between Celebration and classic company towns is the fact that most of the people who live there do not work for the company who owns it, and the town does not host important company buildings. The Novartis headquarters in Basel breaks with the tradition of classic company towns to a greater extent insofar as its founders created a largely secluded and utopian working environment without bothering to build an actual town. The company town is indoors, that is, the town is physically integrated into the company buildings. For a visitor's report listen to the radio transmission 'Novartis Campus—schöne, neue Arbeitswelt' (Fahrländer 2009).
5. Ritzer (2008: xv) explicitly states that there are no relevant differences between McDonald's and Burger King for his argument. The reasons for calling the trend he identifies 'McDonaldization' instead of 'Burger Kingization' is, he says, the nicer ring of the term. Benjamin Barber (1996) deploys a similar term—'McWorld'—to denote the existence of an increasingly homogenized environment of marketing, advertising, and shopping.
6. The peculiarity of 'McItaly' burgers was that they were made of Italian DOP (Protected Designation of Origin) products. The statements by Minister Zaia are taken from Fort (2010) and Ide (2010).
7. Ritzer's idiosyncratic term 'grobalization' is a portmanteau of 'grow' and 'globalization' (Ritzer 2008: 167).
8. Barber (2007: 269) provides a similar argument and warns against upholding the 'laissez-faire assumption' that the exchange between the global and local cultures is free, fair, and to their mutual benefit. This would be like saying that, 'though the python has swallowed the hare, the hare has changed the snake as much as the snake has changed the hare'. In contrast to a fair, reciprocal deal of cultural hybridization, the result is 'the infelicitous preeminence of the dominant culture'.

9. A more detailed version of the following analysis, which investigates Burger King's modification of the erstwhile transformer station on the Nazi Party rally grounds exclusively with a view to nation-building in contemporary Germany, has been published in *Nations and Nationalism* (Beckstein 2013).
10. The first quotation is from a speech given by Hitler on 22 January 1938: 'Wenn Völker große Zeiten innerlich erleben, so gestalten sie diese Zeiten auch äußerlich. Ihr Wort ist dann überzeugender als das gesprochene. Es ist das Wort aus Stein' (Hitler quoted from Weihsmann 1998: 19). The second statement by Hitler is taken from Reither (2000: 6).
11. CT Projektentwicklungsgesellschaft Bochum declined my request to comment further on this issue, as did the chief executive and branch manager of Burger King.
12. I will not pay specific attention to the political significance of Nuremberg in particular. Suffice it to say that the Nurembergian memorialization discourse slightly differs from the broader German one because of the city's legacy from the late Middle Ages. Accordingly, the medieval legacy is an equally important resource for the renegotiation of Nurembergian identity as the National Socialist legacy. It is not a coincidence that Hitler chose Nuremberg to host his Party rallies. Nuremberg, once the city of the Imperial Diet ('die Stadt der Reichstage'), was to become the city of party rallies ('die Stadt der Reichsparteitage'; Dietzfelbinger and Liedtke [2004: 66]). Because Nuremberg in many regards is still a comparatively representative city for the memorial culture of post-war German society, Neil Gregor (2008) used the city as a case study for examining how Germans have dealt with the fraught issue of the nation's Nazi past.
13. It should be noted that not all post-foundational political theorists consider the second qualification of Schmitt's conception of political identities that I make to be valid. Chantal Mouffe, who contributed significantly to a post-foundational revision of Schmitt's friend/enemy-distinction, sticks to the anthropomorphic concretization of collective identities. She insists that collectives of people place themselves in opposition to an empirically-specifiable group of actually existing individuals. In politics, she says, the construction of 'self' and 'other' necessarily means the demarcation of a 'them' from a 'we' (Mouffe 2005: 5, 11). In consequence, theoretically speaking, there could neither be an all-inclusive cosmopolitan consensus nor could a political collective put itself into opposition with its own past by temporal differentiation, as I claim that post-World War II Germany did and continues to do by positing Nazi Germany as its 'other'. However, approaching the question of collective political identities via Jacques Derrida—rather than Carl Schmitt and Chantal Mouffe—, we come to a divergent conclusion (Abizadeh 2005: 54–8, Beckstein 2011: 41–3, Fritsch 2008: 188). The 'other', then, is literally other; it can be human or otherwise. For the 'concreteness' of the 'other' it makes no difference what is opposed to the 'self' because the 'other' (just as the 'self') is always an unfixed, porous, and somewhat phantasmatic projection (Derrida 1997: 11).
14. Given the nature of the discursive source that is the centre of interest of the present discussion, I will concentrate on material (counter-)monumental culture in Nuremberg and elsewhere in Germany. Historians of the culture of remembrance notably emphasize the importance of non-verbal, namely architectural, sources for the construction of the German nation after World War II (Niven and Paver 2010: 1, Young 1992: 268). For historical accounts of the construction of German identity after World War II, see also Frei (2003), Fulbrook (1999), and Herf (1997). For seminal works on national identity and its construction, see Anderson (1983), Gellner (1983), and Smith (2005).

15. Another good case in point, which also concerns a fast-food chain, is the Burger King outlet that opened in 1999 in Maale Adumim and which, in so doing, embroiled itself in Middle Eastern politics. Maale Adumim is an Israeli settlement in the West Bank that is, like all settlements built on occupied territory, widely regarded by the international community as illegal under international law (Berg 2005). The entrepreneurial act immediately unleashed a harsh political dispute: Arab groups interpreted it as a legitimization of the Israeli occupation and settlement policies. Once Burger King International signalled its willingness to cancel the franchise contract for the outlet in Maale Adumim, Jewish protests broke out. Accusing the company of capitulating to Arab pressure, a boycott was threatened. Seeking to contain the damage, Burger King International claimed that the conflict was 'too complex for us to get involved in', and—hoping for a quick resolution of the whole issue—decided that the outlet should be removed. However, the Israeli franchise-holder, Rikamor Ltd, was ready for confrontation. Rikamor Ltd refused to remove the company's brand name and 'proudly defend[ed] its right to proffer kosher Whoppers at a food court in disputed territory'. Three months later, Burger King International succeeded in proving a breach of contract and cancelled the franchise (Sontag 1999).

8 Faraway, So Close

The preceding chapters developed and tested a micropolitical approach to economic matters through an exploration of opportunities for politics in the marketplace. The virtue of this approach, as compared with incomparably more popular macropolitical approaches, is that it brings the inner life of the 'economic system'—the practices and concrete acts of work, consumption, production, and entrepreneurship—into sight. Macropolitical approaches have their virtues, too, which is why the approaches should, as I argued in Chapter 2, be considered two different tools rather than antagonistic rivals, not least because they will usually be of different interest to scholars. Nevertheless, there is a lesson to be learnt from this study for scholars of politics more generally: the economic sphere should not be written off as a far-off enemy territory. The 'othering' of anything related to the economy—certainly one of the more tenacious discursive conventions in the discipline of political theory—is, without doubt, of great analytical value in virtue of its facilitating the clarification of concepts and disambiguation of ideal types, in virtue of its reducing complexity and producing manageable objects of study, and many things more. Yet this analytical value appears to be frequently mistaken for an invitation to essentialize the theoretically constructed difference between the economic and the political. Not everything that happens in the economic sphere is economics and nothing else (just as not everything that happens in the political sphere is politics and nothing else). Likewise, the economy is not just something that is and ought to be politically regulated. Instead, occurrences in the marketplace exhibit various aspects, economic, political, and still more, depending on what we scrutinize within them; given their overdetermined nature, they are also a part of the political forces that regulate society. Economic practices of work, consumption, production, and entrepreneurship, once scrutinized for their political potential, turn out to be much more similar to political practices such as voting, demonstrating, legislating, and running for office than is often suggested. This last chapter spells out this invitation to liberate political theory from its latent anti-economic bias by summarizing and systematizing general insights gained in this study and by providing a tentative suggestion regarding the place that the politics of economic life does and should have in 21st-century democracies.

8.1 Unconventional, Yet Politics

Numerous traces of the political can be found in economic life. Various practices of work, consumption, production, and entrepreneurship lend themselves to political—verbal or non-verbal—statements and performances. The resulting forms of worker and entrepreneurial politics, political consumer activism, and political (by-)production intervene in the process of reinstituting society at logically earlier or later moments than conventional forms of politics, and in a more direct or indirect fashion. To recall, in Chapter 3 we took from the disambiguation of micro-components of political conduct the idea that practices may feed the reinstitution of society at different stages. Thus, in the political sphere, for instance, demonstrations and voting in elections precede governmental policy-making and parliamentary legislation, while the implementation and coercion of law brings a political process to its close.

Many ways of contributing to the process of reinstituting society by economic means fall into the category of early and indirect forms of politics. While not themselves part of the official political process (on the stage of politics), early and indirect forms of politics are still geared towards parliamentary legislation. A consumer boycott, for instance, may mobilize public support for a stricter regulation of producer practices, or a whistle-blower may raise public awareness of some (perceived) injustice, add an item to the agenda of parliamentary debate, and exert pressure on governments to rethink their policies. And if so, boycotters and whistle-blowers thus serve the function of a 'weak public' (Brunkhorst 2002: 676, Frazer 1992: 192–4, Habermas 2004: 307) in virtue of exerting 'communicative power' without relying on the backup of 'administrative power'. But market-based activism may also become politically significant without taking a detour through legislative bodies in virtue of promoting social rather than legal norms. Consumer buycotts, antipreneurialism, slowdowns, or producers' politics behind the product may catalyse the diffusion of certain consumer, producer, or entrepreneurial practices or prefigure novel ones. The Body Shop's refusal to rely on animal testing accordingly constituted an impulse to de-legitimize a traditional business practice of the cosmetics industry. Fast-food chains, to give a second example, triggered the de-contestation of the view that there is nothing wrong with employing consumers as their own unpaid waiters. And the Jane Collective—regardless of whether it additionally aimed at legal reform—provided a (then illegal) abortion service. Not least, labelling and certification schemes may serve as substitutes for law, and while the norms established by labelling and certification schemes cannot be enforced by the police, market-based social ostracism and shaming strategies do some of the job, while socially-responsible shopping may contribute to their implementation.

Functionally considered, marketplace-based politics bears remarkable similarities with conventional forms of politics. Yet a comparison reveals differences as well, and a notable one—besides the obvious point that politics in the marketplace cannot directly access the governmental apparatus of power—reveals itself in Leo Strauss's statement that 'buying a shirt, as distinguished from casting a vote, is not in itself a political action'. Strauss is right in the sense that the vote is an equal share of sovereignty and as such constitutively linked to administrative power, whereas buying a shirt is a market transaction without a guaranteed political impact. Because of this, I argued in Chapter 4 that a micropolitical approach to economic life requires a conception of micropolitics that facilitates a differentiation between individual acts that have no palpable political impact and matter only in the aggregate on the one hand, and individual acts that unfold political impact with a multiplicative arithmetic on the other. Only such a conception of micropolitics enables us to deny that every recalcitrant behaviour at the workstation is already an act of resistance, that each adaptation of lifestyle or corporate policy, every refusal to consume, or any decision to consume less or differently, encroaches on the process of reinstituting society or even the reinstitution of one's lifeworld to an interesting extent. In order to qualify as political, then, political consumer activism (and the other forms of politics of economic life) must not imitate the logic of democratic elections. Instead of secretly adding a single unit to the collective count of aggregate demand, which is not constitutively linked with administrative power, the goal must be to motivate other agents to modify their consumption behaviour, to influence how business actors provide which products and services, or mobilize policy-makers.

By implication, however, this means that the politics of economic life differs from voting, the paradigmatic form of conventional politics in a democracy, in an important way. In contrast to voting, the politics of economic life does not obviate the amplification of one's voice. Perhaps, therefore, declining voter turnouts and the oft-lamented emigration of citizens from the stage of politics to other sites such as the marketplace in Western democracies testifies not so much to a general disenchantment with traditional channels of political articulation; it might not even primarily stem from a general perception that non-conventional forms of political activism are less bureaucratic, have a lower threshold for engagement, and better allow for experiencing 'the thrills of participation' (Micheletti 2003: 24). Perhaps it just testifies to a growing awareness of the structures and strategies of political opportunity. Exerting greater influence than others is a reasonable yardstick for political ambition, after all.

8.2 A Challenge to Democracy?

Yet if the politics of economic life essentially aims at violating the one-person-one-vote formula, and if some of its forms do not only serve as an 'informal prologue to democratic lawmaking' (Hussain 2012: 112) but circumvent the stage of politics, how can it possibly be compatible with democracy? Does it not constitute another challenge to democracy in the 21st century? More than a few think that it does. An early critic of the politics of economic life was Milton Friedman. In the 1970 speech mentioned in Chapter 6, Friedman castigated business people not only for pursuing social ends in addition to economic ones, but also, by so doing, for surrendering to an 'unadulterated socialism', and 'seeking to attain by undemocratic procedures what they cannot attain by democratic procedures' (Friedman 1970: 124–5). Against the backdrop of the increasing popularity of corporate social responsibility initiatives in the past four decades, it must be concluded that Friedman's criticism was unsuccessful in discouraging business actors from acquainting themselves with political roles and joining in the polyarchic regimen as a corporate citizenry. Besides Friedman, Michael Walzer (1983; 1984: 322) made a famous case for 'walling in' more effectively the economic sphere and preventing transformational processes of 'social alchemy' by which economic power is converted into political power. More recently, Waheed Hussain (2012: 112) has characterized political consumer activism that goes beyond contributing to informal deliberations in the run-up to formal democratic law-making as an 'impermissible form of vigilantism' that cannot claim 'a rightful place in the practices of a liberal democratic society'.[1]

Politics in the marketplace is certainly not conducive to democracy in the sense that Ludwig von Mises imagined, namely 'that the market becomes a democracy with each penny being a ballot' (Mises 1940: 260).[2] If pennies are the votes of the economic sphere, we must conclude that the marketplace is a plutocratic, not democratic, order that entails the government of money, for money, and by money. Given the unequal distribution of purchasing power, any attempt to justify politics in the marketplace via analogy to the one-person-one-vote formula must be cynical.[3] However, the question is whether the analogy is not also flawed in regard to what are assumed to be the relevant power resources of the two domains (sphere of politics: votes; economic sphere: money). More generally, we will have to inquire more thoroughly whether the opportunities to influence political outcomes through marketplace-based activism are really substantially less equal than the opportunities to influence political outcomes through conventional forms of political participation on the stage of politics.

The procedural value of political equality delegitimizes a number of ways and means by which privileged actors could (and sometimes do) try to shape political outcomes. At the same time, the procedural value of political equality does not prescribe equal influence. 'Democracy,' as Michael Walzer (1983: 309) puts it, 'requires equal rights, not equal power. Rights here are guaranteed opportunities to exercise minimal power (voting rights) or to try to exercise greater power (speech, assembly, petition rights)'. Citizens may legitimately aim to 'amplify' their voice and 'appropriate' other persons' votes by engaging in discussions and demonstrations or organizing campaigns in the run-up to elections. The disproportionate exertion of political influence is a necessary and desirable result as long as opportunities are to be granted. While the economic sphere does not offer a guaranteed opportunity to exercise minimal power, it offers plenty of opportunities to exercise greater power, and formally speaking, those opportunities are offered to everybody in equal measure. Due to the grossly uneven shares of wealth it is certainly true that the well-off can more easily seize opportunities to exercise political power, such that there is no *fair* equality of opportunity. However, in the official process of democratic politics citizens are also unevenly endowed with the power resources necessary for exerting disproportionate influence, such as rhetorical talent, networking skills, free time, access to officials, education (i.e. the various stocks of individual, human, and social capital), and, mutually reinforcing, wealth. There is plenty of reason to alleviate poverty of all kinds of capital, and more should be done to curb respective oligopolies; yet the difference between forms of participation in the political sphere and in the marketplace is one of degree in regard to the unequal distribution of power resources, not one of kind.

The questions of whether financial and productive capital is more suitable to distorting democratic processes than individual, human, or social capital, and whether a premium on the latter might be more easily justifiable than a premium on the former, exceed the scope of the present inquiry by far. The present outlook may, however, serve as a warning against falling prey to an anti-materialist prejudice that overrates the influence of money in politics as compared to other resources of power and considers it independent from them. That one can buy an election with money in Western affluent societies is an obvious oversimplification of complex processes, and accepting the kernel of truth that lies in this proposition it is still to be remembered that it is usually more efficient to raise money for an election campaign than investing one's own. Analogously, an 'ethical' product is better promoted by organizing a boycott than by privately purchasing it in bulk. And boycotts, again, are usually more about sending warning signals that enable producers to alter their course than about inflicting financial harm. As we touched upon in Chapter 5, the most promising route to a boycott's success is for boycotters to act as 'alert customers,' much in the way Hirschman (1981: 24) describes the exit function from a management perspective: 'The alert customers provide the firm with a feedback mechanism which starts the effort at recuperation while the inert customers provide it with the time and dollar cushion needed for this effort to come to fruition'. If boycott callers' hope were to mobilize all customers to withdraw at once, the activism would be bound to fail, because the relevant firm would be ruined before it could identify and amend the contested business practice. And the aim of any moral, ethical, or environmental agenda must be to eliminate a business practice rather than a specific firm, because otherwise activism would not serve political causes but at best satisfy personal desires for revenge.

To be added for consideration is also that, historically, political activism in the economic sphere has primarily been associated with the less privileged strata of society. According to Machiavelli (2001: 15, I.4), one of the most efficient ways for the commons in Ancient Rome and Renaissance city states to make themselves heard consisted in disturbing the ordered life of the marketplace. Boycotts, too, were first systematically organized by the then (in effect) disenfranchised African Americans (e.g. the boycott of slave-produced goods in 1830, or the Montgomery Bus Boycott in 1955). In the face of these experiences, it might be a problematic aspect of the marketplace that it offers people opportunities for political activism that are not in the possession of full citizenship rights, such as adolescents and transnational activists.

These considerations serve as an invitation to conduct more research into the politics of economic life, asking whether it suffers from substantially greater normative deficits than conventional forms of democratic participation. Yet in so doing, it should also be taken into account that the politicization of economic life contributes to the pluralization of channels for political articulation, which might be seen as valuable in itself. Democracy, after all, should not be reduced to a formalized decision mechanism that seeks to guarantee majority rule. Democracy might be described as a form of government, a method, or a way of life, yet most would consider a ready availability of genuine opportunities for participation an important feature of it. In Ancient Greece, in fact, these opportunities were considered more important than formal decision-making mechanisms. According to the advocates of democracy at the time, the accomplishment of democracy consisted in supplying citizens with 'a capacity to do things', as Josiah Ober shows.[4] The pluralization of channels for political articulation is certainly one of the more auspicious methods of augmenting this capacity—especially if we believe that established liberal democracies require further democratization or acknowledge that political systems, in a changing world, must reinvent themselves in order to remain faithful to their principles. And if it is true that parliaments have decreased in importance due to globalization, that agonism has been displaced from the stage of politics due to an ideological centripetalism among parties, and that voting is decreasingly perceived by citizens as an attractive form of political engagement, then the politicization of economic life might well afford an opportunity to foster the renewal of liberal democracy.

Notes

1. For a more extensive discussion of the seeming incompatibility of marketplace-based forms of political activism with the procedural norms of democratic morality, see Beckstein (2014).
2. Mises's original quotation (in context) reads: 'dass der Markt eine Demokratie bilde, bei der jeder Pfennig einen Stimmzettel darstelle. [. . .] Die demokratische Wahlordnung mag eher als ein unzugänglicher Versuch angesehen werden, im politischen Leben die Marktverfassung nachzubilden. Auf dem Markt geht keine Stimme verloren'.
3. This is, of course, not to say that wealth would not have positive functions in democratic societies, for instance in virtue of promoting faction and serving as a countervailing force to government (Bobbio 1990: 16, Dahl 1998: 48). One need not, however, go as far as the claims made in the *Money in Politics Handbook* (Office of Democracy and Governance 2003: 1), where political financing is put on the same level as free speech: 'Without money in politics, competitive multi-party democracies could not function, nor could their governments operate. Like a form of free speech, political finance is linked to the health and strength of a democracy. Laws and regulations to control political finance risk stifling the basic right of citizens to provide funding to the candidate or party of their choice'.
4. Josiah Ober (2008: 3, 8) argues that, in its original form, the composite of *demos* and *kratos* translates best as 'capacity to do things'. 'Majority rule', in contrast, 'was an intentionally pejorative diminution, urged by democracy's critics' in Ancient Greece 'to rebrand *demokratia* as the equivalent of a tyrannical "*polloi-archia*"'.

References

Abizadeh, Arash (2005) 'Does Collective Identity Presuppose an Other. On the Alleged Incoherence of Global Solidarity', *American Political Science Review* 99, 45–60.

Ackroyd, Stephen and David Collinson (2005) 'Resistance, Misbehavior, and Dissent', in S. Ackroyd, R. Batt, P. Thompson, and P. Tolbert (eds), *The Oxford Handbook of Work and Organization*, pp. 305–26. Oxford: Oxford University Press.

——— and Paul Thompson (1999) *Organizational Misbehaviour*. London: Sage.

Adorno, Theodor W. and Max Horkheimer (1997) *Dialectic of Enlightenment*. London: Verso.

Agamben, Giorgio (2007) 'The Power and the Glory', 11th B. N. Ganguli Memorial Lecture, 11 January, Turin. Centre for the Study of Developing Societies. Available from <www.pubtheo.com/page.asp?pid=1566> accessed 25 August 2014.

——— (2011) *The Kingdom and the Glory. For a Theological Genealogy of Economy and Government*. Stanford: Stanford University Press.

Alinsky, Saul D. (1989) *Rules for Radicals. A Practical Primer for Realistic Radicals*. New York: Vintage.

Almond, Gabriel A. (1991) 'Capitalism and Democracy', *Political Science and Politics* 24/3, 467–74.

Althusser, Louis (1969) *For Marx*. London: Penguin.

Ambrose, Maureen L., Seabright, Mark A., and Marshall Schminke (2002) 'Sabotage in the Workplace. The Role of Organizational Injustice', *Organizational Behavior and Human Decision Processes* 89, 947–65.

Anders, Günther (2009) *Die Antiquiertheit des Menschen*. Vol. I: 'Über die Seele im Zeitalter der zweiten industriellen Revolution'. München: Beck.

Anderson, Benedict (1983) *Imagined Communities. Reflections on the Origin and Spread of Nationalism*. London: Verso.

Antle III, James W. (2010) 'It's Their Party', *The Spectator*, 2 October, 22.

Arditi, Benjamin (2003) 'The Becoming-Other of Politics. A Post-Liberal Archipelago', *Contemporary Political Theory* 2, 307–25.

Arendt, Hannah (1998) *The Human Condition*. With an introduction by M. Canovan, 2nd edn, Chicago and London: University of Chicago Press.

Ariely, Gal (2012) 'Globalisation and the Decline of National Identity? An Exploration Across Sixty-three Countries', *Nations and Nationalism* 18/3, 461–82.

Arlidge, John (2009) 'I'm Doing "God's Work". Meet Mr Goldman Sachs', *The Sunday Times*, 8 November. Available from <www.thesundaytimes.co.uk/sto/news/world_news/article189615.ece> accessed 1 December 2014.

Augé, Marc (2008) *Non-Places. An Introduction to Supermodernity*. London: Verso.

Avineri, Shlomo (1981) *The Making of Modern Zionism. The Intellectual Origins of the Jewish State*. New York: Basic Books.
Axtmann, Roland (2007) *Democracy. Problems and Perspectives*. Edinburgh: Edinburgh University Press.
Bain, Peter and Phil Taylor (2003) 'Subterranean Worksick Blues. Humour as Subversion in Two Call Centres', *Organization Studies* 24/9, 1487–509.
Bang, Henrik P. (2009) '"Yes We Can". Identity Politics and Project Politics for a Late-modern World', *Urban Research & Practice* 2/2, 117–37.
Banzhaf, John F. (1968) 'One Man, 3.312 Votes. A Mathematical Analysis of the Electoral College', *Villanova Law Review* 13, 304–32.
Barber, Benjamin R. (1984) *Strong Democracy. Participatory Politics for a New Age*. Berkeley and Los Angeles: University of California Press.
——— (1996) *Jihad vs. McWorld. Terrorism's Challenge to Democracy*. New York: Ballantine.
——— (2007) *Consumed. How Markets Corrupt Children, Infantilize Adults, and Swallow Citizens Whole*. New York and London: Norton.
Bard, Alexander and Jan Söderqvist (2002) *Netocracy. The New Power Elite and Life After Capitalism*. London: Reuters.
Baringhorst, Sigrid, Kneip, Veronica, März, Annegret, and Johanna Niesyto, eds (2007) *Politik mit dem Einkaufswagen. Unternehmen und Konsumenten als Bürger in der globalen Mediengesellschaft*. Bielefeld: Transcript.
Bastiat, Frederic (2006) *That Which Is Seen and That Which Is Not Seen. The Unintended Consequences of Government Spending*. West Valley City: Waking Lion.
Bauman, Zygmunt (1999) 'The Self in a Consumer Society', *The Hedgehog Review* 1, 35–40.
——— (2007) *Consuming Life*. Cambridge: Polity.
Beck, Ulrich (1996) Th*e Reinvention of Politics. Rethinking Modernity in the Global Social Order*. Cambridge: Polity.
——— (2000) *The Brave New World of Work*. Cambridge: Polity.
——— (2009) *Risk Society. Towards a New Modernity*. London: Sage.
Becker, Gary S. (2008) *The Economic Approach to Human Behavior*. Chicago: University of Chicago Press.
Beckert, Jens (2003) 'Economic Sociology and Embeddedness. How Shall We Conceptualize Economic Action?', *Journal of Economic Issues* 37/3, 769–87.
Beckstein, Martin (2011) 'The Dissociative and Polemical Political: Chantal Mouffe and the Intellectual Heritage of Carl Schmitt', *Journal of Political Ideologies* 16/1, 33–51.
——— (2013) 'Nation Building in Contemporary Germany: The Strange Transformation of Hitler's "Word Made of Stone"', *Nations and Nationalism* 19/4, 761–80.
——— (2014) 'Political Consumer Activism and Democratic Legitimacy' *Studies in Social and Political Thought* 24, pp. 41–64.
Bélanger, Jacques and Christian Thuderoz (2010) 'The Repertoire of Employee Opposition', in P. Thompson and C. Smith (eds), *Working Life. Renewing Labour Process Analysis,* pp. 136–58. Basingstoke: Palgrave Macmillan.
Berg, Raffi (2005) 'Israel's "Linchpin" Settlement', *BBC News*, 12 November. Available from <http://bbc.co.uk/1/hi/world/middle_east/4419046.stm> accessed 28 June 2014.
Berger, Peter L. and Thomas Luckmann (1991) *The Social Construction of Reality. A Treatise in the Sociology of Knowledge*. London: Penguin.
Bermes, Christian (2002) 'Lebenswelt (1836–1936). Von der Optik des Lebens zur Inszenierung des Erlebens', *Archiv für Begriffsgeschichte* 44, 175–97.
Best, Michael H. and Connolly, William E. (1982) *The Politicized Economy*. 2nd edn. Lexington: Heath.

Bewes, Timothy (2002) *Reification. Or the Anxiety of Late Capitalism*. London: Verso.

Bircham, Emma and John Charlton (2001) *Anti-Capitalism. A Guide to the Movement*. London: Bookmarks.

Blühdorn, Ingolfur (2006) 'Self-Experience in the Theme Park of Radical Action? Social Movements and Political Articulation in the Late-modern Condition', *European Journal of Social Theory* 9/23, 23–42.

Bobbio, Noberto (1990) *Liberalism and Democracy*. London: Verso.

Botton, Alain de (2009) *The Pleasures and Sorrows of Work*. London: Penguin.

Bourdieu, Pierre (1984) *Distinction. A Social Critique of the Judgement of Taste*. Cambridge, Mass.: Harvard University Press.

Bowles, Samuel and Herbert Gintis (1990) 'Contested Exchange. New Microfoundations of the Political Economy of Capitalism', *Politics and Society* 18, 165–222.

Braunberger, Gerald (2011) 'Der Verkäufer als Bösewicht', *Frankfurter Allgemeine Zeitung*, 13 August. Available from <www.faz.net/ aktuell/finanzen/der-verkaeufer-als-boesewicht-alles-wichtige-ueber-leerverkaeufe-11112526.html> accessed 21 August 2014.

Breslau, Daniel (2003) 'Economics Invents the Economy. Mathematics, Statistics, and Models in the Work of Irving Fisher and Wesley Mitchell', *Theory and Society* 32/3, 379–411.

Brint, Michael, Weaver, William G., and Meredith Garmon (1995) 'What Difference Does Antifoundationalism Make to Political Theory?', *New Literary History* 26, 225–37.

Brunkhorst, Hauke (2002) 'Globalising Democracy Without a State. Strong Public, Weak Public, Global Constitutionalism', *Millennium* 31/3, 675–90

Buchanan, Mark (2011) 'With High-Speed Trading, the Market Cannot Hold'. *Bloomberg Businessweek*, 4 October. Available from <www.bloombergview.com/articles/2011–10–05/with-high-speed-trading-market-cannot-hold-commentary-by-mark-buchanan> accessed 13 October 2014.

Buder, Stanley (1967a) 'The Model Town of Pullman. Town Planning and Social Control in the Gilded Age', *Journal of the American Planning Association* 33/1, 2–10.

——— (1967b) *Pullman. An Experiment in Industrial Order and Community Planning 1880–1930*. New York: Oxford University Press.

Burnham, Peter (2001) 'New Labour and the Politics of Depoliticisation', *British Journal of Politics and International Relations* 3/2, 127–49.

Burns, Tom (1962) 'Micropolitics. Mechanism of Institutional Change', *Administrative Science Quarterly* 6, 257–81.

Butler, Judith (1997) 'Further Reflections on Conversations of Our Time', *Diacritics* 27/1, 13–15.

Caldwell, Melissa L. (2004) 'Domesticating the French Fry. McDonald's and Consumerism in Moscow', *Journal of Consumer Culture* 4/5, 5–26.

Cameron, Jenny and J. K. Gibson-Graham (2003) 'Feminising the Economy. Metaphors, Strategies, Politics', *Gender, Place & Culture* 10/2, 145–57.

Caruana, Robert and Andrew Crane (2008) 'Constructing Consumer Responsibility. Exploring the Role of Corporate Communications', *Organization Studies* 29, 1495–519.

Celent. (2007). *Socially Responsible Investing in the US and Europe. Same Goals but Different Paths*. Paris: Celent. Available at <www.celent.com/reports> (accessed 27 August 2012).

Certeau, Michel de (1984) *The Practice of Everyday Life*. Berkeley and Los Angeles: University of California Press.

Clark Muntean, Susan (2006) 'Resurrection of the Robber Barons. Reassessing the Theory of the Firm', *Business and Economic History* (BEH on-line) 4,

1–25. Available from <www.thebhc.org/sites/default/files/clarkmuntean.pdf> accessed 16 October 2014.

Collins, Randall (1981a) 'Micro-Translation as a Theory-building Strategy', in K. Knorr-Cetina and A. V. Cicourel (eds), *Advances in Social Theory and Methodology. Toward an Integration of Micro- and Macro-Sociologies*, pp. 81–108. Boston: Routledge.

——— (1981b) 'On the Micro-Foundations of Macro-Sociology', *American Journal of Sociology* 86/5, 984–1014.

Collinson, David (1994) 'Strategies of Resistance. Power, Knowledge and Subjectivity in the Workplace', in J. M. Jermier, D. Knights and W. R. Nord (eds), *Resistance and Power in Organizations*, pp. 25–68. London: Routledge.

Connolly, William E. (1995) *The Ethos of Pluralization*. Minneapolis: University of Minnesota Press.

——— (1999) *Why I Am Not a Secularist*. Minneapolis: University of Minnesota Press.

——— (2005) *Pluralism*. Durham and London: Duke University Press.

Conze, Werner (1972a) 'Arbeit', in O. Brunner, W. Conze, and R. Koselleck (eds), *Geschichtliche Grundbegriffe. Historisches Lexikon zur politisch-sozialen Sprache in Deutschland*, Bd. 1, A-D, pp. 154–215. Stuttgart: Klett.

——— (1972b) 'Beruf', in O. Brunner, W. Conze, and R. Koselleck (eds), *Geschichtliche Grundbegriffe. Historisches Lexikon zur politisch-sozialen Sprache in Deutschland*, Bd. 1, A-D, pp. 490–507. Stuttgart: Klett.

Cowe, Roger and Simon Williams (2000) *Who Are the Ethical Consumers?* Manchester: Co-operative Bank.

Crouch, Colin (2004) *Post-Democracy*. Cambridge: Polity.

Dahl, Robert A. (1985) *A Preface to Economic Democracy*. Berkeley: University of California Press.

——— (1989) *Democracy and Its Critics*. New Haven: Yale University Press.

——— (1998) *Polyarchy. Participation and Opposition*. New Haven: Yale University Press.

——— (2000) *On Democracy*. New Haven: Yale University Press.

——— and Lindblom, Charles E. (1976) *Politics, Economics and Welfare. Planning and Politico-Economic Systems Resolved into Basic Social Processes*. Chicago: University of Chicago Press.

Dalton, Russell J., Scarrow, Susan E., and Bruce E. Cain (2003) 'New Forms of Democracy? Reform and Transformation of Democratic Institutions', in B. E. Cain (ed.), *Democracy Transformed? Expanding Political Opportunities in Advanced Industrial Democracies*, pp. 1–22. Oxford: Oxford University Press.

Darwin, Charles (1872) *The Origin of Species*. London: Murray. Available from <http://darwin-online.org.uk> accessed 14 November 2013.

Deleuze, Gilles and Félix Guattari (2009) *A Thousand Plateaus. Capitalism and Schizophrenia*. With a foreword by B. Massumi, 13th reprint. Minneapolis and London: University of Minnesota Press.

Derrida, Jacques (1997) *Politics of Friendship*. London: Verso.

Dewey, John (1999) *The Public and Its Problems*. Athens: Swallow.

Dietzfelbinger, Eckhart and Gerhard Liedtke (2004) *Nürnberg—Ort der Massen. Das Reichsparteitagsgelände*. Berlin: Links.

Diskin, Jonathan and Blair Sandler (1993) 'Essentialism and the Economy in the Post-Marxist Imaginary. Reopening the Sutures', *Rethinking Marxism* 6/3, 28–48.

Domask, Joseph (2003) 'From Boycotts to Global Partnership. NGOs, the Private Sector, and the Struggle to Protect the World's Forests, in J. P. Doh and H. Teegen (eds), *Globalization and NGOs. Transforming Business, Government, and Society*, pp. 157–86. Westport: Praeger.

Doosry, Yasmin (2002) *Wohlauf, laßt uns eine Stadt und einen Turm bauen . . . Studien zum Reichsparteitagsgelände in Nürnberg*. Tübingen and Berlin: Wasmuth.

Douglas, Mary and Baron Isherwood (1996) *The World of Goods. Towards an Anthropology of Consumption*. London: Routledge.

Downs, Anthony (1957) *An Economic Theory of Democracy*. New York: Harper.

Dryzek, John S. (1996) *Democracy in Capitalist Times. Ideals, Limits, and Struggles*. New York: Oxford University Press.

Dubois, Pierre (1979) *Sabotage in Industry*. Harmondsworth: Penguin.

Dunn, John (2007) 'Capitalist Democracy. Elective Affinity or Beguiling Illusion?', *Daedalus* 136/3, 5–13.

Eberle, Thomas S. (1984) *Sinnkonstitution in Alltag und Wissenschaft. Der Beitrag der Phänomenologie an die Methodologie der Sozialwissenschaften*. Bern: Haupt.

Edwards, Paul K. and Hugh Scullion (1982) *The Social Organisation of Industrial Conflict. Control and Resistance in the Workplace*. Oxford: Blackwell.

Edwards, Tim (2000) *Contradictions of Consumption. Concepts, Practices, and Politics in Consumer Society*. Buckingham: Open University Press.

Ehmer, Josef (2001) 'History of Work', in N. J. Smelser and P. B. Baltes (eds), *International Encyclopedia of the Social and Behavioral Sciences,*, pp. 16569–75. Amsterdam: Elsevier.

Elkin, Stephen L. (2006) 'Political Theory and Political Economy', in J. S. Dryzek and B. Honig (eds), *Oxford Handbook of Political Theory*, pp. 791–809. Oxford: Oxford University Press.

Ely, Richard T. (1885) 'Pullman. A Social Study', *Harper's Monthly* 70 (February), 452–66.

Engels, Frederick [Friedrich] (1972) *The Origin of the Family, Private Property and the State*. Edited and with an introduction by E. B. Leacock. New York: International Publishers.

Fahrländer, Madeleine (2009) *Novartis Campus—schöne, neue Arbeitswelt*. Schweizer Radio DRS (Kontext), 19 January 2009. Available from <www.srf.ch/sendungen/kontext/novartis-campus-schoene-neue-arbeitswelt> accessed 20 January 2004.

Fairtrade International (2011) *Facts and Figures. A Success Story*. Available from <www.fairtrade.net/facts_and_figures.html> (accessed 6 July 2012).

Farrar, Margaret E. (2008) *Building the Body Politic. Power and Urban Space in Washington*, D.C. Urbana: University of Illinois Press.

Fernández-Kelly, Patricia and Jon Shefner, eds (2006) *Out of the Shadows. Political Action and Informal Economy in Latin America*. University Park: Pennsylvania State University Press.

Figueroa, Victor (2007) 'Venezuela's Chavez. An Alternative Democracy in Latin America?', in R. A. Dello Buono and J. Bell Lara (eds), *Imperialism, Neoliberalism and Social Struggles in Latin America*, pp. 195–220. Leiden: Brill.

Fine, Ben (2001) 'Economics, Imperialism and Intellectual Progress. The Present as History of Economic Thought?', *History of Economics Review* 32/1, 10–36.

Fiske, John (2009) 'The Popular Economy', in J. Storey (ed.), *Cultural Theory and Popular Culture*. A Reader, 4th edn, pp. 564–80. Harlow and New York: Pearson Longman.

Fleming, Peter and André Spicer (2007) *Contesting the Corporation. Struggle, Power and Resistance in Organizations*. Cambridge: Cambridge University Press.

Fligstein, Neil (1996) 'Markets as Politics. A Political-Cultural Approach to Market Institutions', *American Sociological Review* 61, 656–73.

Fontaine, Philippe and Alain Marciano (2007) 'The Political Element in Economic Thought', *History of Political Economy* 39/4, 567–70.

Fort, Matthew (2010) 'McDonald's Launch McItaly Burger', *The Guardian* online edition, 28 January. Available from <www.theguardian.com/lifeandstyle/wordofmouth/2010/jan/28/mcdonalds-launch-mcitaly-burger> accessed 22 June 2013.

Foucault, Michel (1986) 'Of Other Spaces', *Diacritics* 16/1, 22–7.

Fowler, Alys (2010) 'Incredible Edible. Todmorden's Local Food Revolution', *The Guardian* online edition, 19 October. Available from <www.guardian.co.uk/lifeandstyle/video/2010/oct/19/incredible-edible-todmorden> accessed 20 October 2013.

Franke, Ulrich and Ralph Weber (2012) 'At the Papini Hotel. On Pragmatism in the Study of International Relations', *European Journal of International Relations* 18/4, 669–91.

Frazer, Nancy (1992) 'Rethinking the Public Sphere', in Craig Calhoun (ed.) *Habermas and the Public Sphere*, pp. 109–42. Cambridge, Mass.: MIT Press.

Freeden, Michael (2002) 'The Ideology of New Labour', *The Political Quarterly* 70/1, 42–51.

——— (2011) 'The Politics of Ceremony. The Wootton Bassett Phenomenon', *Journal of Political Ideologies* 16/1, 1–10.

——— (2013) *The Political Theory of Political Thinking*. Oxford: Oxford University Press.

——— and Andrew Vincent (2013) *Comparative Political Thought*. London: Routledge.

Frei, Norbert (2003) *Vergangenheitspolitik. Die Anfänge der Bundesrepublik und die NS-Vergangenheit*. 2nd edn. München: Dtv.

Friedländer, Saul (2007) *Das Dritte Reich und die Juden*. Vol 1: 'Die Jahre der Verfolgung 1933–1939'. 3rd edn. München: Beck.

Friedman, Milton (1962) *Capitalism and Freedom*. Chicago: University of Chicago Press.

——— (1970) 'The Social Responsibility of Business Is to Increase Its Profits', *The New York Times Magazine*, 13 September, 122–6.

Friedman, Monroe (1999) *Consumer Boycotts. Effecting Change Through the Marketplace and the Media*. New York: Routledge.

——— (2006) 'Using Consumer Boycotts to Stimulate Corporate Policy Changes. Marketplace, Media, and Moral Considerations', in M. Micheletti, A. Føllesdal, and D. Stolle (eds), *Politics, Products, and Markets. Exploring Political Consumerism Past and Present*, pp. 45–62. New Brunswick and London: Transaction Publishers.

Fritsch, Matthias (2008) 'Antagonism and Democratic Citizenship. (Schmitt, Mouffe, Derrida)', *Research in Phenomenology* 38, 174–97.

Fuchs, Doris and Markus Lederer (2007) 'The Power of Business', *Business and Politics* 9/3, 1–17.

Fulbrook, Mary (1999) *German National Identity After the Holocaust*. Cambridge: Polity.

Fuss, Diana (1990) *Essentially Speaking. Feminism, Nature and Difference*. London: Routledge.

Gabriel, Yiannis and Tim Lang (2006) *The Unmanageable Consumer*. London: Sage.

Galbraith, J. Kenneth (1983) *The Anatomy of Power*. Boston: Houghton Mifflin.

Gambetta, Diego (1996) *The Sicilian Mafia. The Business of Private Protection*. Cambridge, Mass.: Harvard University Press.

Geis, Gilbert, Meier, Robert F., and Lawrence M. Salinger, eds (1995) *White-Collar Crime. Classic and Contemporary Views*. New York: Free Press.

Gellner, Ernest (1983) *Nations and Nationalism*. Ithaca: Cornell University Press.

Gibson-Graham, J.K. (2002) 'Beyond Global vs. Local. Economic Politics Outside the Binary Frame', in A. Herod and M.W. Wright (eds), *Geographies of Power. Placing Scale*, pp. 25–60. Malden: Blackwell.

——— (2006a) *A Postcapitalist Politics*. Minneapolis: University of Minnesota Press.

——— (2006b) *The End of Capitalism (As We Know It). A Feminist Critique of Political Economy.* Minneapolis: University of Minnesota Press.

Giddens, Anthony (1986) *The Constitution of Society. Outline of the Theory of Structuration*. Berkeley: University of California Press.

——— (1995) *Beyond Left and Right. The Future of Radical Politics*. Cambridge: Polity.

——— (1997) *Modernity and Self-Identity. Self and Society in the Late Modern Age*. Stanford: Stanford University Press.

——— (2002) *Runaway World. How Globalization is Reshaping Our Lives*. London: Routledge.

Gilpin, Robert (1987) *The Political Economy of International Relations*. Princeton: Princeton University Press.

Ginsberg, Benjamin and Martin Shefler (1990) *Politics by Other Means*. New York: Basic Books.

Ginsborg, Paul (2005) *The Politics of Everyday Life. Making Choices, Changing Lives*. New Haven: Yale University Press.

Glaser, Hermann (1989) 'Rumpelkammern im deutschen Kolosseum', *Rheinischer Merkur*, 16 June, 15.

Gledhill, Ruth (2009) 'Bishop: Church of England Must Be Less M&S and More Like Aldi', *The Times*, 22 September. Available from <www.thetimes.co.uk/tto/faith/article2100715.ece> accessed 29 September 2013.

Glimmel, Hans (2005) 'Grand Visions and Lilliput Politics. Staging the Exploration of the "Endless Frontier"', in D. Baird, A. Nordmann, and J. Schummer (eds), *Discovering the Nanoscale,* pp. 231–46. Amsterdam: IOS Press.

Goethe, Johann Wolfgang von (2008) *Elective Affinities. A Novel*. Oxford: Oxford University Press.

Goldberg, David J. (1996) 'A.D. Gordon. The Religion of Labour', in David J. Goldberg, *The Promised Land. A History of Zionist Thought,* pp. 137–46. New York: Penguin.

Goodman, David (2002) 'Rethinking Food Production–Consumption', *Sociologica Ruralis* 42/4, 271–7.

Goodwin, Neva R., Nelson, Julie A., Ackerman, Frank, and Thomas Weisskopf (2006) 'Essential Economic Activities', in *Encyclopaedia of Earth*. Global Development and Environment Institute, Tufts University. Available from <www.eoearth.org/view/article/152667/> accessed 12 July 2012.

Göran, Ahrne (1988) 'Labour Theory of Consumption', in Per Otnes (ed.), *The Sociology of Consumption. An Anthology*, pp. 49–64. Oslo: Solum.

Gordon, Aaron D. (1929) *Erlösung durch Arbeit. Ausgewählte Aufsätze*. Berlin: Zionistischer Bücher-Bund.

——— (1938a) *Selected Essays*. New York: League for Labor Palestine.

——— (1938b) 'The Simple Truth', in *Selected Essays*, pp. 58–64. New York: League for Labor Palestine.

——— (1959) 'Some Observations', in A. Hertzberg (ed.), *The Zionist Idea. A Historical Analysis and Reader*, pp. 375–79. Garden City: Doubleday and Hertzl.

Gosselin, Peter G. and Warren Vieth (2001) 'As Markets Reopen, U.S. Seeks to Prop Up Economy', *Los Angeles Times*, 17 September. Available from <http://articles.latimes.com/2001/sep/17/news/mn-46648> accessed 20 September 2013.

Gould, Carol C. (1991) 'Claude Lefort On Modern Democracy', *Praxis International* 3/4, 337–45.

Graaf, John de, Wann, David, and Thomas H. Naylor (2005) *Affluenza. The All-Consuming Epidemic.* San Francisco: Berrett-Koehler.

Gramsci, Antonio (1971) *Selections From the Prison Notebooks of Antonio Gramsci.* Edited by Q. Hoare and G.N. Smith. New York: International Publishers.

Greenblatt, Stephen (2006) 'Resonance and Wonder', in I. Karp and S.D. Lavine (eds), Exhibiting Cultures. *The Poetics and Politics of Museum Display*, pp. 42–56. Washington, D.C.: Smithsonian Books.

Grefe, Christian (2011) 'Wir sind vom Konsumismus infiziert. Ein Interview mit Carlo Petrini', *Die Zeit*, 19 May, 'ZeitWissen', 18–19.

Gregor, Neil (2003a). '"Is He Alive, or Long Since Dead?". Loss, Absence and Remembrance in Nuremberg, 1945–1956', *German History* 21/2, 183–203.

——— (2003b) '"The Illusion of Remembrance." The Karl Diehl Affair and the Memory of National Socialism in Nuremberg, 1945–1999', *The Journal of Modern History* 75/3, 590–633.

——— (2008) *Haunted City. Nuremberg and the Nazi Past.* New Haven: Yale University Press.

Grossberg, Lawrence (1992) *We Gotta Get Out of this Place. Popular Conservatism and Postmodern Culture.* New York: Routledge.

Habermas, Jürgen (2004) *Between Facts and Norms. Contributions to a Discourse Theory of Law and Democracy.* Cambridge: Polity.

——— (2005) *The Theory of Communicative Action.* Vol. 2: 'Lifeworld and System. A Critique of Functionalist Reason'. Boston: Beacon.

Hardy, Lee (1990) *The Fabric of This World. Inquiries into Calling, Career Choice, and the Design of Human Work.* Grand Rapids: Eerdmans.

Hay, Colin (2007) *Why We Hate Politics.* Cambridge: Polity.

Hayek, Friedrich August von (1956) *The Road to Serfdom.* Chicago: University of Chicago Press.

Heath, Joseph and Andrew Potter (2006) *The Rebel Sell. How the Counterculture Became Consumer Culture.* Chichester: Capstone.

Heinsohn, Gunnar and Otto Steiger (1999) 'Birth Control. The Political Economic Rationale Behind Jean Bodin's "Démonomanie"', *History of Political Economy* 31/3, 423–48.

Heller, Agnes (1978) *Renaissance Man.* London: Routledge.

Herf, Jeffrey (1997) *Divided Memory. The Nazi Past in the Two Germanys.* Cambridge, Mass.: Harvard University Press.

Herod, Andrew (2007) 'The Agency of Labour in Global Change. Reimaging the Spaces and Scales of Trade Union Praxis Within a Global Economy', in J.M. Hobson and L. Seabrooke (eds), *Everyday Politics of the World Economy*, pp. 27–45. Cambridge: Cambridge University Press.

Hertz, Noreena (1999) 'Better to Shop Than to Vote', *New Statesman*, 21 June. Available from <www.newstatesman.com/node/135018> accessed 1 December 2014.

——— (2002) *The Silent Takeover. Global Capitalism and the Death of Democracy.* London: Arrow.

Heyer, Thomas (2006) 'Hitlers Trafohaus', *Deutschlandfunk* (Corso), 4 August.

Hickman, Leo (2009) 'Burger King Outlet's Global Warming Signs Were to "Raise Awareness"', *The Guardian* online edition, 11 June. Available from <www.guardian.co.uk/environment/ethicallivingblog/2009/jun/11/climate-change-burger-king-baloney> accessed 28 June 2014.

Hilton, Matthew (2007) 'Social Activism in an Age of Consumption. The Organized Consumer Movement', *Social History* 32/2, 121–43.

——— and Martin J. Daunton (2001) 'Material Politics. An Introduction', in M.J. Daunton and M. Hilton (eds), *The Politics of Consumption. Material Culture and Citizenship in Europe and America*, pp. 1–32. Oxford: Berg.
Hirschman, Albert O. (1981) *Exit, Voice, and Loyalty. Responses to Decline in Firms, Organizations, and States*. Cambridge, Mass. and London: Harvard University Press.
Hitzler, Ronald (1994) *Der gemeine Machiavellismus. Beiträge zu einer Soziologie politischen Handelns*. Habilitationsschrift Fachbereich Philosophie und Sozialwissenschaften, Freie Universität Berlin.
——— (2000) 'Die Wiederentdeckung der Handlungspotentiale. Problemstellungen politischer Soziologie unter den Bedingungen reflexiver Modernisierung', *Zeitschrift für Politik* 47/2, 183–200.
Hobsbawm, Eric J. (2009) *Globalisation, Democracy and Terrorism*. London: Abacus.
Hobson, John M. and Leonard Seabrooke (2007) 'Everyday IPE. Revealing Everyday Forms of Change in the World Economy', in J.M. Hobson and L. Seabrooke (eds), *Everyday Politics of the World Economy*, pp. 1–24. Cambridge: Cambridge University Press.
Hobson, Kersty (2004) 'Sustainable Consumption in the United Kingdom. The "Responsible" Consumer and Government at "Arm's Length"', *Journal of Environment and Development* 13/2, 121–39.
Holcomb, John M. and S. Prakash Sethi (1992) 'Corporate and Executive Criminal Liability', *Business and the Contemporary World* 4/3, 81–105.
Holst, Insa and Peter Bräunlein (2008) 'Made in Germany. Wie deutsche Produkte die Welt eroberten', *Spiegel Online*, 27 April. Available from <www.spiegel.de/wissenschaft/mensch/0,1518,549197-2,00. html> accessed 10 May 2014.
Holtzhausen, Derina R. (2000) 'Postmodern Values in Public Relations', *Journal of Public Relations Research* 12/1, 93–114.
Holzer, Boris (2006) 'Political Consumerism Between Individual Choice and Collective Action. Social Movements, Role Mobilization and Signalling', *International Journal of Consumer Studies* 30/5, 405–15.
——— and Mads P. Sørensen (2001) *Subpolitics and Subpoliticians*. Working Paper 4, SFB 536 'Reflexive Modernization'. University of Munich. Available from <www.sfb536.mwn.de/arbeitspapiere/ap4-holzer.pdf> accessed 27 July 2011.
——— (2003) 'Rethinking Subpolitics. Beyond the "Iron Cage" of Modern Politics?', *Theory, Culture & Society* 20/2, 79–102.
Hoover, Kenneth R. (2003) *Economics as Ideology. Keynes, Laski, Hayek, and the Creation of Contemporary Politics*. Lanham: Rowman & Littlefield.
Howe, Richard H. (1978) 'Max Weber's Elective Affinities. Sociology Within the Bounds of Pure Reason', *American Journal of Sociology* 84/2, 366–85.
Hume, David (2006) 'Of the Original Contract', in *Political Essays*. Edited by K. Haakonssen, pp. 186–201. Cambridge: Cambridge University Press.
Humphery, Kim (2010) *Excess. Anti-Consumerism in the West*. Cambridge: Polity.
Humphreys, Ashlee and Kent Grayson (2008) 'The Intersecting Roles of Consumer and Producer. A Critical Perspective on Co-Production, Co-Creation and Prosumption', *Sociology Compass* 2/3, 963–80.
Hussain, Waheed (2012) 'Is Ethical Consumerism an Impermissible Form of Vigilantism?' *Philosophy and Public Affairs* 40/2, 111–43.
Husserl, Edmund (1984) *The Crisis of European Sciences and Transcendental Phenomenology. An Introduction to Phenomenological Philosophy*. Evanston: Northwestern University Press.
Hutt, William H. (1940) 'The Concept of Consumers' Sovereignty', *Economic Journal* 50, 66–77.

Hyman, Richard (1989) *Strikes*. Houndmills: Maximilian.

Ide, Ella (2010) 'Critics Trash McDonald's Nationalist Food Bid', *Reuters*, 5 February. Available from <www.reuters.com/article/idUSTRE6143WS20100205> accessed 22 June 2013.

Inayatullah, Naeem and David L. Blaney (1997) 'Economic Anxiety. Reification, De-Reification, and the Politics of IPE', in K. Burch (ed.), *Constituting International Political Economy*, pp. 59–77. Boulder: Lynne Rienner.

Ingham, Geoffrey K. (2008) *Capitalism*. Cambridge: Polity.

Jackisch, Samuel (2009) 'Gratis dienen, Geld verdienen', *Spiegel Online*, 27 December. Available from <www.spiegel.de/wirtschaft/unternehmen/0,1518,667881,00.html> accessed 9 December 2013.

James, William (1996) 'What Pragmatism Means', *Writings 1902–1910*, pp. 505–22. New York: Library of America.

Jay, Antony, ed. (1996) *The Oxford Dictionary of Political Quotations*. Oxford and New York: Oxford University Press.

Jensen, Hans R. (2005) 'What Does Political Consumerism Mean for Marketers?', in M. Boström, A. Føllesdal, et al. (eds), *Political Consumerism. Its Motivations, Power, and Conditions in the Nordic Countries and Elsewhere*, pp. 439–55. Copenhagen: Nordic Council of Ministers.

Jensen, Michael (2002) 'Value Maximization, Stakeholder Theory, and the Corporate Objective Function Business', *Business Ethics Quarterly* 12, 235–56.

Jessop, Bob (1978) 'Capitalism and Democracy. The Best Possible Political Shell?', in G. Littlejohn, B. Smart, J. Wakeford, and N. Yuval-Davis (eds), *Power and the State*, pp. 10–51. London: Croom Helm.

Joas, Hans (1996) *The Creativity of Action*. Chicago: University of Chicago Press.

Jones, Dan (2009) 'The Good, the Bad, and the Intentional', *The Psychologist* 22/8, 666–9.

Kaplan, Laura (1997) *The Story of Jane. The Legendary Underground Feminist Abortion Service*. Chicago: University of Chicago Press.

Kellaway, Lucy (2010) 'Listening to Your Customers Can Be Bad for Business', *Financial Times*, 18 October, 16.

Kelley, David (2007) 'The Capitalist Ideal. The Moral Vision of "Atlas Shrugged"'. Speech given to commemorate the 50th anniversary of the publication of "Atlas Shrugged" to the Objectivist Society, 12 October. Available from <http://newmedia.ufm.edu/gsm/index.php?title=The_Capitalist_Ideal:_The_Moral_Vision_of_Atlas_Shrugged> accessed 3 July 2013.

Kellner, Douglas (1998) 'Foreword. McDonaldization and Its Discontents—Ritzer and His Critics', in M. Alfino, J.S. Caputo, and R. Wynyard (eds), *McDonaldization Revisited. Critical Essays on Consumer Culture*, pp. vii–xiv. Westport: Praeger.

Kelly, John (2005) 'Labor Movements and Mobilization', in S. Ackroyd, R. Batt, P. Thompson, and P. Tolbert (eds), *The Oxford Handbook of Work and Organization*, pp. 283–304. Oxford: Oxford University Press.

Kerkvliet, Benedict J. (2005) *The Power of Everyday Politics. How Vietnamese Peasants Transformed National Policy*. Ithaca: Cornell University Press.

Key, Wilson B. (1974) *Subliminal Seduction*. New York: Signet.

Khalil, Elias L. (1996) 'What Is Economic Action? From Marshall and Robbins to Polanyi and Becker', *Journal of the History of Economic Thought* 18, 13–36.

Khan, Gulshan A. (2008) 'Pluralisation. An Alternative to Hegemony', *British Journal of Politics and International Relations* 10/2, 194–209.

Kirchgässner, Gebhard (2010) *Homo Oeconomicus. The Economic Model of Behaviour and Its Applications in Economics and Other Social Sciences*. New York: Springer.

Kittner, Michael (2005) *Arbeitskampf. Geschichte, Recht, Gegenwart*. München: Beck.

Klein, Naomie (2010) *No Logo*. 10th anniversary edn. London: Fourth Estate.

Kneip, Veronika and Johanna Niesyto (2007) 'Politischer Konsum und Kampagnenpolitik als nationalstaatliche Steuerungselemente? Das Beispiel der Kampagne Echt gerecht. Clever kaufen', in S. Baringhorst, V. Kneip, et al. (eds), *Politik mit dem Einkaufswagen. Unternehmen und Konsumenten als Bürger in der globalen Mediengesellschaft*, pp. 155–80. Bielefeld: Transcript.

Kley, Roland (1994) *Hayek's Social and Political Thought*. Oxford: Clarendon.

Knobe, Joshua (2003) 'Intentional Action and Side Effects in Ordinary Language', *Analysis* 63/3, 190–4.

Kogl, Alexandra (2007) 'Dislocating Politics, Embedding Economics. An Aristotelian Critique of Arendt's Depoliticized Economics'. Paper presented at the Annual Conference of the American Political Science Association, 30 August.

——— (2008) *Strange Places. The Political Potentials and Perils of Everyday Spaces*. Lanham: Lexington Books.

——— (2009) 'A Hundred Ways of Beginning. The Politics of Everyday Life', *Polity* 41/4, 514–35.

Kondo, Dorinne K. (2002) *Crafting Selves. Power, Gender, and Discourses of Identity in a Japanese Workplace*. Chicago: University of Chicago Press.

Kraus, Björn (2006) 'Lebenswelt und Lebensweltorientierung. Eine begriffliche Revision als Angebot an eine systemisch-konstruktivistische Sozialarbeitswissenschaft', *Kontext—Zeitschrift für Systemische Therapie und Familientherapie* 37, 116–29.

Kunda, Gideon (2006) *Engineering Culture. Control and Commitment in a High-Tech Corporation*. Philadelphia: Temple University Press.

Lachmann, Werner (2006) *Volkswirtschaftslehre*. Berlin: Springer.

Laclau, Ernesto (1999) 'Hegemony and the Future of Democracy', in G. A. Olson and L. Woshma (eds), *Race, Rhetoric, and the Postcolonial*, pp. 129–64. Albany: State University of New York Press.

——— and Chantal Mouffe (1985) *Hegemony and Socialist Strategy. Towards a Radical Democratic Politics*. London: Verso.

Lane, Marc J. (2005) *Profitable Socially Responsible Investing? An Institutional Investor's Guide*. London: Institutional Investor Books.

Langley, Paul (2007) 'Everyday Investor Subjects and Global Financial Change. The Rise of Anglo-American Mass Investment', in J. M. Hobson and L. Seabrooke (eds), *Everyday Politics of the World Economy*, pp. 103–19. Cambridge: Cambridge University Press.

Large, David C. (2001). *Hitlers München. Aufstieg und Fall der Hauptstadt der Bewegung*. München: Dtv.

Lasn, Kalle (2000) *Culture Jam. How to Reverse American's Suicidal Consumer Binge—and Why We Must*. New York: Quill.

——— (2010) 'I. Revolution', *Adbusters Magazine* 91. Available from <www.adbusters.org/magazine/91> accessed 23 November 2013.

Lawrence, Felicity (2010) 'McDonald's and PepsiCo to Help Write UK Health Policy', The *Guardian* online edition, 13 November. Available from <www.guardian.co.uk/politics/2010/nov/12/mcdonalds-pepsico-help-health-policy> accessed 6 May 2013.

Lazear, Edward P. (2000) 'Economic Imperialism', *Quarterly Journal of Economics* 115/1, 99–146.

Lears, T. J. Jackson (1994) *Fables of Abundance. A Cultural History of Advertising in America*. New York: Basic Books.

Lefebvre, Henri (2009) *The Production of Space*. Oxford: Blackwell.

Lefort, Claude (1988) *Democracy and Political Theory*. Cambridge: Polity.
Leidner, Robin (2006) *Fast Food, Fast Talk. Service Work and the Routinization of Everyday Life*. Berkeley: University of California Press.
Lerner, Abba (1972) 'The Economics and Politics of Consumer Sovereignty', *The American Economic Review* 62/1–2, 258–66.
Lewis, Roger K. (2002) 'Will Forces of Globalization Overwhelm Traditional Local Architecture?', *The Washington Post*, 2 November, 20.
Liddle, Roger K. (2010) 'I Refuse to Buy Meat From Supermarkets Until They Ban Halal Slaughter', *The Spectator*, 2 October. Available from <www.spectator.co.uk/essays/6319003/i-refuse-to-buy-meat-from-supermarkets-until-they-ban-halal-slaughter.thtml> accessed 15 October 2013.
Lie, John (1991) 'Embedding Polanyi's Market Society', *Sociological Perspectives* 34/2, 218–35.
Lindblom, Charles E. (1982) 'The Market as Prison', *Journal of Politics* 44, 324–36.
Lindsey, Almont (1939) 'Paternalism and the Pullman Strike', *The American Historical Review* 44/2, 272–89.
Littler, Jo (2009) *Radical Consumption. Shopping for Change in Contemporary Culture*. Berkshire: Open University Press.
Locke, John (1988) *Two Treatises of Government*. Cambridge: Cambridge University Press.
Lukács, Georg (1999) 'Reification and the Consciousness of the Proletariat', in Georg Lukács, *History and Class Consciousness*, pp. 83–222. London: Merlin Press.
Lübbe, Hermann (1983) 'Der Nationalsozialismus im deutschen Nachkriegsbewusstsein', *Historische Zeitschrift* 236, 579–99.
Lütge, Gunhild (2011) 'Alles wahr oder was?', *Die Zeit* 20, 12 May, 29.
Machiavelli, Niccolò (2001). *The Prince*. Trans. by G. Bull. London: Penguin.
Macdonald, Sharon (2006a) 'Undesirable Heritage. Fascist Material Culture and Historical Consciousness in Nuremberg', *International Journal of Heritage Studies* 12/1, 9–28.
——— (2006b) 'Words in Stone? Agency and Identity in a Nazi Landscape', *Journal of Material Culture* 11/1, 105–26.
MacKenzie, Donald, Muniesa, Fabian and Luicia Siu, eds (2007) *Do Economists Make Markets? On the Performativity of Economics*. Princeton: Princeton University Press.
Magnusson, Lars and Bo Stråth (2001) 'Introduction', in L. Magnusson and B. Stråth (eds), *From the Werner Plan to the EMU. In Search for a Political Economy for Europe*, pp. 23–48. Brussels: Peter Lang.
Marchand, Roland (2008) *Advertising the American Dream. Making Way for Modernity, 1920–1940*. Berkeley: University of California Press.
Marchart, Oliver (2007) *Post-Foundational Political Thought. Political Difference in Nancy, Lefort, Badiou and Laclau*. Edinburgh: Edinburgh University Press.
——— (2010) *Die politische Differenz. Zum Denken des Politischen bei Nancy, Lefort, Badiou, Laclau und Agamben*. Berlin: Suhrkamp.
Marcuse, Herbert (2007) *One-Dimensional Man. Studies in the Ideology of Advanced Industrial Society*. London: Routledge.
Margolis, Howard (1983) 'The Banzhaf Fallacy', *American Journal of Political Science* 27/2, 321–26.
Margolis, Joshua D. and James P. Walsh (2003) 'Misery Loves Companies. Rethinking Social Initiatives by Business', *Administrative Science Quarterly* 48/2, 268–305.
Marshall, Alfred (1920) *The Principles of Economics*. London: Macmillan.

Marx, Karl (1989) 'Critique of the Gotha Program', *Marx and Engels 1874–83*, MECW Vol. 24, 75–99. Available from <www.marxists.org/archive/marx/works/1875/gotha/index.htm> accessed 1 December 2012.

——— (1990) *Capital. A Critique of Political Economy*, Volume 1. With an introduction by E. Mandel. London: Penguin.

——— (1992a) *Capital. A Critique of Political Economy*, Volume 2. With an introduction by E. Mandel. London: Penguin.

——— (1992b) 'Economic and Philosophical Manuscripts', in *Early Writings*. With an introduction by L. Coletti, pp. 279–400. London: Penguin.

——— (1993a) *Capital. A Critique of Political Economy*, Volume 3. With an introduction by E. Mandel. London: Penguin.

——— (1994) *Economic Manuscripts of 1861–1864. A Contribution to the Critique of Political Economy*, MECW Vol. 34. Available from <www.marxists.org/archive/marx/works/1861/economic/ch38.htm> accessed 1 December 2012.

——— and Friedrich Engels (2002) *The Communist Manifesto*. With an introduction by G. Stedman Jones. London: Penguin.

——— (2004) *The German Ideology*. Edited, with an introduction by C.J. Arthur. New York: International Publishers.

Massey, Doreen (1998) 'I'm Not an Economist, But . . .', *Soundings* 10, 7–10.

——— (2005) *For Space*. London: Sage.

Massumi, Brian and Erin Manning (2008) 'History Through the Middle. Between Macro and Mesopolitics', *Inflexions* 3, 1–16.

Mayer, Robert (2001) 'Michael Walzer, Industrial Democracy, and Complex Equality', *Political Theory* 29/2, 237–61.

McLean, Fiona (2006) 'Introduction: Heritage and Identity", *International Journal of Heritage Studies* 12/1, 3–7.

Merrifield, Andy (1993) 'Place and Space. A Lefebvrian Reconciliation', *Transactions of the Institute of British Geographers* 18, 516–31.

Merton, Robert K. (1936) 'The Unanticipated Consequences of Purposive Social Action', *American Sociological Review* 1/6, 894–904.

Micheletti, Michele (2003) *Political Virtue and Shopping. Individuals, Consumerism, and Collective Action*. New York: Palgrave Macmillan.

——— Føllesdal, Andreas, and Dietlind Stolle, eds, (2006a) *Politics, Products, and Markets. Exploring Political Consumerism Past and Present*. New Brunswick and London: Transaction Publishers.

——— (2006b) 'Introduction', in M. Micheletti, A. Føllesdal and D. Stolle (eds), *Politics, Products, and Markets. Exploring Political Consumerism Past and Present*, pp. ix–xxvi. New Brunswick and London: Transaction Publishers.

——— (2006c) 'Conclusion', in M. Micheletti, A. Føllesdal and D. Stolle (eds), *Politics, Products, and Markets. Exploring Political Consumerism Past and Present*, pp. 289–300. New Brunswick and London: Transaction Publishers.

Miliband, Ralph (2004) *Marxism and Politics*. London: Merlin.

Miller, David (2000). *Citizenship and National Identity*. Cambridge, Polity.

Miller-Idriss, Cynthia and Rothenberg, Bess (2012). 'Ambivalence, Pride and Shame. Conceptualisations of German Nationhood', *Nations and Nationalism* 18/1: 132–55.

Mills, Charles W. (2000) *The Power Elite*. London: Oxford University Press.

Milne, Seumas (2010) 'The Corporate Grip on Public Life Is a Threat to Democracy', *The Guardian*, 18 November, 39.

Mises, Ludwig von (1940) *Nationalökonomie. Theorie des Handelns und Wirtschaftens*. Genf: Union.

Moeller, Robert G. (2003). *War Stories. The Search for a Usable Past in the Federal Republic of Germany*. Berkeley and Los Angeles: University of California Press.

Möller, Ute (2006a) 'Ärger um Fastfood im Nazi-Bau. Historiker kritisieren Einzug von Burger King in das Trafohaus aus dem Jahr 1936', *Nürnberger Nachrichten*, 7 June, 'Nürnberger Stadtanzeiger', 3.
——— (2006b) 'Einkehren in Hitlers Trafo-Haus. Scharfe Kritik: Im NS-Bau an der Regensburger Straße hat ein Burger King eröffnet', *Nürnberger Nachrichten*, 14 July, 'Nürnberger Stadtanzeiger', 2.
——— (2006c) 'Fastfood im Trafohaus: Gesellschaft kaufte Gebäude unweit des Stadions', *Nürnberger Nachrichten*, 3 May, 'Nord-Anzeiger', 4.
Mouffe, Chantal (2005) *On the Political*. London and New York: Routledge.
Murphy, Verity (2003) 'Mecca Cola Challenges US Rival', *BBC News* world edition, 8 January. Available from <http://news.bbc.co.uk/2/hi/middle_ east/2640259.stm> accessed 24 November 2013.
Nava, Mica (1991) 'Consumerism Reconsidered. Buying and Power', *Cultural Studies* 5/2, 157–73.
Néron, Pierre-Yves (2010) 'Business and the Polis. What Does It Mean to See Corporations as Political Actors?', *Journal of Business Ethics* 94, 333–52.
Niven, William J. and Chlose E.M. Paver (2010) 'Introduction', in W.J. Niven andC.E.M.. Paver (eds), *Memorialization in Germany Since 1945*, pp. 1–14. Basingstoke: Palgrave Macmillan.
Norris, Trevor (2005) 'Consuming Signs, Consuming the Polis, Hannah Arendt and Jean Beaudrillard on Consumer Society and the Eclipse of the Real', *International Journal of Baudrillard Studies* 2/2. Available from <www.ubishops.ca/baudrillardstudies/vol2_2/norris.htm> accessed 20 September 2013.
Nozick, Robert (2003) *Anarchy, State, and Utopia*. New York: Basic Books.
Oakeshott, Michael (1990) *On Human Conduct*. Oxford and New York: Oxford University Press.
Ober, Josiah (2008) 'The Original Meaning of "Democracy": Capacity to Do Things, Not Majority Rule', *Constellations* 15/1, 3–9.
Ozselcuk, Ceren (2009) *Post-Marxism After Althusser. A Critique of the Alternatives*. PhD Thesis, University of Massachusetts.
Packard, Vance (2007) *The Hidden Persuaders*. Introduction by M.C. Miller Brooklyn: Ig Publishers.
Pattie, Charles, Seyd, Patrick, and Paul Whiteley (2003) 'Citizenship and Civic Engagement. Attitudes and Behaviour in Britain', *Political Studies* 51/3, 443–68.
——— (2004) *Citizenship in Britain: Values, Participation and Democracy*. Cambridge: Cambridge University Press.
Pendergrast, Mark (2004) *For God, Country and Coca-Cola*. New York: Basic.
Peretti, Jonah (2006) 'The Nike Sweatshop Email. Political Consumerism, Internet, and Culture Jamming', in M. Micheletti, A. Føllesdal and D. Stolle (eds), *Politics, Products, and Markets. Exploring Political Consumerism Past and Present*, pp. 127–42. New Brunswick and London: Transaction Publishers.
Pitkin, Hanna F. (1987) 'Rethinking Reification', *Theory and Society* 16, 263–93.
——— (1998) *The Attack of the Blob. Hannah Arendt's Concept of the Social*. Chicago: University of Chicago Press.
Polanyi, Karl (1957) *The Great Transformation*. Boston: Beacon Press.
——— (1971) 'The Economy as Instituted Process', in G. Dalton, *Primitive, Archaic, and Modern Economies. Essays of Karl Polanyi*, pp. 139–74. Boston: Beacon Press.
——— (1977) *The Livelihood of Man*. New York: Academic Press.
Postles, Dave (2004) 'The Market Place as Space in Early Modern England', *Social History* 29/1, 41–58.
Prinz, Michael (2003) '"Konsum" und "Konsumgesellschaft". Vorschläge zu Definition und Verwendung', in M. Prinz (ed.), *Der lange Weg in den Überfluss*.

Anfänge und Entwicklung der Konsumgesellschaft seit der Vormoderne, pp. 11–34. Paderborn: Schöningh.
Przeworski, Adam (1993) *Capitalism and Social Democracy.* Cambridge: Cambridge University Press.
Pullman Company (1893) *The Story of Pullman.* Chicago: Blakely and Rogers.
Punch, Maurice (1996) *Dirty Business. Exploring Corporate Misconduct.* London: Sage.
Putnam, Robert D. (2007) *Bowling Alone. The Collapse and Revival of American Community.* New York: Simon & Schuster.
Quittner, Jeremy (2008) 'Meet the Antipreneurs', *Bloomberg Businessweek*, 20 June. Available from <www.bloomberg.com/bw/stories/2008–06–19/meet-the-antipreneurs> accessed 29 October 2013.
Radnitzky, Gerard and Peter Bernholz, eds (1987) *Economic Imperialism. The Economic Approach Applied Outside the Field of Economics.* New York: Paragon House.
Rand, Ayn (1999) *Atlas Shrugged.* New York: Plume.
Reichel, Peter (1999). *Politik mit der Erinnerung. Gedächtnisorte im Streit um die nationalsozialistische Vergangenheit.* Frankfurt a.M.: Fischer.
Reiff, Janice L. (2000) 'Rethinking Pullman. Urban Space and Working-Class Activism', *Social Science History* 24/1, 7–32.
——— and Susan E. Hirsch (1989) 'Pullman and Its Public. Image and Aim in Making and Interpreting History', *Public Historian* 11, 99–112.
Reither, Ingmar (2000) *'Worte aus Stein' und die Sprache der Dichter. Das Reichsparteitagsgelände als poetische Landschaft.* Nürnberg: Sandberg.
Rembold, Elfie and Peter Carrier (2011) 'Space and Identity. Constructions of National Identities in an Age of Globalisation', *National Identities* 13/4, 361–77.
Resnick, Stephen A. and Richard D. Wolff (1989) *Knowledge and Class. A Marxian Critique of Political Economy.* Chicago: University of Chicago Press.
Richtel, Matt and Verne G. Kopytoff (2011) 'Amazon Backs End to Online Sales Tax in California', *The New York Times*, July 12, B7.
Richter, Karl Th. (1875) *Die Fortschritte der Cultur. Einleitung in das Studium der Berichte über die Weltaustellung 1873.* Prag: Dominicus.
Ricoeur, Paul (1977) 'The Model of the Text. Meaningful Action Considered as a Text', in F.R. Dallmayr and T.A. McCarthy (eds), *Understanding Social Inquiry*, pp. 316–34. London: University of Notre Dame Press.
Riehl, Wilhelm H. (1862) *Die deutsche Arbeit.* Stuttgart: Cotta.
Riera, Monica (2006). 'How Should We Build? Architecture, History and the Post-cold War Context in Germany', *National Identities* 8/4: 383–400.
Ritzer, George (2008) *The McDonaldization of Society.* 5th edn. Los Angeles: Pine Forge Press.
——— Goodman, Douglass, and Wendy Wiedenhoft (2007) 'Theories of Consumption', in G. Ritzer and B. Smart (eds), *Handbook of Social Theory*, pp. 410–27. London: Sage.
——— and Nathan Jurgenson (2010) 'Production, Consumption, Prosumption. The Nature of Capitalism in the Age of the Digital "Prosumer"', *Journal of Consumer Culture* 10/1, 13–36.
Robbins, Lionel Ch. (1935) *An Essay on the Nature and Significance of Economic Science.* London: Macmillan.
Robinson, Sandra L. and Rebecca J. Bennett (1995) 'A Typology of Deviant Workplace Behaviors. A Multidimensional Scaling Study', *The Academy of Management Journal* 38/2, 555–72.
Robinson, William I. (2000) *Promoting Polyarchy. Globalization, US Intervention, and Hegemony.* Cambridge: Cambridge University Press.

Rochefort, David A. and Roger W. Cobb (1994) 'Problem Definition. An Emerging Perspective', in D.A. Rochefort and R.W. Cobb (eds), *The Politics of Problem Definition*, pp. 1–31. Lawrence: University of Kansas Press.
Rodrigues, Suzanna B. and David L. Collinson (1995) 'Having Fun? Humour as Resistance in Brazil', *Organization Studies* 16/5, 739–68.
Rorty, Richard (1988) 'The Priority of Democracy to Philosophy', in M.D. Peterson and R.C. Vaughan (eds), *The Virginia Statute for Religious Freedom*, pp. 257–88. Cambridge: Cambridge University Press.
Roy, Donald (1952) 'Quota Restriction and Goldbricking in a Machine Shop', *The American Journal of Sociology* 57/5, 427–42.
Rüsen, Jörn (2005) *History. Narration, Interpretation, Orientation*. Oxford: Berghahn.
Ryback, Timothy W. (1999) *The Last Survivor. Living in a Town Called Dachau*. New York: Pantheon Books.
Sack, Robert D. (1986) *Human Territoriality. Its Theory and History*. Cambridge: Cambridge University Press.
Sapiro, Virginia (2000) 'Economic Activity as Political Activity'. Paper presented at the Annual Conference of the American Political Science Association, Washington, D.C.
Sartori, Giovanni (1973) 'What Is "Politics"?', *Political Theory* 1/1, 5–26.
Scammel, Margaret (2000) 'The Internet and Civic Engagement', *Political Communication* 17/4, 351–5.
Schattschneider, Elmer E. (1975) *The Semisovereign People. A Realist's View of Democracy in America*. Boston: Wadsworth.
Schimmelfennig, Frank (2001) 'The Community Trap. Liberal Norms, Rhetorical Action, and the Eastern Enlargement of the European Union', *International Organization* 55/1, 47–80.
Schippers, Brigit (2009) 'Judith Butler, Radical Democracy and Micro-politics', in A. Little and M. Lloyd (eds), *The Politics of Radical Democracy*, pp. 73–91. Edinburgh: Edinburgh University Press.
Schlosser, Eric (2002) *Fast Food Nation. What the All-American Meal Is Doing to the World*. London: Penguin.
Schmidt, Alexander, ed. (2002) *Geländebegehung. Das Reichsparteitagsgelände in Nürnberg*. Nürnberg: Sandberg.
Schmitt, Carl (1956) *Hamlet oder Hekuba. Der Einbruch der Zeit in das Spiel*. Düsseldorf: Eugen Diedrichs.
——— (1996) *The Concept of the Political*. With an introduction by G. Schwab. Chicago: University of Chicago Press.
——— (2002) *Der Begriff des Politischen*. Text von 1932 mit einem Vorwort und drei Corollarien. Berlin: Duncker & Humblot.
Schumpeter, Joseph A. (2006) *Capitalism, Socialism and Democracy*. New York: Harper Perennial.
Schutt, Jeff (2007) '"Die erfrischende Pause". Marketing Coca-Cola in Hitler's Germany', in P.E. Swett, S.J. Wiesen, and J.R. Zatlin (eds), *Selling Modernity. Advertising in Twentieth-Century Germany*. With a foreword by V. de Grazia, pp. 151–81. Durham and London: Duke University Press.
Schütz, Alfred and Thomas Luckmann (1973) *The Structures of the Life-World*. Vol. 1. Evanston: Northwestern University Press.
Scott, James C. (1990) *Domination and the Arts of Resistance. Hidden Transcripts*. New Haven: Yale University Press.
——— (2000) *Weapons of the Weak. Everyday Forms of Peasant Resistance*. New Haven: Yale University Press.
——— (2008) *Seeing Like a State. How Certain Schemes to Improve the Human Condition Have Failed*. New Haven: Yale University Press.

Sen, Amartya K. (1977) 'Rational Fools. A Critique of the Behavioral Foundations of Economic Theory', *Philosophy and Public Affairs* 6/4, 317–44.

Shover, John L. (1965) *Cornbelt Rebellion. The Farmers' Holiday Association.* Urbana: University of Illinois Press.

Simon, Roger I. and Susan L.T. Ashley (2010) 'Heritage and Practices of Public Formation', *International Journal of Heritage Studies* 16/4–5, 247–54.

Simons, Jon (2005) 'The Radical Democratic Possibilities of Popular Culture', in L. Tønder (ed.), *Radical Democracy. Politics Between Abundance and Lack*, pp. 149–66. Manchester: Manchester University Press.

Sion, Brigitte (2010) 'Affective Memory, Ineffective Functionality. Experiencing Berlin's Memorial to the Murdered Jews of Europe', in W.J. Niven, C.E.M. Paver (eds), *Memorialization in Germany Since 1945*, pp. 243–52. Basingstoke: Palgrave Macmillan.

Slater, Don (2005) *Consumer Culture and Modernity*. Cambridge: Polity.

Smethurst, Paul (2000) *The Postmodern Chronotype. Reading Space and Time in Contemporary Fiction*. Amsterdam: Rodopi.

Smith, Adam (2009) *An Inquiry into the Nature and Causes of the Wealth of Nations*. Project Gutenberg EBook. Produced by C. Muir and D. Widger. Available from <www.gutenberg.org/ebooks/3300> accessed 20 August 2014.

Smith, Anthony D. (2005) *National Identity*. 6th reprint. Reno: University of Nevada Press.

Smith, David M. (2000) *Moral Geographies. Ethics in a World of Difference.* Edinburgh: Edinburgh University Press.

Social Investment Forum Foundation (2007) *Socially Responsible Investing in the US and Europe. Same Goals But Different Paths*. Available from <www.celent.com/reports/socially-responsible-investing-us-and-europe-same-goals-different-paths > accessed 7 May 2014.

Sontag, Deborah (1999) 'Burger King Outlet in West Bank Becomes a Political Dispute', *The New York Times*, 30 August. Available from <www.nytimes.com/1999/08/30/world/burger-king-outlet-in-west-bank-becomes-a-political-dispute.html> accessed 28 June 2014.

Speer, Albert (1995) *Inside the Third Reich*. London: Phoenix.

Staten, Henry (1986) *Wittgenstein and Derrida*. Lincoln: University of Nebraska Press.

Stolle, Dietlind and Marc Hooghe (2006) 'Consumers as Political Participants?', in M. Micheletti, A. Føllesdal and, D. Stolle (eds), *Politics, Products, and Markets. Exploring Political Consumerism Past and Present*, pp. 265–88. New Brunswick and London: Transaction Publishers.

——— and Michele Micheletti (2005) 'Politics in the Supermarket. Political Consumerism as a Form of Political Participation', *International Political Science Review* 26/3, 245–69.

Strauss, Leo (1988) *What Is Political Philosophy? And Other Studies*. Chicago: University of Chicago Press.

Streeck, Wolfgang (2012) 'Citizens as Customers: Considerations on the New Politics of Consumption', *New Left Review* 76, 27–47.

Swanson, Jacinda (n.d.) 'The Economic (and Artistic and Political) Practice of Gleaning'. Working Paper. Available from <www3.nd.edu/~econrep/papers/swanson.html> accessed 3 December 2013.

——— (2002) *Politicizing the Economic*. PhD Thesis, University of Notre Dame.

——— (2005) 'Recognition and Redistribution. Rethinking Culture and the Economic', *Theory, Culture & Society* 22/4, 87–118.

——— (2007a) 'The Economy and Its Relation to Politics', *Polity* 39/2, 208–33.

——— (2007b) 'Power and Resistance. Perpetuating and Challenging Capitalist Exploitation', *Contemporary Political Theory* 6, 4–23.

——— (2008) 'Economic Common Sense and the Depoliticization of the Economic', *Political Research Quarterly* 61/1, 56–67.
Swedberg, Richard (2000) *Max Weber and the Idea of Economic Sociology*. Princeton: Princeton University Press.
——— and Ola Agevall (2005) *The Max Weber Dictionary. Key Words and Central Concepts*. Stanford: Stanford University Press.
Tauber, Alfred and Sahotra Sarkar (1993) 'The Ideology of the Human Genome Project', *Journal of the Royal Society of Medicine* 86, 537–40.
Taylor, Frederick W. (2007) *The Principles of Scientific Management*. Sioux Falls: NuVision Publications.
——— (2008) *Shop Management*. Sioux Falls: NuVision Publications.
Teivainen, Teivo (2002) *Enter Economism, Exit Politics. Experts, Economic Policy and the Damage to Democracy*. London: Zed Books.
Thomason, Burke C. (1982) *Making Sense of Reification. Alfred Schutz and Constructionist Theory*. Atlantic Highlands: Humanities Press.
Thompson, Noel (2001) 'Social Opulence, Private Asceticism. Ideas of Consumption in Early Socialist Thought', in M.J. Daunton and M. Hilton (eds), *The Politics of Consumption. Material Culture and Citizenship in Europe and America*, pp. 51–68. Oxford: Berg.
Thompson, Paul and Stephen Ackroyd (1995) 'All Quiet on the Workplace Front? A Critique of Recent Trends in British Industrial Sociology', *Sociology* 29/4, 615–33.
Throsby, C. David (2003) *Economics and Culture*. Cambridge: Cambridge University Press.
Thumfart, Alexander and Arno Waschkuhn (2005) *Staatstheorien des italienischen Bürgerhumanismus. Politische Theorie von Francesco Petrarca bis Donato Giannotti*. Baden-Baden: Nomos.
Tilly, Charles (1995) *Popular Contention in Great Britain (1758–1834)*. Cambridge, Mass.: Harvard University Press.
——— and Sidney Tarrow (2007) *Contentious Politics*. Boulder and London: Paradigm Publishers.
Tocqueville, Alexis de (2003) *Democracy in America. And Two Essays on America*. With an introduction by I. Kramnick. London: Penguin.
Toffler, Alvin (1980) *Future Shock*. New York: Morrow.
Tomberger, Corinna (2010) 'The Counter-Monument. Memory Shaped by Male Post-war Legacies', in W.J. Niven, C.E.M. Paver (eds), *Memorialization in Germany Since 1945*, pp. 224–32. Basingstoke: Palgrave Macmillan.
Touraine, Alain (2000) *Can We Live Together? Equal and Different*. Stanford: Stanford University Press.
Tuan, Yi-Fu (2008) *Space and Place. The Perspective of Experience*. Minneapolis: University of Minnesota Press.
Unger, Roberto Mangabeira (1997) *Politics. The Central Texts*. Edited and introduced by Z. Cui. London: Verso.
——— (2004) *Social Theory. Its Situation and Its Task*. London and New York: Verso.
——— and Cornel West (1998) 'Progressive Politics and What Lies Ahead', *The Nation* 267, November 23, 11–15.
United States. Agency for International Development. Office of Democracy and Governance (2003) *Money in Politics Handbook*. Washington. Available from <http://aceproject.org/ero-en/topics/election-integrity/pnacr223.pdf> accessed 11 November 2013.
Urry, John (1996) 'How Societies Remember the Past', in: S. Macdonald and G. Fyfe (eds), *Theorizing Museums*, pp. 45–68. Oxford: Blackwell.

Usunier, Jean-Claude and Julie Anne Lee (2009) *Marketing Across Cultures*. Harlow: Pearson.

Varese, Federico (2010) 'General Introduction. What Is Organized Crime?', in F. Varese (ed.), *Organized Crime*, pp. 1–35. London: Routledge.

Verba, Sidney and Norman H. Nie (1972) *Participation in America: Political Democracy and Social Equality*. New York: Harper & Row.

Viboonchart, Nalin (2008) 'Mecca-Cola Introduced to Thailand', *The Nation*, 21 January. Available from <www.nationmultimedia.com/2008/01/21/business/business_30062839.php> accessed 24 November 2013.

Vihinen, Lea and Hyung-Jong Lee (2005) 'Fair Trade and the Multilateral Trading System', *OECD Papers* 5/2, 1–14.

Walras, Léon (2003) *Elements of Pure Economics. Or the Theory of Social Wealth*. London: Routledge.

Walser, Martin (1998) *Rede zur Verleihung des Friedenspreises des Deutschen Buchhandels*. Available from <www.hdg.de/lemo/html/dokumente/WegeInDieGegenwart_redeWalserZumFriedenspreis/index.html> accessed 30 June 2012.

Walzer, Michael (1981) 'Philosophy and Democracy', *Political Theory* 9, 379–99.

——— (1983) *Spheres of Justice*. New York: Basic Books.

——— (1984) 'Liberalism and the Art of Separation', *Political Theory* 12/3, 315–30.

——— (1999) 'Deliberation, and What Else?', in S. Macedo (ed.), *Deliberative Politics. Essays on Democracy and Disagreement*, pp. 58–69. Oxford: Oxford University Press.

Warf, Barney and Santa Arias (2009) 'Introduction. The Reinsertion of Space in the Humanities and the Social Sciences', in B. Warf and S. Arias (eds), *The Spatial Turn. Interdisciplinary Perspectives*, pp. 1–10. London: Routledge.

Watkins, Evan (1998) *Everyday Exchanges. Marketwork and Capitalist Common Sense*. Stanford: Stanford University Press.

Watson, James L., ed. (2000) *Golden Arches East. McDonald's in East Asia*. Stanford: Stanford University Press.

Watson, Sophie (2009) 'The Magic of the Marketplace. Sociality in a Neglected Public Space', *Urban Studies* 46/8, 1577–91.

Weber, Max (1906) 'Zur Lage der bürgerlichen Demokratie in Russland', *Archiv für Sozialwissenschaft und Sozialpolitik* 22, 234–353.

——— (1978) *Economy and Society*. New York: University of California Press.

——— (2002a) *The Protestant Ethic and the Spirit of Capitalism*. Oxford: Blackwell.

——— (2002b) 'Suffrage and Democracy in Germany', in P. Lassman (ed.), *Political Writings*, pp. 80–129. Cambridge: Cambridge University Press.

——— (2002c) 'The Profession and Vocation of Politics', in P. Lassman (ed.), *Political Writings*, pp. 309–68.Cambridge: Cambridge University Press.

Weihsmann, Helmut (1998) *Bauen unterm Hakenkreuz. Architektur des Untergangs*. Wien: Promedia.

Weiß, Wolfgang W. (1992) 'Chronologie der Versäumnisse. Der Umgang mit dem Reichsparteitagsgelände nach 1945', in Centrum Industriekultur Nürnberg (ed.), *Kulissen der Gewalt. Das Reichsparteitagsgelände in Nürnberg*, pp. 163–75. München: Hugendubel.

Weitzman, Martin L. (2004) 'Capitalism and Democracy. A Summing Up of the Arguments', in S. Bowles, H. Gintis, and B. Gustafsson (eds), *Markets and Democracy. Participation, Accountability, and Efficiency*, pp. 306–15. Cambridge: Cambridge University Press.

Wenman, Marc A. (2003) 'What Is Politics? The Approach of Radical Pluralism', *Politics* 23/1, 57–65.

West, Patrick (2004) *Conspicuous Compassion. Why Sometimes It Really Is Cruel to Be Kind.* London: Civitas.

Whitehead, Laurence (2002) *Democratization. Theory and Experience.* Oxford: Oxford University Press.

Williams, Raymond (2009) *Keywords. A Vocabulary of Culture and Society.* New York: Oxford University Press.

Willmott, Hugh (1993) 'Strength Is Ignorance, Slavery Is Freedom. Managing Culture in Modern Organizations', *Journal of Management Studies* 30/4, 515–52.

Wissenburg, Marcel L. J. (2009) *Political Pluralism and the State. Beyond Sovereignty.* London and New York: Routledge.

Yan, Yunxiang (2000) 'McDonald's in Beijing. The Localization of Americana', in J. L. Watson (ed.), *Golden Arches East. McDonald's in East Asia*, pp. 39–76. Stanford: Stanford University Press.

Yarden, Ophir (1998) 'The Sanctity of Mount Herzl and Independence Day in Israel's Civil Religion', in A. Houtman (ed.), *Sanctity of Time and Space in Tradition and Modernity*, pp. 317–48. Leiden: Brill.

Yates, Frances A. (1999) *Giordano Bruno and the Hermetic Tradition.* Chicago: University of Chicago Press.

Young, James E. (1992) 'The Counter-Monument. Memory Against Itself in Germany Today', *Critical Inquiry* 18/2, 267–96.

Zimmermann, Benedicte (2001) 'Work and Labour: History of the Concept', in N. J. Smelser and P. B. Baltes (eds), *International Encyclopedia of the Social and Behavioral Sciences*, pp. 16561–5. Amsterdam: Elsevier.

Žižek, Slavoj (2002) 'A Plea for Leninist Intolerance', *Critical Inquiry* 28/2, 542–66.

——— (2008) *For They Know Not What They Do. Enjoyment as a Political Factor*. London: Verso.

——— (2010) *Living in the End Times.* London: Verso.

Zoglin, Richard (2005) 'Fast Food Speeds Up the Pace', *Time Magazine*, 21 June. Available from <www.time.com/time/magazine/article/0,9171,1074756,00.html> accessed 30 June 2013.

Index

Note: Page numbers with *f* indicate figures.

For Product Safety Concerns and Information please contact our EU
representative GPSR@taylorandfrancis.com
Taylor & Francis Verlag GmbH, Kaufingerstraße 24, 80331 München, Germany

www.ingramcontent.com/pod-product-compliance
Ingram Content Group UK Ltd.
Pitfield, Milton Keynes, MK11 3LW, UK
UKHW022120190926
475702UK00013B/1557
* 9 7 8 0 8 1 5 3 7 0 2 2 2 *